HOW TO MAKE
MONEY FROM
PROPERTY

Visit our How To website at www.howto.co.uk

At **www.howto.co.uk** you can engage in conversation with our authors – all of whom have 'been there and done that' in their specialist fields. You can get access to special offers and additional content but most importantly you will be able to engage with, and become a part of, a wide and growing community of people just like yourself.

At **www.howto.co.uk** you'll be able to talk and share tips with people who have similar interests and are facing similar challenges in their lives. People who, just like you, have the desire to change their lives for the better – be it through moving to a new country, starting a new business, growing their own vegetables, or writing a novel.

At **www.howto.co.uk** you'll find the support and encouragement you need to help make your aspirations a reality.

You can go direct to **www.how-to-make-money-from-property.co.uk** which is part of the main How To site.

How To Books strives to present authentic, inspiring, practical information in their books. Now, when you buy a title from **How To Books,** you get even more than just words on a page.

HOW TO MAKE
MONEY FROM
PROPERTY

Authoritative, comprehensive and
authentic advice on investing in property,
whatever the state of the market

Ajay Ahuja

howtobooks

I dedicate this book to Hana,
who has helped me all the way through this book from
endless cups of tea to providing ideas and inspiration.
Thank you.

Published by How To Books Ltd,
Spring Hill House, Spring Hill Road,
Begbroke, Oxford OX5 1RX, United Kingdom
Tel: (01865) 375794 Fax: (01865) 379162
info@howtobooks.co.uk
www.howtobooks.co.uk

How To Books greatly reduce the carbon footprint of their books by sourcing their typesetting and printing in the UK.

British Library Cataloguing in Publication Data.
A catalogue record for this book is available from the British Library.

ISBN 978 1 84528 411 4

Produced for How To Books by Deer Park Productions, Tavistock
Typeset by PDQ Typesetting, Newcastle-under-Lyme, Staffordshire
Printed and bound by Cromwell Press Group, Trowbridge, Wiltshire

NOTE: The material contained in this book is set out in good faith for general guidance and no liability can be accepted for loss or expense incurred as a result of relying in particular circumstances on statements made in the book. The laws and regulations are complex and liable to change, and readers should check the current position with the relevant authorities before making personal arrangements.

CONTENTS

Introduction   1

Part One: Getting Started

1   **Deciding whether to be a full-time, part-time or hobby investor**   7
    The pros of being employed   7
    The cons of being employed   10
    The pros and cons of being self-employed   14
    You decide   17

2   **Deciding whether you are a trader or investor**   18
    Understanding the difference between a trader and an investor   18
    Types of trader   19
    Types of investor   19
    Are you a trader or an investor?   21

3   **Raising the starting capital**   22
    Minimize your fixed costs of living   22
    Raise your initial investment   24
    Maintain your fixed costs of living   25
    Cash is king   28

Part Two: The Property Clock

4   **Understanding the property price cycle**   31
    The property clock's existence   31
    Understanding growth   37
    Understanding yield   43
    Property prices – actual prices, real prices and bubbles   50
    12 p.m. to 3 p.m. – the hot spot   55
    3 p.m. to 6 p.m. – the cooling spot   57
    6 p.m. to 9 p.m. – the cold spot   62
    9 p.m. to 12 p.m. – the warm spot   67
    Strategy summary   71
    The lifetime property clock   74
    How the property clock and the lifetime property clock interact   78

Part Three: Types of Property Business

5	**Residential owner (rent a room)**	**83**
	Vital statistics	83
	The formula	83
	Choosing the right property	84
	Financing the property	86
	Getting the property ready	88
	Finding and choosing the right tenants	90
	Profit forecasting	93
	Lodger agreement	94
6	**Residential owner (bed and breakfast)**	**98**
	Vital statistics	98
	The formula	98
	The numbers	99
	Building the anticipated revenue figure	100
	Finding the right property	103
	Choosing the USP/theme/niche	105
	Maximizing revenue	106
	Complying with regulations	108
7	**Property trader (traditional)**	**110**
	Vital statistics	110
	The formula	111
	Determining market value	113
	Finding the property	114
	Financing the deal	118
	Selling the property	121
8	**Property trader (enhance)**	**123**
	Vital statistics	123
	The formula	124
	Refurbishment, conversion or extension?	124
	How to make money from refurbishment	126
	How to make money from conversion	128
	How to make money from extending a property	129
	Financing the project	132
	Getting planning permission	134
	Selling the property	134
9	**Property trader (options)**	**136**
	Vital statistics	136
	Options explained	136

	Valuing options	137
	Finding property option deals	139
	Negotiating the best deal	140
	Selling options	141
	Exercising options	142
	Power of attorney	142
	Summary	143
10	**Property investor (serviced apartments)**	**144**
	Vital statistics	144
	Choosing the right property	145
	Equipping the property	147
	Finding customers	148
	Running the business	150
11	**Property investor (buy to let)**	**153**
	Vital statistics	153
	The formula	154
	Deciding what you want	154
	Maximizing starting capital	158
	Investing wisely	158
	Remortgaging and investing aggressively	162
12	**Property investor (student/HMO lets)**	**164**
	Vital statistics	164
	University towns = students = £££!	164
	Finding the right property	165
	Finding the right student tenant	170
13	**Property investor (pension)**	**177**
	Vital statistics	177
	Traditional pension vs property pension	178
	How a traditional pension works	181
	How a property pension works	183
	Comparisons between traditional and property pensions	188
	Some assumptions about each type of pension	191
	Risks vs returns	197
	Your profile	200
	The strategies	205
14	**Property investor (lease options)**	**209**
	Vital statistics	209
	Lease options explained	209
	Buy properties for 50p	211

	Say goodbye to purchasing costs	212
	Your and the vendor's responsibilities	213
	Finding the right properties	214
	Renting out the property	214
	Grooming yourself for purchase	214
15	**Property sourcer (client facing)**	**216**
	Vital statistics	216
	What is a property sourcer?	216
	Finding the right clients	217
	Finding suitable properties	219
	Presenting the deals	222
	Finding a match	223
	Keeping hold of your client base	224
16	**Property sourcer (property facing)**	**225**
	Vital statistics	225
	Getting the leads	226
	Turning leads into deals	228
	Monetizing the deals	230
	Finding buyers	232

Part Four: Business Advice

17	**Starting your own property business**	**237**
	Getting the tools	237
	Getting educated	239
	Promoting your business	239
	Informing the authorities	240
	Controlling cash	241
	Understanding your competitors	243
	Understanding your customers	244
	Building alliances	244
18	**Don't give up! Methods of motivation**	**246**
	Fear and greed method	246
	Negative positive method	248
	Competition method	252
	Goal setting method	253
19	**Staying in business**	**256**
	Increasing cash inflow (business)	256
	Controlling cash outflow (personal)	260
Index		**262**

INTRODUCTION

I left my full-time job ten years ago at age 27. At the time I had no strategy of how I was going to quit. All I knew was that I'd had enough at work. I did, however, have three key attributes which you will need whatever strategy you employ:

- □ courage;
- □ motivation;
- □ foresight.

COURAGE

I think leaving my job was the bravest thing I have ever done. Not only did I have a job, I had a *career*. A career as a chartered accountant with one of the most prestigious accountancy firms in the world. I was earning £30k+ which ten years ago was not bad for a 27-year-old. My family were very proud of me and among my peers I was considered a success. However, inside I felt like a failure. A failure to myself. I was clearly doing something that I didn't want to do.

So you can guess their reaction when I said I was going to leave my safe, secure, well-paid job – 'You must be mad!' Not mad, but brave. Brave enough to do what most people are scared to do, brave enough to try to do things my way, prepared to forgo life's little luxuries and to expect no less than 100% effort from myself.

It is likely that you will not get much support from the people around you if and when you decide to leave your job. It's not because they are malicious. They will just be scared for you. This is why *you* need to be courageous. You will *never* be 100% sure that leaving your job is the right thing to do and the people around you will only further erode your confidence. If you are looking for certainties then leaving your job will always remain a dream.

MOTIVATION

A successful property business will not land in your lap! I've come up with over a hundred business ideas, implemented about ten of them and succeeded with only a few of them (all property related). It's no good just having an idea, you have to believe in the idea and take it to the next level. You need to find out whether the idea will work and the only way to do that is to actually implement it. This all requires effort!

I'm sure you've heard half-baked business ideas from people claiming that they're guaranteed to work. Well, if they were guaranteed why don't they do it! It's easy to say 'I don't have the time' or 'I don't have the money' but if it is such a good idea you'll find the time or get the finance. The reason they don't do anything about it is because they are lazy!

I'm no brain of Britain but the beauty of business is that you don't have to be. It's the laws of probability. If you try enough times you will succeed. But to try takes effort. I've come up with some good ideas and some really stupid ideas. I didn't know whether they were good or stupid until I had chatted with people and/or implemented them. With hindsight I would never have bothered with some of them!

FORESIGHT

Now I'm not asking you to predict the future. What I'm asking you to do is to *think* about the future. You need to have some idea of where you want to be. Having a mental picture of where you want to be tomorrow, next week, next month, next year and next decade. Having this picture then helps you determine your actions.

When I left work my goal was to replace my salary with self-employment. I knew I wanted to earn £1,700 per month within three years. I also wanted this income without me having to do too much, so I chose property investment. I refined my strategy so I could earn my target income. Within a year I got my target income. I was able to think about what I wanted, when I wanted it, how involved I wanted to be and what I was willing to do. I used my powers of foresight to help me determine what, when and how. Armed with these thoughts it was a lot easier to get what I wanted as I knew what I was aiming for!

HOW THIS BOOK CAN HELP YOU

I have a portfolio of 200 properties, and I run a property sourcing business providing buy-to-let property deals for clients. My two core businesses are in property. I come into contact with virtually every type of business that is property related. As a natural entrepreneur I am always thinking 'Is that a good business to get in to?'

Now most are owner operated. That is to say, these businesses require heavy input of time from the owner. This I do not have. However, what I do have is time to share with you my evaluation of these businesses from a property entrepreneur's viewpoint. This is very powerful as you get my opinion as (1) a chartered accountant, (2) an entrepreneur and (3) a potential customer.

So, if you love property and are looking to get involved but do not know which angle to come in at then read every page of this book! Every type of property business worth getting into is in here. You have to evaluate what is right for you. I can present you with each type of business and its merits and pitfalls but it is up to you to marry yourself with the right one. Pick the right business and nothing can stop you. Pick the wrong one and it becomes all a bit messy!

HOW THE BOOK IS STRUCTURED

Part One is designed to help you decide whether you want to invest as a hobby or to make it a career, whether full time or part time. It will also help you decide what type of property business you want to be in. Whether you are a trader or an investor.

Once you've made these decisions Part One will go on to show you how to get some cash together to start in business.

Part Two explains the whole cyclical nature of the property market.

Part Three goes into detail about the 12 hottest property businesses you could go into. Each business will include its **vital statistics**, which will give you a snapshot of the business in numbers and very few words. For example:

Earning potential before tax	Example: £5,000 to £25,000
	The range of the average to the most you can make. So most people will earn £5,000 but those who really go for it can expect to earn up to £25,000. I purposely ignore the lower amounts as these will obviously be around, zero or even a loss!
Capital required	Example: £10,000 to £50,000
	A range of the least to the most you will need: the amount of money you need to get started.
Skills required	The skills that will be needed to be good at this business.
Qualifications preferable	These will be qualifications that would be handy to have to be successful in this type of business.
Competitiveness: low/medium/high	The level of competitiveness in this market.
Risk: low/medium/high	The level of risk in this business.
The business model in a nutshell	A concise summary of the business. The whole business model will be described in one sentence.
Potential gaps in the market and suggested USPs	Angles and unique selling propositions (USP) that could lead to success in this business.

The final part of the book will give general business advice specific to the property market. It will help you to stay in business and hopefully become a supplier or customer to me one day – or even a competitor to keep me on my toes!

I am really looking forward to opening up the world of property to show you what it can really offer you. But before we dive in I want to help you determine what property business is right for you. So let's start with Part One: Getting Started.

PART ONE: GETTING STARTED

1

DECIDING WHETHER TO BE A FULL-TIME, PART-TIME OR HOBBY INVESTOR

The lifestyle I have now is worth more to me than money can buy – even though it makes me more money than any employment could ever give me! I wake up when I want and I go to bed when I want and in between I do whatever I want. It's as simple as that.

Ironically I work harder now than when I was employed. This is because I love my work and the line between work and pleasure is very blurred. I find myself researching things out of my own interest that become relevant to my work. Writing this book and sharing my knowledge is an interest of mine. It just so happens that writing books falls under the definition of work!

If you are wondering whether to get into the property game on a full-time, part-time or hobby basis let's look at the pros and cons of being employed. So let's start with the pros of being employed.

THE PROS OF BEING EMPLOYED

1. Regular fixed income

You receive a fixed salary at the end of the week or month regardless of your input level. There is little or no risk. This regular income allows you to take on fixed costs of living which determine your lifestyle.

Food for thought

When you got your first pay cheque you probably had some idea what you were going to do with it. I imagine it was something similar to what other people do. The need to maintain your lifestyle soon takes over and becomes the reason why you work. You become a slave to this lifestyle.

Is this regular income enough? OK, it's relatively risk free, but is it or will it ever amount to what you are worth? Can you do all the things you want to with your current or projected salary? And how long will this regular income last? Maybe your firm is in financial trouble and is looking to make redundancies.

2. Separation

Work life and out-of-work life, in theory, can be separate. When your work commitments end you can focus on your out-of-work life. You need not worry if some trouble hits your employer as there will always be someone else to deal with it.

Food for thought

Should there be a distinction between the two lives? Wouldn't it be more sane to have one life rather than two? You can then be assured of who you are all of the time.

Does it serve any purpose to separate these two lives? Just because it turns 5 p.m. should you end your working day?

Separation, invariably, is not clear cut. If you have an overbearing boss, a heavy workload or job insecurity then work life can taint your out-of-work life. Would it not be more beneficial for your working life and your social life to be blurred? That is to say that working is socializing and socializing is working?

3. Enjoyment

Working for your current employer puts you in situations that you enjoy. Situations such as working with children and animals, which you might not get the opportunity to do otherwise.

Food for thought

You may enjoy your job but your ability to choose your hours is limited and the salary might not be enough.

If you enjoy your job this can be a great starting point for your new business. Even though you forgo certain opportunities, other equally enjoyable ones may present themselves when you enter an industry that you enjoy.

Why not set up as a competitor to your employer? Several people I know have done just that. They enjoyed their job but left their employer and set up as a direct competitor – and won!

4. Status

With your job comes a certain status in society which helps contribute to your self-esteem.

Food for thought

You may enjoy the status the job brings but your ability to choose your hours is limited and the salary might not be enough.

Personally I think status is all about self-importance. Some people work hard to acquire status and as a result they rely on it in order to feel better about themselves and compared with others. Once you forget about what others think of you and you focus on yourself and what's right for you then the importance of status diminishes to nothing.

5. Social contact

Your job exposes you to a wide variety of people or certain types of people whom you enjoy meeting and who form part of your social circle.

Food for thought

Nothing stops you meeting these people out of work. You can maintain your existing network of friends and build new networks through your existing friends, especially if you are a sociable person anyway.

However, you may find that through self-employment you tend towards different people compared with when you were employed. Your attitudes will change and your existing network of friends might not change with you.

6. Education

You may benefit from valuable training and education. Some employers spend a lot of money training up individuals so that they are more informed and hence better at their job. These skills are transferable and really help to boost your CV.

Food for thought

Some of the best training you'll ever receive is through experience. Experience is unconscious learning and is easier to digest. Through self-employment you will find yourself in situations that no textbook will help with. These experiences will be more valuable than any training programme!

Look at these pros. How many are applicable to you? Are they sufficient to keep you in employment? Before you answer the last question, compare your pros with the cons of being employed.

THE CONS OF BEING EMPLOYED

1. Your time is not yours

You have to be in work at the hours dictated to you by your employer. Even if you work flexi-time you still have to work a certain number of hours every week.

You are expected to get to your place of work on time regardless of what you did last night or want to do in the day, and to stay at work for a set number of hours. If you need to be home for whatever reason it's not your employer's problem – and nor should it be! Your employer pays you a wage so that you are there to take their orders during their specified work hours.

Food for thought

This is the single and most important reason why I left work. It's not about the money, as money can only be spent; it's about time, which spent wisely can be precious.

If you work a 40-hour week, take an hour to get ready for work and commute for one hour each way then work takes up 55 hours per week. This equates to well over half your waking hours! And usually at the end of the day you're too knackered to do anything else. If you do overtime then this statistic gets even worse.

Were you put on this planet to live for two days a week – Saturday and Sunday? Or would you like to work when you want, dictating your own hours rather than having someone else do it for you? Would you like to do things while other people are at work?

I never go shopping on a Saturday. I go in the week when the queues are small or non-existent, you can find a parking space and you can get there without getting stuck in a traffic jam.

2. Minimum retirement age is 60

If you have no outside source of income other than your salary then your pension is all you've got to look forward to. Your financial commitments will probably mean you need either a salary or a pension, so you cannot afford to retire till age 60 or over.

Food for thought

What a thought! I do not even know whether I will reach the age of 60. You may die never knowing what it's truly like to not have to work to live.

Do you want to work until you are 60 or over? Do you have ideas or things you want to achieve before you're too old? It's a big world out there and knowing you spent half your life in an office building, shop or factory may leave you feeling a little bit hollow. You may even have to work beyond 60 if your pension fund is not big enough to provide for you. Age 60 is only a minimum!

3. Retirement income is unknown

Unless you have a very expensive defined benefit pension policy (and this is being phased out now) you will have no idea what your retirement income will be. Your pension depends on the performance of the stock market and the annuity rates being offered at the time. Neither of these will be known at the time of retirement.

Food for thought

How can you plan for retirement if you do not know how much you will have to spend? It can be very unnerving not knowing whether you will simply have enough especially when pension companies have performed so badly.

Owning a business opens up other opportunities that provide you with a defined retirement income, such as non-executive directorships, consultancy, licences and royalties, part sale deals, complete liquidation and much more. If you do go into business you will find out all about these opportunities in good time!

4. Effort does not always equal reward

Your salary is largely fixed. You may receive a bonus but this will be a fraction of your salary and may be dependent on the performance of others which you have no control over. So however much effort you put in, your reward will never mirror that effort. Your salary will fit within a predefined scale and will also rely on the performance of your peers.

Recognition of effort can also be lacking. If you have an all-the-glory boss who loves to take the credit, or you are only one of many in a team that has done well, then direct assignment of credit can be blurred. More often than not it's the more popular members of the team as opposed to the harder-working ones that get the credit – how unfair!

Food for thought

Wouldn't it be nice to know that all of your effort directly benefits you? I think this is how people operate when it comes to work. They will work hardest when they know they will get *all* the benefits from their efforts.

Employees largely fall into one of two categories:

1. **Driven** – working beyond their allocated duties because of the promise of promotion or more pay.

2. **Workshy** – who do the least they need to keep their job as they are demotivated, due to lack of either interest for the job or promotional prospects.

Employees tend to start off as driven, turn to workshy and then move jobs. They repeat this process for the duration of their working life, never finding their true vocation. Do you find yourself changing jobs every few years? Do you find yourself jumping into a job that you think will be interesting, later finding out that the same old feelings surface?

5. You will never be rich!

If you look at this year's *Sunday Times* Rich List 1,000 you will not find one single employee among them. OK, the CEO or chairman of a company is technically an employee, but their wealth is derived from the *ownership* of the company rather than from their salary. The rich own businesses and the poor work for businesses – it's as simple as that.

But I'm not only talking money here. You will never be rich with time, which for me was my main motivation for becoming self-employed. The abundance of money has diminishing returns. But time spent with your children and family is priceless.

Food for thought

There is no limit to what you can earn being self-employed, unlike being employed. It's quite disheartening to know that the only way you can be rich is by winning the lottery.

Even if you earn or have the capacity to earn large sums of money this will only last as long as you work there. You may experience a high salary for a few years before you retire or the market changes. If you set up your own business properly then the large sums can continue indefinitely – whether you do the work or not!

6. You cannot choose who you work with

I think we've all come across this one! A boss or colleague may be brilliant at what they do but you simply don't get on with them. Whether it's a personality clash, a cultural difference or opposite working styles, whatever the problem is, you can't stand them! And there may be nothing you can do about it.

This reason alone can cause a lot of stress. Having an overbearing boss who is always in your face, giving you impossible deadlines to meet and never appreciating your work can make you feel quite low.

Food for thought

Do you have feelings of hatred towards any of your colleagues? These intense feelings are not good for you. Wouldn't it be better to surround yourself with people you like being around *all* of the time?

You can choose whom you work with or do business with if you are self-employed. You won't have to 'put on a face' for anyone you don't like. You will find that you will become a 'straight talker' as a result because there will be no need to do otherwise.

When I started in business a few contacts were a bit rude and condescending to me, probably because I was younger than them and they thought they knew better. I simply refused to do business with them. Because money was not the motivation, but freedom was, I was confident enough to say to myself that there is no need for these people to be in my life.

7. You will always be under someone else's control

Unless you're the CEO or chairman then there is always someone above you. So if they want you to work out of your area or to change department then that is their choice, not yours – and so it should be, as they pay your wages! Even if you are a manager and you think you have control, the reality is something else. Your promotion, pay, benefits and authority levels are all set from above.

Food for thought

Taking orders from someone else in exchange for a pittance means that you are merely a slave. I found the whole concept of work like being back at school. It seems very patronizing for someone else to tell you when you should be working and checking that you stick to *their* regime.

8. You will always have job insecurity

There is no such thing as a job for life. In our cut-throat business environment employers make redundancies if it makes economic sense. Having a job is, ironically, more risky than having a business as the employees are the first to go when there is financial trouble. If you own a business then no one can get rid of you because it's yours! I'm not saying that you won't get into financial trouble but if you do you won't be the first to go.

Food for thought

You will have a better idea of your security if you know everything about the business. The only way for you to know everything about the business is to make sure you own the business!

If you remain focused then you can ensure that you will always be self-employed. In this book I show you not only how to build your position but also how to *maintain* your position so that you never go back to employment.

THE PROS AND CONS OF BEING SELF-EMPLOYED

In part, the pros and cons of self-employment are a reversal of the pros and cons of employment. But there are others. Let's look at the reversal in summary first and then at the others.

Pros

1. **Your time is yours**. No one tells you when to work apart from you. If you want to work late or get to work early then that is your choice. If you want to work all night then do so. Or if you don't want to work one day then don't!

2. **No minimum retirement age**. If you do well, then you can sell up or step down and let your business pay for your retirement. There is no law stopping you spending your profits in order to do nothing – even if you are only 21!

3. **Retirement income can be predicted**. Again, if you have done well you have explored the options available to you to ensure a guaranteed income from your business to keep you in retirement.

4. **Effort does always equals reward**. If you do nothing you'll receive nothing. If you do something you'll receive something. But whatever you do you can be assured that you will receive 100% of the benefits flowing from your effort.

5. **You can be rich**! There is no law to say that you cannot earn £1 trillion a year. There are no limits. The only thing that limits you is YOU!

6. **You can choose whom you work with**. You decide whom you deal with and who you employ. You have 100% control over who enters your life.

7. **You will never be under someone else's control**. Of course not – it's your business. Whatever your choice of markets it will be solely your decision. It's a highly responsible position to be in, you determine the success of your business.

8. **You will always have job security**. Part Four of the book deals with this in more detail.

Cons

1. **Irregular income**. It's true that your income will be irregular. Hopefully you will prepare for this: minimize your fixed costs of living so that you can weather the bad times. Once you are through these times then having an irregular income of £10k one month to £30k the next won't be such a problem!

2. **No separation**. Who needs separation? Why not have a life that is not split between work and social life? If you're interested in something – turn it into a business!

3. **No enjoyment**. If you will miss the enjoyment you got from your job then look to do something similar, or within the supply chain of this environment. Always look to do something that you think you will enjoy. To ensure success you must have an interest in the product/service you are selling.

4. **Loss of status**. Status means absolutely nothing! It may get you a table in a restaurant, but is it really worth working 40+ hours a week for this privilege?

5. **Lack of social contact**. If your time is yours then it's up to you to maintain social contact. At least you can socialize only with the people you want to socialize with.

6. **No normal education**. The best education is experience. The best training in life from school, university and work doesn't compare with the real-life experiences of setting up a business.

These are the reversals, but here are some others that I have found through experience. I am sure there must be more.

Other pros and cons

1. Administration

People think that there is a lot of red tape in running a business – and they're right! The admin grows with the business: the more trade you do the more paperwork. However, it's a small price to pay for the increase in business.

You will have to do everything when you start out, but if your business grows then you can pay someone to do the admin, and the other things you don't want to!

2. Tax

People become more focused on how to avoid tax rather than on how to make a profit. Only profits are taxed, so first make a profit, then worry about tax.

Self-employed people have to be responsible for their own tax but the amount you pay is the same for the self-employed as for the employed.

3. Responsibility

Yes, you do have to be responsible – but do you have a problem with this? Being responsible is part of being an adult.

It's easy to delegate responsibility when you are employed – it's not our problem. However, there is a lot of personal reward to be had knowing that the buck stops with you. When things go right then you can take full credit. When things go wrong you learn important lessons that no course or training programme could ever teach you.

4. Jealousy

If you achieve success with your own business then you will get jealousy from some – it's only natural. You simply have to be thick-skinned. Being self-employed teaches you a lot about how to ignore negativity and just get on with things.

Don't repeat the mantra, 'Well, if they're jealous then they weren't friends in the first place'. Becoming self-employed is hard not just for you but can be for others around you too.

5. Apathy

It's completely normal when you become your own boss to have bouts of apathy. But if you are determined to make your business work then you will ensure that they are only bouts and don't last long.

It is your right to do nothing if you do not want to. But if you have set goals within your business plan you will not allow yourself to do this. Apathy comes from when you don't *have* to do things – and this is one of the perks of being self-employed!

6. Invest rather than spend

When you enter the world of business you understand that every £1 you have could either buy you something you want now, or buy you something you want at a later date that's even better if you invest it. Knowing this means that you will spend carefully, investing enough, so that you can acquire things that you never thought possible.

Think whether the things you actually buy make you feel better about yourself. Isn't your time more important than any material good? So would it not be better to invest in business knowing that you will then have more time for yourself, your family and friends?

YOU DECIDE

I hope I have given you food for thought. One strategy could be to start off the business as a hobby, then progress to part time, once you have proved it to be semi-successful, really go for it, jack in the job and go full time. At that point I welcome you aboard!

2

DECIDING WHETHER YOU ARE A TRADER OR INVESTOR

It is important to decide whether you are a trader or an investor. It is advisable to be either one or the other so you have clarity of goals and aims. You can be both, but your strategy would need to be even more crystal clear than if you were just one or the other.

UNDERSTANDING THE DIFFERENCE BETWEEN A TRADER AND AN INVESTOR

First let me define what traders and investors are.

Definition of a trader

My definition of a trader is someone who buys and sells within one year. They buy a commodity and look to derive a profit from selling it. Examples include supermarkets, retailers, and car dealers. These businesses make money by buying something with the knowledge that they can sell it for more than they paid for it within a reasonable amount of time, usually less than a week.

They are bargain-hunters. They need to strike a good deal at the start in order to get their profit. So if a good purchase price is obtained then all the hard work has been done. It is all about the deal for a trader.

Definition of an investor

An investor is someone who buys and holds for a period longer than ten years and enjoys the fruits that ownership brings. Investors want to build up what they own to get larger and larger fruits. Examples include Warren Buffet, the Duke of Westminster, and me!

Investors evaluate the potential fruits to be gathered from owning the asset before buying. They have to look to the long term to obtain value from the asset, as opposed to the trader who just needs to know what they can sell an asset for in the short term.

TYPES OF TRADER

B2B

B2B means Business to Business. A B2B trader sells direct to another business. They are also known as **wholesale** traders, or **in the trade**.

These traders do not have a department called 'Customer Service'! They like the fact that there is no touchy feely required. A business deals with another business with a view to trade long term. Maintaining relationships with business customers is very important as you will have very few customers, sometimes only one.

B2C

A B2C trader sells to the end user. The person they are selling to is a consumer of their product or service. Other names for such traders are **retailers**, **shop front**, **front facing**.

There is more glitter to these businesses. Presentation has to be tip-top and they need to adopt an attitude of 'the customer is always right'. Customers may be referred to as 'clients' and a well-structured customer service department is often necessary.

TYPES OF INVESTOR

So you want to invest in property, but for what reason, and how are you going to do this? Well, there are many ways to invest in property but we have narrowed these down to five types relative to London. Investors can be broadly categorized into one of the following seven types and it is up to you to decide which category you fit into.

1. Cash and equity investor

Objective: To maximize rental income and capital growth combined. Will sell the property when this further achieves this objective.

This investor's approach is a semi-business approach. The investor has no love for the property and is only interested in the overall money the property is going to make. He will sell if the market is high or hold if the rental income is good. His intentions are to reinvest any monies gained into other property. This type of investor will have a good degree of interest in the property market and will stay abreast of developments and trends.

2. Pension investor

Objective: To cover all costs involved with the house by the rental income and to have paid off the mortgage by retirement age. The rental income (or return on sale) thus provides a retirement income.

This investor will be at least 15 years off retirement age. He will look for a property with good rental demand if he intends to live off the rental income on retirement. If he is also considering selling the property in order to purchase an annuity he will also look for a high capital growth area. As good practice this type of investor should evaluate whether their equity in the property will purchase an income greater than the rental income being generated currently.

3. Holiday investor

Objective: To cover some of the costs of owning the house by letting it out; ultimately to get a holiday home.

Typically an investor with a family who wishes to save on holiday costs and eventually pass down the property to his children, or release the value of his nest-egg. Saving money rather than making money is the motivation for this investor. He will seek non-conventional investment properties such as cottages, away from city centres and amenities, and restricted occupancy homes.

4. Retirement investor

Objective: To cover all costs involved with the house by the rental income and to have paid off the mortgage by retirement age. Then sell own home to move into the investment home.

Non-typical investment properties may be sought, possibly in a surrounding village or near to a main town or city. The major concern for this investor is tenant demand so choice of location is key. The investor will use the proceeds from the sale of his original home to clear outstanding mortgages and purchase an annuity.

5. University investor

Objective: To provide a home for offspring while they are at university. Will either sell or hold after the three years.

This investor is likely to purchase a four-bed (or more) home near the university; the son or daughter will live in one room and rent the others to their friends. The rental income will cover all costs involved; the property will then be sold for profit or held and rented out again through the university. The overall profit on the investment is the boarding fees saved in those three years and the gain on the sale of the property.

6. Downshifter investor

Objective: To sell existing home and buy a lifestyle property with no outstanding mortgage.

This investor will realize the gain in their home free from tax and purchase a property that will change both their location and their job. Typical properties are B&Bs and shops with living accommodation above.

7. Business investor

Objective: To maximize rental income to replace salary from full-time employment.

The investor will look for high-yielding properties and invest in high tenant demand areas, as he relies on this income. He will be interested in the property market and be abreast of the latest prices, mortgage rates and rental figures. This way he can ensure that his net income is maximized.

ARE YOU A TRADER OR AN INVESTOR?

I hope you will now be able to decide if indeed you want to be an investor, what type of investor, and more importantly what you want to get from your investment. The whole process becomes easier when you are clear exactly what you are looking for.

Are you a trader or an investor? Are you doing this full-time or part-time? From reading the first chapters I hope you can confidently say you are one of the following.

- ☐ Full-time investor.
- ☐ Full-time trader.
- ☐ Part-time investor.
- ☐ Part-time trader.
- ☐ Hobby investor.
- ☐ Hobby trader.

I am a full-time investor. I am in it with all my heart and for the long term. I am so convinced that property investment is my path to wealth and freedom that it is my first priority. My other property businesses are supporting businesses to feed capital into my long-term investment plans with regards to property investment. Now since I have mentioned capital it brings me nicely on to the next chapter.

3

RAISING THE STARTING CAPITAL

Living like a pauper will prepare you for your property business. Why? Well, you have to do three things to get into self-employment. You have to:

1. Minimize your fixed costs of living.
2. Raise your initial investment to start your own business.
3. Maintain your fixed costs of living.

MINIMIZE YOUR FIXED COSTS OF LIVING

The most important factor in business is cash. The biggest cash drain anyone has is their cost of living. If you can control that and reduce it to the bare minimum then you are more likely to survive in the initial stages of self-employment.

There are really only two core ways of minimizing your fixed costs of living: **going without** (i.e. not spending!) and **cutting costs** (i.e. spending less!).

Going without – not spending

When you get paid, put a certain amount aside so you can't get at it. Put it in a separate deposit account, give it to a family member or hide it under your mattress – whatever you do, don't spend it! You'll soon adjust to the new level of spending that you have at your disposal.

Always ask yourself – do I really *need* this item that I'm buying now or do I just *want* it? When I was setting up my business I went without a number of things that I used to spend money on regularly. These included newspapers and magazines, CDs, designer clothes, meals at restaurants, and nights out in London bars and nightclubs. I also moved into lodgings to save money.

I knew that if I went without now I would gain in the future, and that is what happened. I hope this inspires you. Saving for a route out can be very rewarding. When you do start your own business the positive results can be immediate: the labours of your scrimping and saving will result in you having enough time for your family, friends and yourself.

Spending less

There are really only five things you generally spend your money on: food and consumables, shelter, travel, entertainment and clothing, and loans and savings plans. Here are some tips on how to cut back on spending on each of these categories.

1. Food and consumables

Apart from the savings, it is probably healthier. Go round to your mum's! Your family may be more than willing to help. But always remember those who helped you when you get to the top.

Try non-branded goods. Often the quality is as good as the branded ones. And don't forget buy one get one free. Every supermarket does this. If you have time visit different ones and take advantage of their deals.

2. Shelter

Rent a room rather than a flat or house. You could improve your social life as well as save money.

Switch utilities suppliers. Be constantly on the lookout for new tariffs for gas, electricity, telephone and mobiles.

Shop around for contents insurance. Never renew a premium without looking for a better deal.

Consider purchasing second-hand furniture. Don't be tempted by 0% finance deals – save the cash and buy new later.

3. Travel

Sell the car. Calculate whether the amount you spend a month on the car is greater than if you walked, cycled, took the train or bus and took taxis. If it is – then it's time to sell the car!

Or, downsize your car so that the costs are reduced. Consider third party only insurance. Shop around for cheap service deals.

Try walking or get a bike. You will save money *and* get fit!

4. Entertainment and clothing

Shop in the sales, markets and charity shops. You may be surprised how well stocked some market traders are now. And is it a need or a want? If you master making this decision alone then half the battle is won.

When you go out – don't stay out late. Go home early! You'll find that you will still have some cash in your pocket.

Look out for deals offered in bars, clubs, cinemas and restaurants such as two for one meals or tickets.

5. Loans and savings plans

Switch credit cards and loans to obtain the best deals. Some deals can really save you money. And make an effort to clear those balances!

Cash in endowment policies. Freeze payments to pension plans. You need as much cash available as possible.

RAISE YOUR INITIAL INVESTMENT

Apart from saving part of your current income, there are other quick ways of raising your initial investment to start your business. How much that is depends on the type of business but below is a list of inventive ways of raising cash fast. The items are listed in order of the 'cost' to you, starting with the cheapest first. By cost I mean the effective interest rate being paid on the initial investment. BOE means current Bank of England base rate.

Sources of cash

Personal assets

Cost: 0%

Sell some of your assets to realise some cash. This may be jewellery, cars, furniture, pieces of art, electrical equipment. Look in the garage or attic – you may be surprised!

Savings

Cost: BOE

Cash in your savings in deposit accounts or cash ISAs. The cost will be that year's lost interest.

Endowment policies or company shares

Cost: BOE + 3%

You could surrender an endowment policy or liquidize a current share portfolio. However, talk to your financial adviser or stockbroker before taking this action. It could be time to let go of some poorly performing stocks and enter the property arena, as many share market investors are doing now.

The cost of this is roughly equivalent to the average return delivered on the stock market. This, of course, will depend on the type of policy or stocks you hold. You could be better off if you do sell now to avoid a loss in the future.

Borrow from family

Cost: BOE + 4%

Do you have a family member who has cash sitting in the bank and is willing to lend it to you? Offer them a better rate of return than any deposit account could. If you are lucky they may lend it to you at 0%, but if you offer a return of BOE + 4% you might get quite a few positive responses.

Could you access your inheritance early? Many families do this to avoid inheritance tax. As long as the donor lives seven years beyond the date of the gift no inheritance tax is payable.

Secured borrowings

Cost: BOE + 2–7%

For this you must already own a property. The cheapest way is to remortgage the whole property and release the equity tied up in your home. It pays to shop around. A good mortgage broker could probably beat the current rate that you are paying and even reduce your monthly payments while still raising you some cash on top.

The other way is to get a second charge loan where you keep your existing mortgage and borrow on the remaining equity on the house. You've probably seen the TV ads promising you a new car or holiday. Well, forget that – we're going into business!

Unsecured borrowings

Cost: BOE + 2–15%

The cheapest way to do this is by transferring a current credit card balance to a new credit card with introductory rate offers. You draw out as much cash as you can on your current credit card and then apply for a credit card that has a low introductory rate for balance transfers until the balance is cleared. Once your new credit card has been approved you transfer your existing balance on your old credit card to the new credit card at the introductory rate, typically BOE + 2%. This rate is fixed until you clear the balance.

You may, however, not get this new credit card. The other way is to draw down the cash on your existing credit card at the credit card rate. This can be expensive but if the business has guaranteed customers lined up then you could use the cash on a short-term basis, say one to two years, and use the profits to clear the credit card balance over that period.

You may be able to arrange an overdraft with your bank or a personal loan at around BOE + 6%. You need to speak to your bank manager.

Other unsecured lenders involve high arrangement fees and the interest rate can even go up to BOE + 35%! Shop around, steer clear of anything with an interest rate higher than 25% unless you are really desperate and the business idea is a dead cert.

Get a partner

Another way to raise cash is by taking on a financial partner. The financial risk is borne by the partner but you end up doing all the work. However, the partner will be entitled to a share of your profits and you will not be free to do what you want with the business. The cost to you will depend on how successful the business is as the cost will be the share of profits. This is the most expensive way to finance a business, but it can also be the cheapest, if the whole project fails, as your partner has taken the full financial risk. If this is the only method available to you to get into business I would still advise you to do it – you will still be freeing yourself from the rat race.

This is not an exhaustive list and you may have other good ideas for raising finance but if you can't raise the finance the project can't go ahead. It's as simple as that.

MAINTAIN YOUR FIXED COSTS OF LIVING

In an ideal world as soon as you go in to business it will make a profit and these profits will maintain your fixed costs of living. However, it is more likely that you will make a loss in the first year – but your fixed costs of living still have to be met! So how do we raise this short term cash requirement? Well, it can come from three sources. These are, in the order you should seek from them: you, family and friends, and outside sources.

You

Go part-time at work

This will give you time to start your business to see how well it does. Once you are up and running and getting a satisfactory income you can leave work completely.

Get a flexible part-time contract

If you can, work hours to suit you that won't affect the setting up of your business and allow your fixed costs to be maintained. Examples include handcraft jobs or parcel deliveries, or flexible jobs where you can work for short periods at a time such as temping, strawberry picking or taxi driving. Do not feel that these jobs are beneath you. Once your business takes off you can take pride in the fact that you did them.

Get a complementary job

What better way to find out about running a business than to go and work for that type of business? If you want to run a restaurant, go and get a job in a restaurant! You will acquire tricks and tips and get a feel as to what it would be like to run that type of business. Apart from paying your bills this strategy will help you establish whether that business is right for you.

Family and friends

Gifted contributions

As mentioned earlier, you may be surprised by the support you get from people around you. If you make your family and social circle aware of what you are doing they may well move forward certain cash gifts that were planned. A family member of mine gave me £5,000 in cash to invest that was to be left to me upon their death. It can be very tax efficient if your family members do give you cash early as you can avoid inheritance tax in certain circumstances, usually when the deceased has more than £259,000 to leave. Do seek professional advice on this.

Loans

In certain cultures it is commonplace to borrow from friends. If you are part of a tight-knit community and you know that people trust you, then why not ask? They can only say no!

Ad hoc work

Use your contacts. If a family member or friend can get you a short-term job while you are setting up your business then go for it! Any quick income will help you keep up with your bills.

Outside

Loans

Not the most ideal way to fund your fixed costs of living. If you are thinking of taking a loan try and get 12 months' worth of your shortfall and aim to pay it off over the longest period possible. This way your monthly loan repayments are kept to a minimum. Also, if you can, get a loan that does not penalize you if you pay it off early. If your business does better than expected you can redeem the debt when you want, thus saving on interest.

Overdrafts

Overdrafts may be more suitable as they can be paid off as and when you wish. Apply for an overdraft facility *before* you leave work; you will be unlikely to get one once you have no provable income. With overdrafts you pay interest on the balance outstanding only and on a daily basis. If the business does well at the start the overdraft can be redeemed sooner than planned.

When I left work I had a £10,000 overdraft facility in place. I let it run up to around £5,000 before business picked up but I was thankful that I had such a facility.

Credit cards

I don't care what people say about credit cards – they are great! It's the cardholders that don't know how to use them that give them a bad name. One of my current credit card providers offered me £10,000 in cash at 0.7% APR for four months – so I took it! I will use it to fund property purchases and then redeem it in time when one of my remortgages come through.

As long as you have a plan to repay the credit card company within a set period of time there is nothing to beat a credit card in the speed of raising cash – precisely when you need it.

CASH IS KING

As you can see, you have to be mature in the way you handle cash, be active in raising cash and be inventive when it comes to raising cash fast. Cash is crucial to running a business and ensuring that it survives. It doesn't really matter where it comes from, as long as you can pay your debts when they fall due – then you remain in business. The definition of insolvency, or bankruptcy, is when the debtor is unable to pay his or her debts in full *and* on time. So to remain in the black you always have to have access to cash – fast!

So you've learned how to preserve, earn and raise cash – what are you going to do with it? You need to invest it! Time to identify what business you are going to do.

PART TWO: THE PROPERTY CLOCK

4

UNDERSTANDING THE PROPERTY PRICE CYCLE

THE PROPERTY CLOCK'S EXISTENCE

Property prices follow a cyclical pattern. Property prices rise and then property prices fall. The reasons why this happens will become apparent later. So what is the best time for an investor to become interested? When the prices start to rise, of course!

If we were to speed up this process over a notional 12-hour period, with 12 o'clock being the point at they first rise and 6 o'clock being the point they first start to fall then we would have the diagram in Figure 1.

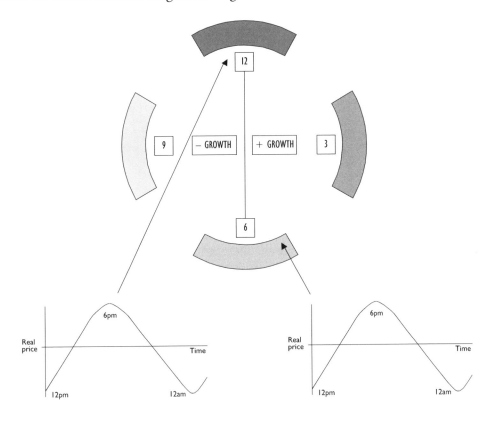

Figure 1.

So at 12 p.m. prices increase until 6 p.m. and then they start to fall. We can see that anyone that has any sense gets interested anywhere between 12 p.m. and 6 p.m. So who buys between 12 p.m. and 6 p.m. and why do they buy?

A **professional property investor** will buy a property that will enable him to buy other properties *and* make money. That is, it will enable him to benefit from capital growth so that he can remortgage and buy further properties. When rented out it will, after voids, letting agent fees, tax and other expenses, provide a positive cashflow.

A **novice/speculative investor** will invest in a growth area because they believe that the trend upwards in price will continue. They are less concerned in fundamentals as they are not aware of them – they simply believe that the trend is upwards.

The **owner-occupier** will buy because if they delay buying it will cost them more. It is in their interest to buy sooner rather than later as their overall purchase price will be higher the longer they leave it.

So who buys between 6 p.m. and 12 p.m.? Prices are falling now, so the novice/ speculative investor loses interest as there are no capital growth prospects and the owner occupier will wait until the prices drop further. The only buyer remaining is the **professional investor**.

The only time a professional property investor will buy in this market is if the investment puts money in his pocket. He will invest in a falling market if the property market is providing him with a better return on his other investments, such as the stock market, other businesses or a bank or building society. It is the professional property investor that prevents the property market falling to nothing, and provides the cushion to the fall.

Based on this information we can see that the professional investor buys on known information, i.e. the property purchase puts money in their pocket. The novice/ speculative investor and owner-occupier buy based only on the fact that the trend of the prices is rising.

So how does the professional investor calculate whether a property will put money in his pocket? Well it's called gross yield. Gross yield, in mathematical terms, is:

$$\frac{\text{Annual rent}}{\text{Property purchase price}}$$

Now annual rent is a pretty static figure. Rents simply rise slowly and steadily, the same way wages do. So in real terms they remain the same. But property prices are far more volatile. They gather momentum far in excess of the rate of wage inflation and hence rise and fall greater than the rate of inflation – but we will get to that later. Assuming we agree with the stability of rental prices and the volatility of property prices, we can show that: *Property prices are inversely related to yield.* That is to say, as property prices rise the yield falls. Let me show you this example:

Annual rent: £10,000
Property price: £100,000

Yield is then:

$$\frac{£10,000}{£100,000} = 10\%$$

Let's say that the property price increases to £110,000 in six months. A professional investor considering the market will now consider the yield to be:

$$\frac{£10,000}{£110,000} = 9.1\%$$

As the property price *increases* from £100,000 to £110,000 the yield *decreases* from 10% to 9.1%.

Now let's say that the property price falls from £100,000 to £90,000 in six months. A professional investor considering the market will now consider the yield to be:

$$\frac{£10,000}{£90,000} = 11.1\%$$

As the property price *decreases* from £100,000 to £90,000 the yield *increases* from 10% to 11.1%.

This is called an inverse relationship as the yield and property price move in different directions. So if we were to create a yield vs time graph then it would be the exact opposite of the real price vs time graph (Figure 1). Fitting the yield curves into the clock we get Figure 2.

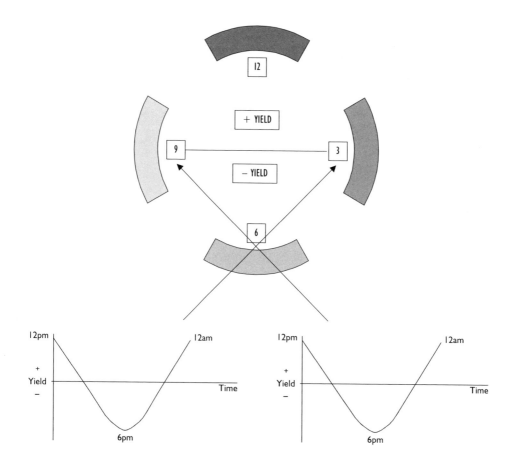

Figure 2.

So if you're a sensible investor then you will invest during 12 p.m. to 3 p.m. and 9 p.m. to 12 p.m. Any investment you make will make money because it's a positive yield.

If we superimpose these two strategies then we come up with the face of the property clock (see Figure 3).

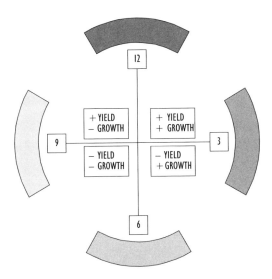

Figure 3.

But every clock needs power to move round the face. For the property clock I call these drivers. Figure 4 shows the drivers that push the property clock round with regularity.

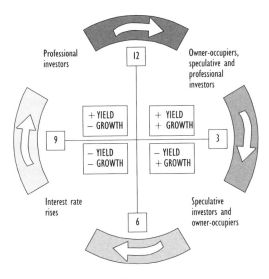

Figure 4.

We can see that:

☐ everybody drives the price from 12 p.m. to 3 p.m.;
☐ speculative investors and owner-occupiers only drive the prices from 3 p.m. to 6 p.m.;

☐ interest rate rises drive the price then downwards from 6 p.m. to 9 p.m.;
☐ professional investors drive the price downwards even further from 9 p.m. to 12 a.m. but prevent the prices from falling to zero.

The clock quarter regions can be named quite specifically as:

12 p.m. – 3 p.m.	Hot spot
3 p.m. – 6 p.m.	Cooling spot
6 p.m. – 9 p.m.	Cold spot
9 p.m. – 12 a.m.	Warm spot

The names will be explained later. Now, we have the complete face, drivers and names for each clock quarter for the property clock (see Figure 5).

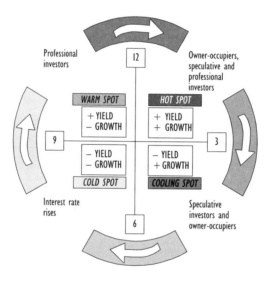

Figure 5.

This clock is relevant to any property market with the following.

☐ A variable interest rate environment.
☐ Easily obtainable buy-to-let mortgage.
☐ A lack of long-term fixed interest rate mortgages (typically greater than ten years).

The UK market fits this model. If any of these conditions are eliminated then the clock slows down. If all conditions are eliminated then the clock STOPS! Assuming that these things don't happen, the strategy is to know when the clock strikes 12 p.m. most importantly, and know when the clock strikes 3 p.m., 6 p.m. and 9 p.m.

I am going to ignore wage inflation. Even though a house may cost twice as much in 20 years' time you can be sure that you will be earning twice as much. I am going to assume real prices. This makes the figures simple. Actual prices rise and fall but real prices remain the same.

UNDERSTANDING GROWTH

Calculating growth

Many investors invest in property solely for the growth. They are not concerned with making a rental profit (and are sometimes happy to make a rental loss!) but with making an above average gain on their initial investment. Annual Capital Growth (ACG) can be determined by:

$$\text{Current Market Value after one year of purchase (CMV}_1) - \text{Purchase Price (PP)}$$
$$= \text{Annual Capital Growth (AGC}_1)$$

Basically it's how much your property has gone up in value in a year of ownership. For future years ACG is:

$$CMV_n - CMV_{n-1} = ACG_n$$

In simple terms it's the difference between the value of the property now and the value one year ago.

Understanding + /- growth

Understanding why property prices rise and then fall is vital if we want to make money! It is property prices that drive yield, *not* the other way round, hence what affects property prices is most important. Property prices are volatile while rents are stable. Experts call the rise and fall in property prices the boom bust cycle. The boom bust cycle will be directly related to two things: the **general economy**, and **land values**. This is because property is (1) *built* on land, and (2) *bought* with money.

So a full understanding of the limited nature of land and the dynamics of the economy will enable you to see where we are in relation to the boom bust cycle. Certain principles need to be explained before we enter the boom bust cycle.

☐ Land is in limited supply.
No matter what we do, nothing can increase the supply of land greater than the surface area of the UK. Undeveloped land belongs predominant to the aristocracy and local councils. Certain areas, such as London, will *always* attract the speculator. Massive profits can be made by simply holding on to a piece of land until the surrounding land gets developed.

☐ The population is growing.
An increase in population means an increase in the number of homes needed, and business premises, which causes a pressure on land requirements. Overall land values *have* to increase.

☐ Increase in land values causes an increase in the development of land sites.
A landowner will happily hold on to a piece of land as there is no cost to this. If land values rise in line with the overall state of the economy, he will be tempted to sell at a profit to a developer who then builds on the land, or the landowner will develop the land himself.

☐ An increase in the development of land causes an increase in infrastructure.
More amenities are required to service the developed areas, such as train stations, better road links, schools, etc. This causes overall land values to increase further.

☐ Due to the rise in land values, saving increases.
Money can only either be spent or reinvested. The general public are attracted to the returns to be had from property developments and increase saving resulting in less spending on the high street and a fall in consumption.

☐ The fall in consumption is hidden by the feel-good factor.
Because home-owners experience an increase in the value of their home they use this security to borrow, and spend on the high street. This increase in borrowing to spend is greater than the amount saved to invest (mentioned above), thus overall consumption increases.

☐ A trade deficit occurs as a result in the rise of consumption.
Imports exceed exports to cope with the rate of consumption. This causes a deficit. The government must raise rates to attract outside investment to finance the deficit.

☐ As rates rise the returns from property look less attractive.
The boom is due to property looking attractive to speculative investors because of capital growth. If rates rise property price growth stabilizes and thus expected growth is no longer factored into the overall return.

If the availability of land was not restricted then real prices would fluctuate as shown in Figure 6. However, the availability of land to be developed is restricted due to speculation, thus real prices fluctuate as shown in Figure 7. Real prices rise and fall to a greater degree and over a shorter period of time.

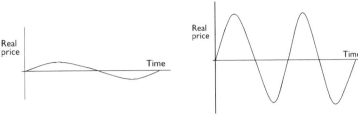

Figure 6.   Figure 7.

The start of the boom

Let's start when everything is at a sensible price. There is no rapid increase or decrease in prices, supply equals demand and so prices are stable. As the population is growing so is the demand by businesses and individuals to buy commercial and residential property. This means that:

- □ properties are knocked down and built even higher (i.e. the number of floors) to accommodate the increase in demand;
- □ properties are built in the undeveloped areas to cope with the increased demand;
- □ infrastructure increases to cope with the increase in population.

This is what is supposed to happen but invariably doesn't! Some landowners do not develop their land and hold out for greater increases in value. This in turn causes:

- □ Development in areas away from the city centre, which puts a strain on the infrastructure. Building in a small village near a city centre means that the road connecting the burgeoning village to the city has to be upgraded and perhaps a train station constructed.

- □ Increased infrastructure surrounding the city, thus creating a continual cycle of surrounding villages becoming overdeveloped and undeveloped land within the centre becoming worth potentially millions.

- □ Commercial and residential property within the city centre becomes over-enhanced (i.e. knocked down and built again to a high spec), which costs a fortune to the investor but with the hope of an even bigger return.

- □ Developers buy sub-prime land for development a long way into the future, thus bypassing greedy landowners with high prices on prime plots. However, the money invested by the developer is removed from the economy.

So in all, due to the limited supply of land, and rising prices (and to any number of property programmes or friends' stories of how they made a small fortune), it's only a matter of time before – the **property speculator** emerges. The speculator assumes that you can buy a property, do nothing and then sell it in a year and make more than the average annual salary!

Middle of the boom

Due to the introduction of the speculator, who is really only a novice investor, property prices are over-predicted. This means that existing buildings can be sold to them at inflated prices, or plots of land sold to developers (who are speculators also) resell the newly built properties to other speculators because the speculator's view is that the property's value is heading in only one direction – UP!

As prices rise artificially high this encourages even more to be spent on them to gain a higher profit. People save more, in order to invest in property, and thus spend less on the high street, lowering overall consumption. However, this is masked temporarily by what's known as the 'feel-good factor'.

Some home-owners feel 'richer' so they spend on the high street by obtaining unsecured debt such as credit cards or loans. They know that the increase in the value of their home can be accessed, by remortgaging, if they struggle to meet the debt. So consumption is maintained by credit provided by the banks.

Towards the end of the boom

Consumption is now fuelled by over-borrowing, and increases to an all-time high. This causes a trade deficit to occur. This is because people save to invest in property, hence money is taken out of the domestic economy and the production of goods at home naturally falls. Importation of goods abroad is the only way we can satisfy the increase in consumption. We also have to export less to further meet consumer demand.

A trade deficit is where imports exceed exports. That is, we buy more from abroad than we do goods produced at home. As a result the government loses revenue through taxes due to companies not producing enough to tax, so the government has to borrow to pay for its spending. The only people that are willing to lend will be from abroad. To attract investors from abroad the government gilt rate has to be increased. Increased gilt rates ultimately results in rising interest rates.

At the peak

It's not a pretty place at the peak! The following misunderstandings and interpretations are occurring.

- ☐ Investments are being made by speculators who are basing their returns on historical growth. Fundamental principles have gone out the window and investment decisions are being based on previous (and successful) speculative trades and success stories of other investors.

- ☐ Consumption is being fuelled by credit cards and second charge secured loans by home-owners feeling good, and the reluctance of the consumer to save due to continued increases in their property values.

- ☐ Lenders are lending on perceived equity to home-owners as a result of speculation.

- ☐ Investing, consuming, lending and borrowing are in excess.

- ☐ Interest rates are rising to cope with the trade deficit, consumer price inflation and to attract people back to saving.

The crash

Something has to cause the crash. They do not happen overnight but they happen a lot quicker than a boom. Think of a roller-coaster: slowly to the top of the slope, then when it tips over the edge . . .

The following will happen, and at a greater pace than the climb.

- ☐ Interest rate rises are increased to hurt! They are set to control inflation as we have been spending too much on the high street.

- ☐ With the increased interest rate the projected positive cashflows fall. This lowers the overall return on uncompleted capital intensive projects such as the erection of skyscrapers or new builds of luxury apartments.

- ☐ The calculation of possible investments now includes the higher rate of interest rate and they no longer look so attractive.

- ☐ The property development market slows.

Now if all this speculation had been done with private money then we wouldn't care. The problem is that it's been done with other people's money, i.e. the bank's! It's the pulling of the plug by the bank that causes the rapid decline in property investment. A clear chain of reactions can be seen in Figure 8.

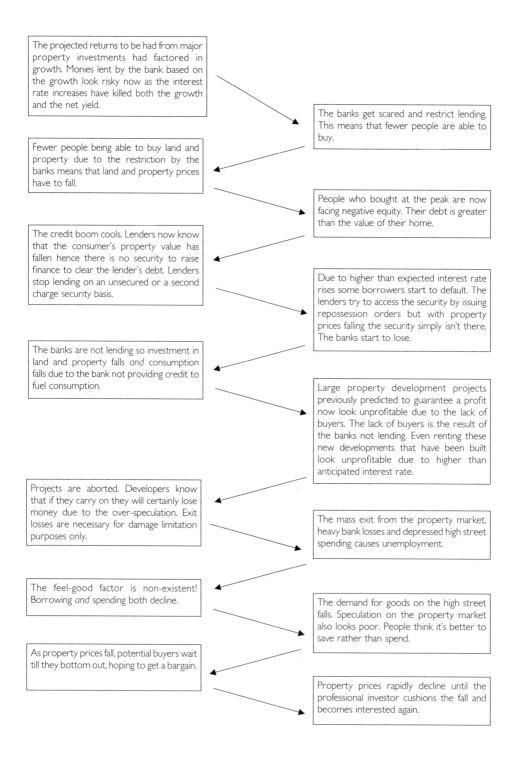

The projected returns to be had from major property investments had factored in growth. Monies lent by the bank based on the growth look risky now as the interest rate increases have killed both the growth and the net yield.

The banks get scared and restrict lending. This means that fewer people are able to buy.

Fewer people being able to buy land and property due to the restriction by the banks means that land and property prices have to fall.

People who bought at the peak are now facing negative equity. Their debt is greater than the value of their home.

The credit boom cools. Lenders now know that the consumer's property value has fallen hence there is no security to raise finance to clear the lender's debt. Lenders stop lending on an unsecured or a second charge security basis.

Due to higher than expected interest rate rises some borrowers start to default. The lenders try to access the security by issuing repossession orders but with property prices falling the security simply isn't there. The banks start to lose.

The banks are not lending so investment in land and property falls *and* consumption falls due to the bank not providing credit to fuel consumption.

Large property development projects previously predicted to guarantee a profit now look unprofitable due to the lack of buyers. The lack of buyers is the result of the banks not lending. Even renting these new developments that have been built look unprofitable due to higher than anticipated interest rate.

Projects are aborted. Developers know that if they carry on they will certainly lose money due to the over-speculation. Exit losses are necessary for damage limitation purposes only.

The mass exit from the property market, heavy bank losses and depressed high street spending causes unemployment.

The feel-good factor is non-existent! Borrowing *and* spending both decline.

The demand for goods on the high street falls. Speculation on the property market also looks poor. People think it's better to save rather than spend.

As property prices fall, potential buyers wait till they bottom out, hoping to get a bargain.

Property prices rapidly decline until the professional investor cushions the fall and becomes interested again.

Figure 8. (Source: www.landvalue.tax.org)

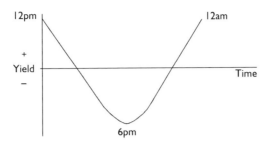

This is why property prices move up and down. If we look at the real price vs time graph, 12 p.m. is the beginning of the boom and 6 p.m. is the beginning of the bust. I *really* want you to understand this boom bust cycle. Understanding these fundamentals will ensure that you *never* lose in property investment. Please reread this section as many times as it takes so you make sense of how the boom bust cycle works. Then we can move on to yield, which is the ultimate tool for any serious property investor.

UNDERSTANDING YIELD

Calculating yield

How does a professional investor know that a property purchase is going to put money in his pocket? Well, it's called yield. Yield is defined as *what you get out relative to what you put in*.

Let's look at this in detail. Yield has two key variables: what you get out, and what you put in. So to calculate yield you simply divide what you get out by what you put in and express it as a percentage.

$$\frac{\text{What you get out}}{\text{What you put in}} \times 100$$

What you get out

What do you get out from property? – RENT! But it's not just as simple as that. You have to consider the *expected* rent and *expected* costs. Does the professional investor include capital growth? No, because it is unknown, even though the professional investor may have an inkling. So the output for a professional investor is the annual rent minus the annual interest cost, expenses and tax.

The annual rent is the amount you expect to receive from your tenant for use of your property only. You do not include payments from your tenant that are considered expenses, such as water rates or council tax, if you do include this in your rent. You calculate it on an annual basis; returns are always calculated annually – it's industry standard. You assume a full year with no void periods. Void periods are dealt with below.

The annual interest cost is the annual amount you pay to the bank as a result of obtaining borrowings to purchase the property. Essentially it is the monthly mortgage payment you pay on an interest-only basis multiplied by 12.

Typical **expenses** will be:

☐ **Service charges and ground rent**. If you rent out a flat you are responsible for the service charges and ground rent. These are the costs to maintain the block and to keep the freeholder happy! These expenses can never be the responsibility of your tenant as non-payment of these charges can result in the loss of your flat as it is leasehold. Consider these costs before you buy a flat as some service charges can be extortionate.

☐ **Insurances**. You need buildings insurance to cover the property against damage or vandalism. Some areas are expensive to insure; get an idea of insurance premiums for the area before buying so you can see how much it will affect the overall output. You may want rent guarantees and maintenance insurances so these premiums will need to be accounted for.

☐ **Letting agent fees**. You may need to use a letting agent if you want to avoid the hassle of renting out the property. Costs vary: some letting agents charge 7% of the rent, others charge 17%! Get an idea first as the charge is applied to the rent so it hits the top line.

☐ **Repairs**. This cost has to be estimated, obviously. This expense alone can make the difference between making a profit or a loss. Over the long term, repairs even out through the life of the property but if you get hit for large repair bills early on it can leave you out of pocket for a while.

☐ **Void periods and bad debts**. If you are investing in a high-demand area then voids will be minimal but it's always good practice to assume one month per year. I invest in medium demand areas and I assume two months for some areas. Remember also that sometimes tenants do not pay! So the non-payment of rent is as good as a void. I charge 1 month as standard. So in total I charge three months worth of rent to this expense which is equivalent to 25% of the annual rent.

☐ **Admin costs**. Letters, tenancy agreements, postage and other office costs need to be estimated. The more properties you have the lower the overall cost as the cost is split between the properties.

□ **Other costs**. These depend on the property. Marketing costs will vary as to the location of the property, as will security costs for the property during void periods. These have to be budgeted for.

It's good to calculate this output as it determines whether it is a good investment. If the output is less than expected then you can walk away from the deal. If it meets your expectation or even surpasses it then it's worth considering. This output is commonly called the expected net profit of an investment. We would hope that this figure is positive!

Tax is an unavoidable expense. Unfortunately we all have to pay tax. Things to consider when taking into account the amount of tax you'll have to pay are:

□ **Allowable expenditure**. You have to check that the expenses above are tax deductible. Expenses have to be incurred necessarily, wholly and exclusively to the business for them to be deductible. If they're not then they will have to be added back when calculating your tax liability which will result in a higher tax charge.

□ **Allowable reliefs**. There will be certain reliefs available to you such as Wear & Tear allowance and capital allowances which the Inland Revenue allow you to apply to the profit. Even though these are not out of pocket expenses (i.e. no money has changed hands) you still can claim these reliefs to lower your overall profit thus reducing your tax charge.

□ **Basic or higher rate tax payer**. Higher rate tax payers are taxed at 40% compared with 20% for a basic rate tax payer. This means that you receive less of the profit. It may be more beneficial to invest in other more tax-efficient investments geared towards higher rate tax payers.

Tax-free investments benefit the higher rate tax payers the most. Investments such as ISAs and private pensions are out there as alternatives to property investments. You have to look at the yields from these investments and compare them with property. I can tell you now that property returns way in excess of any of these investments but ultimately it's up to you where you invest!

What you get out should only ever be assessed by what you put in. So let's look at what you put in.

What you put in

Well, you can be assured that you'll have to put in some of your hard-earned cash! How much depends on what you've got and what you're willing to borrow. There can only ever be two sources for investment – your cash and borrowed cash. You need to decide what type of investor – high, medium or low risk – you are before calculating yield.

High risk investor

What you put in: Nil
Your cash: None
Borrowed cash: Purchase price + acquisition costs = total cost of investment

You borrow the whole of the cost of the investment: the deposit, the mortgage amount, solicitor costs, arrangement fees and valuation fees, by way of a mortgage and unsecured borrowings. On the surface the yield would again be infinity. However, because you have borrowed all the money your ability to service the debt is dependent on the yield so yield becomes very important. The yield of the investment is more important than for the other types of investor as it has to be compared with the average interest rate you're borrowing at. If the yield is lower than the average rate then the investment will lose money. See further below.

Medium risk investor

What you put in: Some
Your cash: Deposit + acquisition costs
Borrowed cash: Purchase price – deposit = mortgage

This is the normal way people invest in property. You put in some but the bank puts in the lion's share. Typical ratios of your money to the bank's money are anywhere between 15:85 to 40:60. So you want to know what return you expect to get on your own money invested. This is called Return On Capital Employed (ROCE), capital being another name for your own personal contribution to the investment.

Low risk investor

What you put in: All
Your cash: Purchase price + acquisition costs
Borrowed cash: None

If only! You are rich enough to fund the whole purchase price and acquisition costs from your own savings. There are no borrowings. You need to calculate the yield so you can make a direct comparison with other investments.

As mentioned above, to calculate yield you simply divide what you get out by what you put in and express it as a percentage (multiply by 100).

Computing your calculation

So the magic calculations that need to be computed, based on what you put in and get out detailed above, are as follows.

High risk investor

$$\frac{(Annual\ rent - Annual\ mortgage\ cost - Annual\ loan\ cost - Expenses - Tax) \times 100}{Deposit + Acquisition\ costs}$$

This is the real cashflow inward to you after every expense including tax relative to what you theoretically put in. It includes the borrowing cost of both the mortgage and the unsecured loan obtained to purchase the property. Even though you have put in nothing you have to assess whether the money you borrowed on an unsecured basis is returning you a good yield.

Medium risk investor

$$\frac{(Annual\ rent - Annual\ mortgage\ cost - Expenses - Tax) \times 100}{Deposit + Acquisition\ costs}$$

Unlike the high risk investor there is no annual unsecured loan cost as you have put in your savings. You need to know whether the yield is better than keeping your money in the bank.

Low risk investor

$$\frac{(Annual\ rent - Expenses - Tax) \times 100}{Property\ purchase\ price + Acquisition\ costs}$$

Unlike both investors above there is no borrowing cost. However, you need to know whether the yield is better than keeping your money in the bank.

The example of Tom, Dick and Harry

Let's look at an example to calculate the yields. Tom, Dick and Harry are all higher rate tax payers but they have very different risk profiles. They see a property advertised for £100,000 but adopt different strategies to buy the property.

☐ **Tom**, a high risk investor, will borrow £27,000 on an unsecured basis to raise the deposit of £25,000 and £2,000 acquisition costs. He will then obtain the other £75,000 by way of a mortgage to purchase the property.

☐ **Dick**, a medium risk investor, will fund the deposit and acquisition costs from his savings. He will then obtain the other £75,000 by way of a mortgage to purchase the property.

47

□ **Harry**, a low risk investor, will fund the property price and acquisition costs with his savings.

They estimate that it can rent out for £1,000 per calendar month. They also estimate the annual expenses to derive a profit and loss account and calculate the yields for each investor (see tables).

Estimated expenses

	Tom	Dick	Harry
Rent	£12,000	£12,000	£12,000
Unsecured borrowing costs (interest only)	£1,750	N/A	N/A
Mortgage costs (interest only)	£4,500	£4,500	N/A
Void periods	£1,500	£1,500	£1,500
Service charges and ground rent	£1,000	£1,000	£1,000
Repairs	£500	£500	£500
Agents' fees	£1,050	£1,050	£1,050
Sundry	£450	£450	£450
Profit	**£1,250**	**£3,000**	**£7,500**
Tax @ 40%	£500	£1,200	£3,000
Net profit	**£750**	**£1,800**	**£4,500**

Calculated yields

Investor Result	Calculation	
Tom (high risk investor)	$\frac{(\text{Annual rent} - \text{Annual mortgage cost} - \text{Annual loan cost} - \text{Expenses} - \text{Tax}) \times 100}{\text{Deposit} + \text{Acquisition costs}}$ $\frac{£750 \times 100}{£27,000}$	2.8%
Dick (medium risk investor)	$\frac{(\text{Annual rent} - \text{Annual mortgage cost} - \text{Expenses} - \text{Tax}) \times 100}{\text{Deposit} + \text{Acquisition costs}}$ $\frac{£1800 \times 100}{£27,000}$	6.7%
Harry (low risk investor)	$\frac{(\text{Annual Rent} - \text{Expenses} - \text{Tax}) \times 100}{\text{Property purchase price} + \text{Acquisition costs}}$ $\frac{£4500 \times 100}{£102,000}$	4.4%

Now all these yields are positive, so the property purchase is expected to put money in the investor's pocket. The level of each of Tom, Dick and Harry's thresholds for investment will determine whether they will buy the property. So if Tom's threshold is 4% then he will not buy as the investment is below his 4% threshold. If Harry's threshold is 4% then Harry will buy as his yield is above his threshold. Their thresholds will be based on their own personal criteria and alternative investments. But you can be assured that if the yields were negative then the professional investor would *not* be interested. This is because the investment will take money out of his pocket.

Understanding + /– yield

It's obvious to see that when the clock strikes 12 p.m. you are winning on both counts. That is to say that:

☐ The yield is positive and at its highest point.
☐ The capital growth is positive and at its highest point.

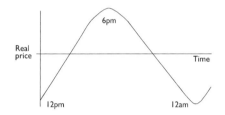 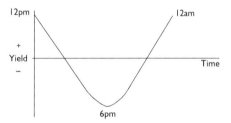

Looking at the real price vs time and yield vs line graphs, we can see that at 12 p.m. the property is at its lowest real price. As a result of this the yield is at its highest. Now due to the fact that rental prices are directly proportional to wages, which rise religiously with inflation, we can show that it's the property price alone that drives the yield. In other words the yield is only high due to the property purchase price being *artificially low* due to market conditions.

You have to draw on your own experiences to really believe what I'm saying. House prices have risen by 20% in a year, but do you ever see rental prices rising accordingly? – probably not. Rental prices are directionally proportional to wages. This makes sense. If you had volatile rental prices people would end up on the streets! So as we have eliminated inflationary influences from this model.

Another good thing about rents is that they are **known** and **predictable**.

They are known in that it is very easy to assess the market rental value for an average property. As long as the property is not unique in any way, then the market rental value will be comparable with similar properties on the market. The market will not entertain a rental property that is overpriced, as tenants will simply go elsewhere. So market rents tend to fall within a small range.

They are predictable in that rental values only increase with wage inflation. So we can assume that they will rise only modestly, and since we are ignoring inflation we can predict that rents will remain the same in real terms.

So we can see that over the four key points on the clock the yield is the inverse to the property purchase price. In other words, as property prices increase, yields decrease (see table).

Yield vs property price

	12 p.m.	3 p.m.	6 p.m.	9 p.m.
Property price	£50,000	£116,667	£233,333	£116,667
Annual rent	£10,000	£10,000	£10,000	£10,000
Annual mortgage cost @ 6% interest				
of property price	£3,000	£7,000	£14,000	£7,000
Other costs	£3,000	£3,000	£3,000	£3,000
Net yield	£7,000	£nil	(£7,000)	£nil

It is property prices that drive yield. In other words, the property price is everything! And knowing that the property price is everything we theoretically can ignore the yield curve as it is simply a result of the property price curve. An analysis of property prices is essential if we want to gain heavily – so read on!

PROPERTY PRICES – ACTUAL PRICES, REAL PRICES AND BUBBLES

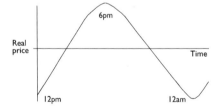

Looking at the property price curve again, at 12 p.m. we can see that the price is at the lowest point below the real price. Now in order to discover if you have found an area that is in the 12 p.m. to 3 p.m. range you need to compare the **real price** with the **actual price** the property can be bought for. If the actual price is less than the real price, then BINGO!

Determining the actual price

This is determined this as being 95% of the advertised price of a property. On average properties sell at 95% of their asking price. So if we see a property advertised for £60,000 then the actual price will be £60,000 × 95% = £57,000.

In reality the actual price is what you have to pay for the property. It could be 95%, 100% or even 105% of the asking price, depending on how competitive the market is. Under normal conditions 95% is about average.

Determining the real price

This is based on fundamental principles. It is the greater of two figures: (1) the price willing to be paid by a professional investor, and (2) the price willing to be paid by a first-time buyer.

Whichever is the greater will be the real price of the property. So we need to calculate both of these prices.

The price willing to be paid by a professional investor

This will be a function of what the investor could get elsewhere in the market. If an investor wishes to take no risk then he can stick his money in the bank and earn interest. If he wants to invest in property he will look for a premium as he is taking on risk. As property is a long-term investment he looks for a comparison investment of the same timescale that is risk free. The best rates you would get would be from a 20-year fixed interest government gilt.

A government gilt is a loan to the government. Assuming the government will not go bankrupt, it is risk free. Property is considered to be the next lowest risk investment. As an average, property investors require a minimum of 2% loading on a 20-year fixed government gilt for them to invest. This determines the yield required and hence sets the real value of the property. Let's look at an example:

Variables:

20-year fixed interest government gilt	5.62%
Property investor loading	2.00%
Annual rental value of property	£5,000

The real value would be: £5,000 × 1/(5.62% + 2.00%) = £65,616

This is the maximum value an investor would be willing to pay for a property with a rental value of £5,000. But the property price *could* be higher due to a first-time buyer being able to *afford* the property.

The price willing to be paid by a **first-time buyer**

This is calculated as follows:

$$\frac{\text{Salary} \times 4}{(0.95)}$$

This assumes that lenders will lend four times the buyer's salary if he puts down a 5% deposit on the property. If a first-time buyer wants the same property as in the above example, and his salary is £21,000, then he could afford a purchase price of: (£21,000 × 4)/(0.95) = £88,421.

So in this example the first-time buyer 'wins' and thus the real value of the property is £88,421.

Actual and real prices compared

If we look at the actual price compared with the real price we see that for both the investor and the owner-occupier the property is undervalued.

	Owner-occupier	Professional investor
Actual price	£57,000	£57,000
Real price	£88,421	£65,616
Undervaluation	**£31,421**	**£8,616**

We can see clearly that we are within the 12 p.m. to 3 p.m. quarter. Both the investor and the owner-occupier are interested as the prices willing to be paid by each are above the actual price. The owner-occupier has more to gain in buying than the investor, so aggressive bidding may occur, pushing the price up quickly and dramatically.

So who drives property prices? We all do! It's our attitude that drives a property price rather than interest rates. Interest rates play a part but its our propensity to borrow, the availability of borrowing, the willingness of lenders to lend and our fear of missing the boat that cause prices to rise.

Bubbles

So what is happening between 3 p.m. and 6 p.m? Effectively, properties are being sold above the asking price. Using the same example above, let's say that asking prices have rocketed to £100,000. Then we would have the actual price as: 95% × £100,000 = £95,000.

Both the professional investor and owner-occupier prices will remain the same as nothing will have changed. That is to say, over the period of rocketing property prices the following would have remained stable: gilt rates, salaries, the rental value of the property and lending criteria by the banks.

So we would have the following overvaluation.

	Owner-occupier	Professional investor
Actual price	£95,000	£95,000
Real price	£88,421	£65,616
Overvaluation	**£6,579**	**£29,384**

This overvaluation is what I call the **bubble** element to the actual property price. Specifically in this case it is £6,579: that is, the lower of the two overvaluations.

So who is buying the property at its actual price, £95,000? Well it certainly isn't the professional investor or standard owner-occupier. The people who are buying at inflated prices are:

☐ **The speculative investor**. This investor is banking on prices rising at the same rate as in the past. Also if the stock market is underperforming then the attraction of the property market is heightened. He buys then sells within a number of months or years to make a tidy profit. This type of investor can make money if he knows when to sell but he will only be selling to another speculative investor, or…

☐ **The scared owner-occupier**. This owner-occupier is scared of prices rising beyond affordability so he buys a property for more than what it is worth. A professional working couple may buy an unsuitable property like a studio flat or an ex-local authority one-bed flat. They *should* wait for prices to fall so that they can get a two-bed flat but fear drives them to buy a smaller property for an inflated price.

☐ **The over borrower**. This buyer will buy by using a deposit that has been raised by borrowing from a bank, credit card or loan company, or may get a self-certified mortgage by lying about their income. Either strategy will result in overborrowing. They also think, like the scared owner-occupier and speculative investor, that if they do not buy now they will miss out.

The bubble element exists when the actual price is greater than the real price and is the difference between the two figures. To spot bubble elements look at:

☐ **Type of property**. If you're buying a studio flat for the price equivalent to five times the salary of the typical purchaser then a bubble element may exist as the property is unaffordable to the typical purchaser. It may not have a bubble element if the rental value stacks up – see below.

- ☐ **Type of purchaser**. For a small one-bed flat in a city centre, consider what the average salary is for a worker in that city. The average city worker will be your main buyer as they invariably pay more than an investor. Could they afford what you are paying? If not then you may be buying at an artificially high price, unless it has a decent rental value – see below.

- ☐ **Rental value**. What does the property yield at? If the property yields greater than a 2% loading on the 20-year gilt rate then it's priced correctly. If it yields below then there may be a bubble element to the price.

- ☐ **Second and third-time buyers**. Bear in mind that people move up the property ladder. The gain from the sale of their original property contributes to the overall purchase price. For a two-bed home the typical purchaser may be a second-time buyer. The real value will be four times their salary *plus* the estimated gain on their previous property. If you are paying more than you calculate they could afford then a bubble element may exist.

Things to be aware of

20-year government gilt figure

Being aware of this will enable you to calculate the real value of the property. The real value is a function of a 2% loading of this rate.

Differential between long-term rate and current rate

If there is a significant difference between the long-term rate and the current rate then the property prices can rise or fall abnormally from their real property value. Close inspection of the differential will keep you ahead of the pack as you will see the lenders react and how property prices change.

Also be aware of heavily discounted mortgage products coming onto the market. If these deals become popular they can distort prices, forcing other lenders to reduce their rates and making the whole mortgage market even more competitive than it already is!

Rental value of property

You need to be aware of the rental values of property. You can then calculate the real value of a property in conjunction with your required return, which you can then compare with the actual asking price. If the real value is in excess of the asking price then take a look at the property!

Current market value of property

You need to be aware of the current market values of property. This involves searching on the net, looking in local papers and talking to estate agents. Based on your real value of property calculations you can see if the current market values look attractive.

We have set out the basis for the property clock. Now let's get on to the detail of each quarter.

12 P.M. TO 3 P.M. – THE HOTSPOT

At the start: 12 p.m.

The clock strikes 12 p.m. – but there's no gong! At this point hardly anyone knows that this area is a goldmine. It's a buyer's market. No one wants these properties and there are plenty of vendors desperate to sell. You walk in to the estate agents saying you want to buy and they roll out the red carpet! You, with your hard earned cash *and* the bank's money, want to buy big time.

The agent shows you details of over 20 properties all yielding in excess of 12%. You ask about the areas and despite reassurance you're not convinced. You're looking at the details of studios and one-bed flats yielding in excess of 20%. You ask to view all the properties and to your surprise the agent immediately books half the day to do so. A lot of them are empty; no one currently wants them as investments and some of the areas look a bit rough. However, you can be assured that it is only a matter of time before other investors follow and regenerate the area to solid rental markets.

You have to be brave to buy at 12 p.m. However, if you are brave you will make a fortune, as you have understood the concept of supply and demand. So you have to go where there is *low* demand for property and wait for the demand to rise. And you can be sure that it will rise.

12pm → 3pm

Yields of 12% to 20% are unsustainable. If a place remained at this level you could be plough all your savings and future income into the area and make a solid £50,000 out of every £100,000 invested if you bought wisely, even more if you took a risk. However, a good thing never lasts for ever. I will show you how it goes from 12 p.m. to 3 p.m. That is to say, the area goes from +growth and +yield to +growth and –yield.

Let's just say that I am alone in having found this magic area that is yielding in excess of 12%. So I buy as much as I can afford from every estate agent in the area, as soon as a property comes on the market that meets my criteria. It won't be long before other professional investors find this area too. So when other professional investors get wind of this magic area a bidding war commences.

It starts with properties being sold within 24 hours of coming onto the market, at full asking price. This sends signals to vendors that they can increase their selling prices. Even then vendors underestimate how much they could put up their prices by (due to the recent stagnation of the market). Professional investors will pay over their asking price. This is because they have set criteria to buy to. For example my criteria include buying at 12% yield. So if a property is selling at £30,000 and I know that it will still yield 12% at £35,000, and it's a competitive market, then I would be silly not to offer £35,000 so as to ensure that I got the property.

What we then see is a rapid increase in prices. It's all about who will accept the lowest yield. The market quickly changes from a buyer's market to a seller's market. All the while the owner-occupier is trying to get a look in – typically first-time buyers. They are struggling as investors are snapping properties up before they've had a chance to even look at them.

The speculative investor now gets wind of what has been going on: stories of dramatic price increases and properties selling for over their asking price. He is thinking that he can buy a property and hold it for a year or two before selling at a massive profit.

The speculative investor is not the most clever of investor. It's unlikely that he does this full-time, but as a secondary source of income. He may never have bought a property before apart from the one he lives in (is this you?). This is where the errors start to occur. The speculative investor is not familiar with net yield and overestimates what the property will return. He overestimates the rent, underestimates the void periods, mortgage payments and repairs. However, blinded by the historic growth the speculative investor will push prices beyond the reach of the professional investor (i.e. to a level of negative yield) and outbid the professional. Say goodbye to the good times because at this point – the clock strikes 3 p.m.

Look at this as a sweeping hand of the clock (see Figure 9).

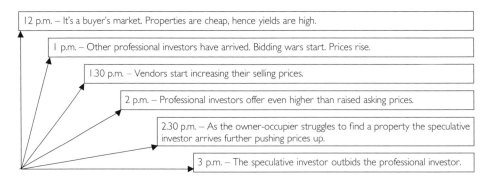

Figure 9.

Strategies within a hotspot

In a nutshell: *borrow from everywhere and buy everything*!

This may seem a bit extreme, but this is the only way you win at this game. You've got to bite the bullet and go for it. Hot spots do not last for long. I've seen hot spots go to cooling spots in three months. I've made £200,000 in capital growth for literally ten days' work of finding the right properties. And the funny thing is that this £200,000 will be accessed to buy in another hot spot and I'll simply repeat the process. This is how I have made a consistent £500,000 per year. So if you lock in to a hot spot early then you can sit back and watch your investments rocket as late entrants to the market bid prices up. The more you buy the more you make. It's as simple as that.

3 P.M. TO 6 P.M. – THE COOLING SPOT

Cooling starts: 3 p.m.

Picking up from the last section – the speculator has outbid the professional. The speculative investors and the owner-occupiers remain both with very different agendas. The speculative investor is looking to make money and the owner-occupier is looking for somewhere to live. Bearing in mind that the speculative investor is essentially a novice, his buying choices will be largely based on his own experiences with property. This will be likely limited to purchases that he has made for himself to live in. So in effect the speculative investor has the same buying requirements as the owner-occupier, but with different agendas! The speculative investor will buy on emotion rather than fundamentals just the same as the owner-occupier. So he will be lured into the same property developer traps as the normal owner-occupier. Common errors made by speculative investors are:

☐ Paying a higher purchase price for a property that conforms to his high standards of décor, disregarding the prospective tenant's lower standards. The standard of décor required for rental properties will be overestimated in the belief that the tenant will pay for this higher standard *and* that the tenant will maintain it so.

☐ A bias towards private up-market areas where the speculative investor feels 'safe'. A speculative investor will be typically earning above the average UK salary and will expect his tenants to be 'young professionals'. What he fails to understand is that the young professional sector may be looking to buy themselves and may very well be a competitor for the type of properties the speculative investor is looking at. They may also have assistance from parents in the buying process.

Private developments can become a fierce bidding ground with only one winner – the property developer!

☐ Taking on properties. Speculative investors look at the past historical growth and consider these types of property another goldmine. They assume that after refurbishment they can make a nice tidy profit *and* have the opportunity to display their interior design skills. Again the speculative investor overestimates the sale price and underestimates the repair work and bids higher than the owner-occupier.

☐ Assuming that tenants will be grateful and less fussy when deciding whether to rent a property. Box rooms may be tolerated by owner-occupiers but not by tenants! There is an arrogance element to the speculative investor for the tenant to be impressed by the high finish of the property even though the property may be undersized.

So as these two types of purchasers walk into the estate agents the red carpet is definitely not rolled out! The estate agent will have seen at least 20 people already saying 'I'm looking for a property to buy to rent out' or 'I'm looking for a property to get me on the property ladder' – change the record! You, as a professional investor, look around at the display of properties on the wall. They are all under offer or sold. You ask what the estate agent has under £100k; there is one, a studio flat, requiring upgrading, on a lease less than 50 years! Any property that looks mildly interesting is above £150k and yielding less than 6.5%. You depart, leaving the speculative investor and the owner-occupier to battle it out.

3 p.m. → 6 p.m.

So what causes an owner-occupier to outbid a speculative investor? Well, an owner-occupier will buy a property based on what they can afford; a speculative investor will pay whatever covers his estimated expenses. So whoever is higher will win. Look at this example, where the advertised property price is £100,000 and the rental value per annum is £7,000.

☐ **The speculative investor**. If the rental value is £7,000 then his mortgage company will allow him £7,000/130% = £5,384. (Any buy-to-let mortgage company will lend only if the rent is 130% or greater than the mortgage payments.) He can now use the rent to pay the mortgage and benefit from the expected capital growth that he estimates at no cost to himself – essentially money for nothing! So at borrowing rates of 5%, the price the speculative investor can go to is:

$$\frac{£5,384}{5\%} = £107,680$$

□ **The owner-occupier**. The typical owner-occupier purchaser for this type of property is earning £20,000. His buying power will be his level of deposit and the mortgage he can raise. Based on a £10,000 deposit and four times the salary lending the owner-occupier could stretch to: £10,000 + (4 × £20,000) = £90,000.

So we can see that the speculative investor wins and thus will outbid the owner-occupier and push the price beyond £90,000. The speculator will get the property at between £90,000 and £100,000. The speculator may then have to battle it out with other speculators, thus pushing the price to £107,680. However, the speculative investor has not factored in void periods; tenant default; interest rate rises; repairs; and an exit strategy.

The only way the price can be pushed beyond the £107,680 mark is by other owner-occupiers joining together to increase their buying power or by an individual seeking high income multiple lenders. If you had two owner-occupiers deciding to buy together, both on the same salary and deposit, then their combined buying power would be (assuming a 2.75 times joint salary which is standard within the mortgage market): £10,000 + £10,000 + (2.75 × £40,000) = £130,000.

Now the property's value has risen to what a couple is willing to pay for it. They can quite comfortably afford it even with expected interest rate rises. Their borrowing has been underwritten to be no more than 2.75 times joint salary.

So there is a point at which even the speculative investor drops out and is outbid by the owner-occupier accepting a lower standard property. Speculative investors that are holding now sell to owner-occupiers as the speculative investors are losing money on a monthly basis due to rents not covering the mortgage and other expenses even though they are gaining on capital growth.

If it had been an individual seeking a high income multiple lender then his buying power could have been: £10,000 + (4.93 x £20,000) = £108,600.

At the time of writing 4.93 times individual salary is the highest income multiple I can find in the mortgage market. This still outbids the speculative investor.

Look at it as a sweeping hand of the clock (see Figure 10).

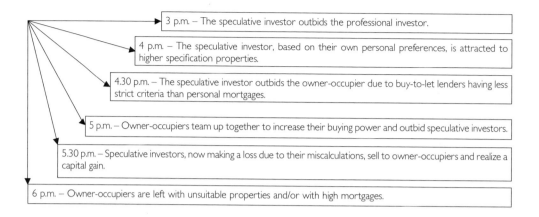

Figure 10

Strategies within a cooling spot

The professional investor has dropped out of the market at this point. Their strategy is not to buy. If you want to make money in a cooling spot then you have no option but to buy and then sell. In other words you have to property trade. Now I am no expert on this – I've never done it! It's a risky game to play. I believe that property is a long-term investment. A lot of money can be made but also can be lost. If you get your figures wrong and the market turns then you can get really stung.

The buyers in a cooling spot

There is no point in selling when your property is currently in a hot spot. This is because there is still room for the price to grow and it's currently profitable thus it's not costing you to hold. It only becomes worth selling when the property becomes unprofitable but the price is still growing. *The highest point in the market can only ever exist within a cooling spot.* This is because the property price has risen to the point that it is unprofitable but it is still on the trend upwards. The professional investor drops out of buying in this market and only owner-occupiers and novice investors remain.

You are able to sell within this market as owner-occupiers are not concerned about the profitability of a property as they are not renting it out. There are also speculative investors banking on the property price to continue growing and the novice investor that doesn't do his sums right. These buyers are able to buy your property at an inflated price above the real price for the following reasons.

Owner-occupier

Self-certified borrowing

In the UK we borrow at the current variable base rate and not at the long term average rate. Currently the long term rate is around 5.7% and the variable base rate is at 4%. This is why we have a boom bust cycle. When rates fall below the long-term rate first time buyers over-borrow, as they can afford it, by obtaining a self-certified mortgage, thus increasing their buying power. Their increase in buying power creates the bubble element as their buying power takes them over the real value of the property.

High income multiple lending

Some lenders offer in excess of four times the salary. This enables a first-time buyer to borrow in excess of the real value of the property, thus creating a bubble element.

Consumer debt

Some people borrow the deposit for the property by way of a loan. This means that you can enter the property market very quickly as you do not have to wait to save up for the deposit. This increases the number of buyers, thus increasing demand for property, hence pushing up the price.

Novice investor and speculative investor

Buy to let

Due to the buy-to-let mortgage also operating under the current variable base rate the same problem occurs here. Instead of demanding a 2% loading over the long-term rate they demand a 2% loading over the current variable base rate. This means that you get novice investors buying at 6% yields and below, hence superseding the first time buyer's highest price.

Due to the poor performance of the stock market in recent years the property market has attracted the traditional stock market investor, who will invest for capital growth and so will be happy to take less than a 2% loading. The speculative investor will make the estimation that the growth experienced in the past will happen in the future over the short term. The speculative investor's bid then supersedes the first time buyer's bid, hence a bubble element will exist.

Find out more

It is these types of buyers that cause the bubble in the property market – so use them to your advantage! To find out about where the hot spots, cooling spots, cold spots and warm spots are in the UK then visit **www.propertyhotspots.net**. This site also has a national yield and capital growth index for over 330 areas in the UK.

Things to be aware of

Ratio of earnings to property value

If property values are in excess of four times the salary then you know that there is a bubble element to the property price. Try to get local data on people's earnings to help you determine the real price of the property.

Lending multiples

Check to see if lending multiples are increasing. Currently the standard is 4 but there is a growing number of lenders offering 4.25, which is causing the real price of property to rise.

Number of first-time buyers

This needs to be a healthy number to keep the market buoyant – especially where investors have refused to invest. If this number drops then prices will fall in that area to the price that an investor would buy at.

6 P.M. TO 9 P.M. – THE COLD SPOT

6 p.m. It's getting cold

So now we have owner-occupiers buying properties that are too small for what they're worth and owner-occupiers with high income multiple mortgages, but not a speculative or professional investor in sight. The market has gone stagnant. Renters are unwilling to buy and live in a property that is smaller than what they are renting, owner-occupiers are stuck in a property that is not growing as before, speculative investors are not interested because on the face of it there is no gain to be had and the professional investor has long gone due to it being unprofitable since 3 p.m. So who is left buying? The owner-occupier! The owner-occupier is overstretching themselves by accepting unsuitable properties or going to high income multiple lenders (the self-certified borrower who has not been honest about his income is also buying but this is a small percentage of the overall buyers at 6 p.m.).

The inevitable is about to happen. Interest rates will rise. This is the only thing that can jolt the market. And it's not a few quarter-point interest rate rises. I'm talking about a 2%+ rise from its lowest point. This is when it begins to hurt.

Two terms then start to rear their ugly heads, in this order: **negative equity**, and **repossession**.

Negative equity

This, in simple terms, is when the mortgage balance is greater than the value of the house. This in itself is not a problem over the long term as the value of the house will recover. It is a big problem for:

- ☐ **owner-occupiers** who wish to move;
- ☐ **lenders** wishing to access their security on defaulting borrowers;
- ☐ **the economy**, due to the loss of the feel good factor, hence a reduction in spending;
- ☐ **the property market**, as fewer property deals are done: estate agents, brokers and other industries surrounding the property market feel the pinch.

Repossession

This is when the lender legally enforces the sale of a property they have lent on due to the borrower defaulting on their mortgage payments. Repossessions occur as a result of interest rate rises, and job losses within the household, both of which make mortgage payments unaffordable.

The number of repossessions occurring every month are directly related to the economy as repossessions are a function of interest rates and job losses. So if interest rates rose to 20% and/or everyone lost their job then everyone would get repossessed and lose their home. If interest rates were 0% and unemployment rates are 0% then no one would lose their home. We are somewhere in between.

6 p.m. → 9 p.m.

So at 6 p.m. only the owner-occupiers are buying. The owner-occupier is buying unsuitable properties at inflated prices or obtaining finance from high income multiple lenders. Property prices now reach their maximum limit. Joint owner-occupiers are unable to buy as lending is restricted to 2.75 times the joint salary and individual owner-occupiers are restricted to 4.93 times salary. Speculative investors are unable to buy as lending is restricted to 130% of the mortgage payment. Buyers at 6 p.m. are buying at the peak. As usual it is the private individual who suffers – buying high and forced to sell low. These buyers have not factored in interest rate rises, as well as owner-occupiers who have previously bought and accessed their equity from high income multiple lenders (greater than four times) and second charge lenders with less strict lending criteria. They have ignored warnings that rates will rise.

Rates begin to rise, but only modestly, in order to attract overseas investment in government gilts to fund the deficit being experienced as a result of overconsumption. Hints appear in the press of negative equity spreading across thousands of households due to the now upward trend of interest rates. Repossession rates are followed closely; if there is an increase you can be sure it's front-page news. A sense of fear sets in even though there has been no real change in property prices. Properties remain for sale with vendors not willing to drop their prices (they don't have to) but no buyers are able to afford what is for sale.

TV ads for loans are in decline. Stories of how people have made a fortune in property now seem stale and unrealistic. Some speculative investors who were breaking even are now losing money due to the slight increase in interest rates. The speculative investor is not forced to sell (as the loss is only small and manageable) but the investment is taking money out of his pocket and he can bank a gain if he sells now. So several properties come on to the market. As they already have a gain locked in, the speculative investor will reduce their price for a genuine quick sale. Property prices start to fall, creeping back to affordable levels. Some speculators are lucky and sell to frustrated owner-occupiers dying to get on the property ladder. Others are not so lucky, as owner-occupiers get wise and decide to wait and see if prices drop further or if a better property comes on to the market.

Rates rise again. And again. Repossession rates have risen for the first time and it's splashed over the press. Certain areas are reported to be in negative equity. The owner-occupier seeking a home is now smiling as he thinks property prices will drop further. Estate agents are convincing their vendors to reduce their prices to attract people through the door. Lenders are losing as a result of repossessions; after all legal and other costs of repossession have been taken into account the monies raised from the sale do not cover the amount they lent. Lenders start to restrict lending. This further stagnates the market. Property prices fall further.

Second charge lenders and unsecured lenders start experiencing defaults due to the borrower choosing to pay their mortgage rather than their other debts. Regret for the holidays and cars that were bought with this money sets in. People begin to restrict spending on the high street and try to liquidize the assets bought with their remortgaged money. Suddenly saving seems better than spending! The feel-good factor has now been lost. Property prices start falling further due to the lack of buyers.

Speculative investors are now happy just to get back what they paid for a property. Some investors actually lose capital to obtain a quick sale, seeing some of their hard-earned savings lost to free them from the bind of poor-performing investment property or properties. Property investment starts to get a bad name.

Rates rise further. Repossession rates rise further. Everyone who bought at 6 p.m. is now in negative equity. The owner-occupiers who overstretched themselves by overborrowing cannot meet the higher repayments that are the result of the interest rate rises. The market gets flooded with properties for sale by desperate vendors. Some are unfortunate and get repossessed. Supply of property is now well in excess of demand. It is neither a buyer's market nor a seller's market. Prices have to fall even further.

The only saviour of this falling market with any kind of buying clout is the professional investor. At 9 p.m. he sees that prices have fallen to a level where if he were to buy, the purchase will put money in his pocket at a rate greater than leaving the money in the bank *even though* property prices are falling. Welcome back the professional investor.

Look at it as a sweeping hand of the clock (see Figure 11).

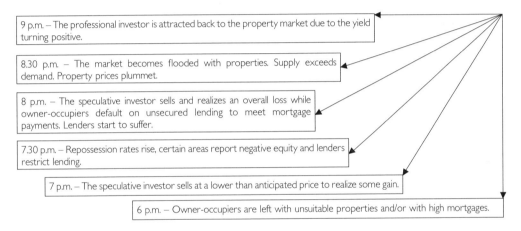

Figure 11.

Strategies within a cold spot

There is no money to be made here. Anything you buy will take money out of your pocket every month – ouch! If an area is a cold spot then simply avoid it. If you own a property in a cold spot and you can get out with a gain then do so. If you can't get out with a gain then you will have a property that is in negative equity and is costing you every month to hold.

You can sell, but it will cost you capital to get out. I would not advise this. Property is a long-term investment and prices *will* recover so there is no point in realizing a loss if can avoid it. But you have to fund the difference every month from your own pocket. This requires cash.

If you are on a repayment mortgage ensure that you switch to an interest-only mortgage as this will lower monthly payments quite dramatically. You want to know how long you're going to have to fund this shortfall and being aware of certain key variables will enable you to gauge the likely damage of being in the cold spot environment and how long and how bad the cold spot will be. These are as follows.

Global rates

Our rates are restricted by global rates. We cannot be out of sync with the rest of the world. This is called interest rate parity. The formula holds:

$$\frac{F}{S} = \left(\frac{1 + R_A}{1 + R_B}\right)^T$$

Where S is the spot exchange rate, expressed as the price in currency A of one unit of currency B. F is the forward rate, R_A and R_B are the interest rates in the respective countries, and T is the common maturity for the forward rate and the two interest rates. It assumes that if interest rates were 10% in Europe then we would convert all our sterling to euros, place them on deposit in a European bank and then convert them back after a year and enjoy the profit. This theory states that the profit would be nil as it would be money for nothing and when you converted back in sterling you would get an inferior exchange rate. So we are all locked within each country's interest rate.

The world has been in a recession. Interest rates have been low in the major economic countries which has kept our rates low even though we are not in a recession. Once rates start moving upwards over the borders then our rates will rise. You need to be aware of the financial indicators of the major economic countries. They will be the same as 'home rates', below.

Home rates

Taking into account the interest rate parity above there will still be some freedom within the UK to set rates. The rate is set by the Bank of England and they use the following reports to set them:

- **Consumer price index**. This measures price inflation. The target for the Bank is 2.5%. If it goes over then rates are expected to be increased by the Bank.

- **Employment cost index**. This measures wages growth. If wages rise above expectations this causes an increase in spending and thus results in inflation. Expect the Bank to put rates up.

- **GDP report**. This measures the overall performance of our economy. If it falls two quarters in a row then we are in a recession and expect rates to be lowered by the Bank.

☐ **Unemployment rate**. This measures the number of people out of work. If it's too low then it causes an increase in spending, thus inflation. Expect the Bank to rise rates.

☐ **House price inflation**. Very underrated by the Bank! I don't know what threshold they set but they are willing to see massive inflation here and do nothing about it. However, be aware that the Bank do consider house price inflation when setting rates.

Keep abreast, where possible, of the UK and global reports surrounding their economies. Here is where you will be able to see the triggers to movements in the UK and global interest base rates.

Negative equity

If there are a significant number of property-owners in negative equity then this reduces the feel-good factor. In turn this reduces spending and productivity. This can trigger a recession which results in higher unemployment and a fall in property prices.

9 P.M. TO 12 P.M. – THE WARM SPOT

9 p.m.: it's getting warm

We have seen a rapid decline in property prices. Repossessions are higher than they've been in the last five years, negative equity has swamped the nation – who would want to get into property investment? The only ones who do are people like me. Professional investors hate having money in the bank. A return is guaranteed but it will certainly be low.

So above the carnage within the property market the vultures, being the professional property investors, hover waiting to swoop. They will know that it's a buyer's market rather than a seller's market. They will accelerate a fall in prices to the level that will put money in their pockets. So, for example, an investor sees a property advertised at £100,000 and knows that it is worth buying at £85,000. As it's a buyer's market he will place a cheeky offer of anywhere between £75,000 to £85,000. If the vendor is desperate he will sell so as to limit the damage of holding this property.

9 p.m. → 12 p.m.

Interest rates have peaked. Property has got a bad name. Property investment is now considered a stupid thing to do. The fortunate people with money who still want to speculate are heading towards their stockbroker to play the stock market. The professional property investor, however, never favouring the stock market, watches property prices on a daily basis to see when the price falls to a level that will put money in his pocket.

So who buys at 9 p.m.? Well, it's the professional property investor who will accept the lowest yield. In my experience this will be a 2% loading on the current borrowing rate on the most desirable rental properties. So if the interest rate is 8% and buy-to-let mortgage rates are 9.5% then the lowest yield acceptable will be 11.5%, being 9.5% + 2% = 11.5%. He chooses the most desirable rental properties because a 2% loading does not allow for long void periods.

For example, say there are two properties for sale. One is an ex-local authority flat advertised at £60,000; the current rent would be £6,000 p.a. The other is a two-bed house, price £100,000, current rent £10,000 p.a. The yields for both would be 10%.

The professional investor will then assess the likely voids of both properties. With the studio flat it will be likely that the tenant will outgrow it quickly due to its size. Also, being ex-local authority, it will only appeal to a limited audience. A two-bed private house will be a decent-sized living space for a single person, couple or one-child family and will appeal to a wider audience with it being in a private area. He will estimate that the voids will be longer with the studio flat compared with the two-bed house.

However, the yield is below his target of 11.5%. He calculates his price to get a 11.5% yield.

$$\frac{£10,000}{11.5\%} = £86,956$$

So the professional investor will go in with a bid of around £80,000 (professional investors do not care if they offer 20% below what the vendor is asking!) and will happily negotiate at a price of around £87,000.

Perhaps the vendor will accept less than £87,000 as they are desperate to sell. This pushes prices down further. An offer of £80,000 might get accepted thus setting the new price levels for two-bed private houses.

Ex-local authority studio flats need to come down even further! At this less desirable end of the market, professional investors may require a loading of 6%. If borrowing rates are 9.5% then a yield of 9.5% + 6% = 15.5% will be needed from the most cautious of investor! This equates to:

$$\frac{£6,000}{15.5\%} = £38,710$$

So a bid of £38,710 is all that the professional investor will pay. So prices have fallen further.

Notice that I have not mentioned the owner-occupier in all of this. The owner-occupier does not operate to fundamentals, focusing solely on the property price itself. His worst fear is buying a property that immediately falls in value. The owner-occupier will wait until prices bottom out. Unfortunately he can't spend every day studying prices, unlike the professional investor who does it as his livelihood. The owner occupier has other things to do – like his job!

Property prices continue to be bid downwards. The best rental properties are bought first, with lower end rental properties having to fall further. New entrant professional investors, with higher loadings on their requirements, cause prices to fall again, but the lower end of the market still has to fall further to attract any interest. There comes a point, however, when prices at the lower end of the market catch the eye of one investor (someone like me!) who thinks – hang on, these properties are CHEAP! They start to buy where the market has bottomed out, and gain fantastic returns. So fantastic that other investors get wind of it and before you know it – the clock strikes 12 p.m.!

So here we have the complete loop. As the clock strikes 12 p.m. then we are simply back to a hot spot. Then all the principles described earlier are applicable.

Look at it as a sweeping hand of a clock (see Figure 12):

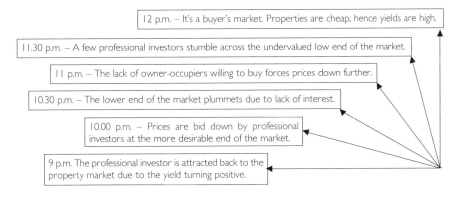

Figure 12.

Strategies within a warm spot

The key strategy is to bid low. Do not be scared of insulting the vendor with your offer. It's up to them to say yes or no. At least your offer is on the table for them to consider. It may get rejected now but accepted a few weeks down the line. Do not wait for the prices to fall to your desired level. It's up to you to drive the price down. If you wait, it is likely that another investor will get there before you.

Making your offer stand out

If you're going to bid low then make sure it's serious. Not seriously low but a serious offer worth considering. A vendor may accept a lower than anticipated offer if it is one of the following:

Cash offer

This means that the sale will theoretically happen quickly as there is no mortgage to be obtained. There may be no survey to highlight potential problems with the property. With no complications with regard to the finance it is likely the vendor will favour this offer. A lower cash offer may be accepted over a higher mortgage offer. It simply eliminates the lender from the transaction and as we all know lenders can be awkward even at the best of times. Back up your offer by showing them your bank statement to prove you have the cash. This will really improve your chances of your bid being accepted.

Backed by a Mortgage In Principle

A Mortgage In Principle (MIP) is where a lender has already credit-checked you and has agreed to lend, subject to the property only. This will show the vendor that you have already done the preliminaries to get the finance. All that is required is that the property gets valued up to the agreed price and that it is suitable security for mortgage purposes.

Flexible offer

If you can be flexible this may help your offer to be accepted. For instance the vendor may want to negotiate moving out in six months' time and you may be in no hurry to acquire the property. Or a vendor may wish to take certain fixtures and fittings with them. You could agree to this, stipulating that they replace items or make good the damage caused as a result of removing these fixtures and fittings.

How to obtain finance

You may well find that obtaining finance in a falling market is not that easy. The banks have got their fingers burned due to defaulters in negative equity. Lending criteria will be stricter and may include:

   □ **A larger deposit**. This lowers the risk to the lender. If, for example, they restrict lending to 50% Loan To Value then the property price will have to fall by 50% before the bank starts to get worried. But this will be a big problem for you as you have to come up with the other 50%!

☐ **Full status**. Instead of the bank lending on the strength of the property to pay the mortgage they may look at the property *and* your status. They may ask that you prove that you earn in excess of £50,000 p.a. This will mean payslips, tax assessments or certified accounts.

☐ **A proven background**. As the banks become more cautious they may restrict lending to professional landlords only. This may be decided on how many years you have been in the business or the number of properties you have.

So to ensure that you are able to buy within a falling market you need:

☐ **Cash**. Cash is needed for a deposit. More cash may be needed than expected. Ensure that you've remortgaged yourself to the hilt! This means that you will have the cash to put down. You do not want to be in the situation where you can get a flat for £25,000, that rents out for £500 pcm (24% yield!) but you can't raise the 50% deposit (£12,500) from one of the few lenders still remaining in the buy-to-let market. Once the market recovers you will be able to re-access the £12,500 (and more!) put down as lenders warm back to the idea of buy to let. Once the flat recovers to £50,000 and lenders are willing to lend 85% Loan To Value then your £12,500 put down will raise an extra £30,000 to buy further properties ((£50,000 x 85%) − (£25,000 x 50%) = £30,000).

☐ **Status**. Make sure you can prove your income. It helps to be in a good job. If you are self-employed ensure that you have been so for three years and you have certified accounts.

☐ **Experience**. Make sure you've got a well-performing portfolio under your belt. The threshold is usually around five properties and three years' experience. This will make you stand out from the rest.

STRATEGY SUMMARY

I have dissected the property cycle into four distinct sections. The strategies within each spot can be simplified as shown in Figure 13.

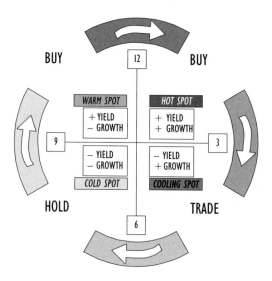

Figure 13.

So we can see that if you are a true professional investor you will only ever be interested in warm and hot spots. The reasons for this are:

- **Hot spot**. You are prompted to buy. Buying is the only true way to participating in the property market. If the strategy was to sell then it is a sure way to get out of the property market. So finding hot spot areas is key if you want to grow within the property market.

- **Cooling spot**. You are prompted to trade. Trading is buying and then selling. So in effect you dip in and out of the market. No professional investor would do this as it exposes you to both massive gains and massive losses. Massive gains are acceptable (and well received!) but massive losses are possible and potentially bankruptable which is definitely unacceptable.

- **Cold spot**. You are prompted to hold. How exciting is that! No buying or selling is required so no real strategy is required here.

- **Warm spot** – you are prompted to buy. Again this is the only way to grow. If you can find a warm spot then it will only turn into a hot spot, so massive gains are inevitable.

So in a nutshell, you should only ever be interested when an area is either a hot spot or a warm spot, as it prompts you to buy. So how do you find both of these?

How to find a hot or warm spot

I have never found a warm spot in my time in property investment. Since I started property investment in 1996 there has always been a hot spot to be found. The principles in finding a warm spot are the same as in finding a hot spot. But one should only ever seek a warm spot when there are no more hot spots. Methods I have used to find hot spots are:

1. Searching on the internet

I owe a substantial amount of my success to the internet. I was able to discover areas that I had never heard of. These unknown areas now form a significant part of my portfolio!

You have to find cheap properties, generally for under £60,000. Visit these four sites:

www.asserta.com
www.home.co.uk.
www.rightmove.co.uk
www.vebra.com

Type in any town or city and search the widest radius possible. Put in a maximum price of £60,000 and see what comes up! If nothing does then the area you entered is not a hot spot. If something comes up then check it out further. If quite a few come up then BINGO!

Once you have found an area then visit www.ukpropertyshop.com, which lists all the individual estate agents in that area. Check their websites. If what they have looks good then go down there and buy everything you can!

2. Looking in agents' windows

Wherever you are, *always* check estate agents' windows. I do this out of habit and interest. It's good to get an idea of property prices in different areas. You never know – you may stumble across a bargain.

3. Getting local press

Scan the property section in the local press. Here you can gauge the whole market in that area. You may find that there is an agent that specializes in low-value properties.

4. Looking for areas that are self-sufficient

Areas with bad transport links or that are a bit isolated make perfect hot spots. They are sometimes valued low due to lack of demand by buyers (there is no point in living there unless you work there) but have high tenant demand due to people wishing to rent there. One of the areas where I have a significant portfolio is Corby which meets these criteria. It has no train station, is 30 miles from anywhere significant but has a large Scottish community who wish to live there.

5. Getting out there!

Go visit places. Look at a map of the UK, pick an area that you like the sound of and go and visit it, stopping off at all the towns on route to check out the estate agents. See it as a mini adventure – have some fun!

If all of that seems like hard work then visit my site, www.propertyhotspots.net, where you will find out about all the current hot spots that I could find and areas that are soon to be hot spots (and a hell of a lot more!).

THE LIFETIME PROPERTY CLOCK

The property clock cycle lasts anywhere between three and ten years. In contrast, our own home ownership goals have a cycle that lasts typically for 40 years and more. If we understand this cycle, which I call the lifetime property clock, we then have a whole understanding of the property market. This is because the property market is made up of investors following the property clock and owner occupiers following the lifetime property clock who look for a home to live and bring up their family in.

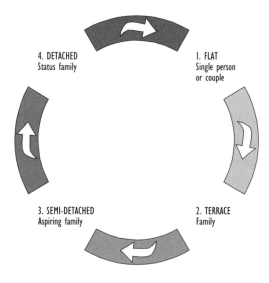

Figure 14.

Figure 14 shows that there is a definitive clock that exists within our own personal property goals over our lifetime. Let's look at the detail of each stage of the clock.

1. Single person or young couple (age 20–30)

We may start our working life while still living in our parents' home! There then comes a point when you want to be independent and your own place. At this time you turn into a first-time buyer.

First-time buyers (single people and young couples) want to preserve as much disposable income as possible so they still have some spending money. They will aim to buy a property that is cheaper than paying rent, is not surplus to their needs, and is easy to maintain.

The properties that meet these criteria will be the cheapest types of property, specifically flats – studio, one and two beds. They will be smaller than other property types and maintained by someone else, typically the freeholder.

An example of a first-time buyer would be Jack. Jack has £8,000 saved and earns £18,000 per year. He sees flats going for around £75,000 and houses for £120,000 plus.

Buying power is calculated as (deposit you actually have) + (mortgage you're able to get).

To calculate what Jack can afford: the deposit is £8,000 and the mortgage he is able to get will be four times his salary. So his buying power is calculated as: £8,000 + (4 × £18,000).

This equates to £80,000, which buys him a nice one-bed flat near the town.

So as nature follows its course, the single first-time buyer meets the love of their life and they decide to have a family. A bigger property is required, preferably with a garden. Therefore a house is needed...

2. Couple with children (age 30–40)

Two things have probably happened to the first-time buyer since they bought.

1. **Equity increase**. The flat will have grown in value. The mortgage balance will now be somewhere around 40–80% of the value, depending on timing and how the market has performed. If they are unfortunate enough to be in negative equity (where the mortgage balance is greater than the property value) they simply have to wait it out until prices recover so that they can move.

2. **Salary increase**. It is likely that the buyer's salary has increased. This means that the buyer can borrow more to acquire his next property.

So the buyer can afford a better property – a house! He has a larger deposit due to an increase in equity and increased borrowing power due to an increase in salary. Using the example above let's say Jack, five years down the line, meets Jill (who owns a similar flat bought at the same time). They get married and decide to sell both their flats, use the equity in their flats and combine their salaries to buy a house.

	Jack	Jill	Total
Value of flat	£100,000	£100,000	£200,000
Mortgage balance	£72,000	£72,000	£144,000
Equity	£28,000	£28,000	£56,000
Salary	£23,000	£23,000	£46,000

Their buying power follows the same equation: (deposit you actually have) + (mortgage you're able to get). The deposit is £56,000 and the mortgage they will be able to get will be 2.75 times their joint salary. So their buying power is calculated as: £56,000 + (2.75 × £46,000).

This equates to £182,500, which buys them a three-bed terrace in the same town.

The majority of the population will stop here. The second-time buy house often meets all a family's basic needs: a room for each child, living and dining space, garden. They aim to clear the mortgage by or before retirement age. A second-time buyer becomes a third-time buyer when:

1. Another child comes along and the family outgrows the house.

2. Household income increases significantly due to success in jobs or business. The household will seek a better house as they can afford it.

3. An inheritance is received which is significant enough to invest in the family's property aspirations.

In the first instance, if the household income has not increased they can only afford a house of the same value, but larger. They may have to forgo such benefits as proximity to the town centre, train station or quality of area to obtain the larger house, for instance moving from a three-bed private terrace to a four-bed ex-local authority property. There is no progression in price. It's more like a sideways move within the lifetime property clock.

In the second and third instance a higher value property is sought. This is a valid third-time buyer as they are progressing upwards in the property market. This is what I call the aspiring family.

3. The aspiring family (age 35–55)

So a household is able to move up the property ladder are when their buying power increases. Looking at the two situations above, a rise in income increases the buyer's **borrowing** power. An inheritance increases the **deposit** amount and therefore their buying power.

Going back to Jack and Jill, suppose they both achieve an 80% increase in their salaries. Their individual pay goes from £23,000 to £41,400. Then the mortgage they are able to get increases from $2.75 \times (£23,000 + £23,000) = £126,500$ to $2.75 \times (£41,400 + £41,400) = £227,700$. That's an increase of £101,200.

So now Jack and Jill can look at houses (assuming property prices have remained at the same level) for £101,200 greater than what their house is worth, which equates to £182,500 + £101,200 = £283,700. This will probably buy them a four-bed semi or three-bed detached in a private area.

Note that the same house could be bought if there was no increase in salary but Jack inherited £101,200 on their death of his remaining parent.

Most third-time buyers will stop here. But some families will want to move again . . .

4. The status family (age 40–60)

So what makes someone want to buy for the fourth time? Status! If the property they live in is meeting all their needs then the mind slowly turns 'wants' into 'needs'. Like I *need* a triple garage to house my three cars; I *need* a swimming pool and gym for my health; I *need* a separate study room for my work.

Buying power will be calculated the same as before, but figures can be anything as houses at this end of the market can start at £500,000 with no upper limit. There are very few executive houses relative to other houses and their worth will be determined by very different fundamentals. Executive homes have few comparables and few buyers. Values of executive homes will be set by holding out for a buyer to fall in love with the house. The vendor simply has to wait. You find that at the top end there are few vendors who require a quick sale.

It can be assumed that once someone is over 60 years of age they will be unlikely to want to move upwards in the property market. Once a spouse dies, the remaining partner often leaves the home to move into a smaller property. Sometimes this is a serviced retirement flat, effectively a move back round to position 1, the single person.

Forced moves

I have ignored forced moves, for instance moving house due to job relocation, divorce or sizing down, in order to keep the model simple. Forced moves have an impact on the market but it is safe to say that generally people strive to move round the lifetime property clock in a clockwise fashion.

HOW THE PROPERTY CLOCK AND THE LIFETIME PROPERTY CLOCK INTERACT

How is the property clock relevant to the lifetime property clock? We can assume that the rental sector will be concentrated in properties in Stages 1 and 2 (see Figure 15).

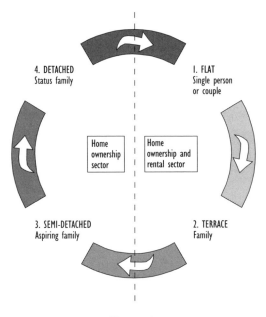

Figure 15.

Check out the rental lists of letting agents. They will predominantly be for flats and terraced houses: 90%, with just a few semis and detached houses. There are two reasons for this:

1. Semis and detached houses are sold at a premium compared with terraced properties with the same number of bedrooms. However, the rent achievable for a semi or detached house will not compensate for the premium paid: this lowers the overall yield of the property, hence making it unprofitable. Professional investors will shy away from such investments.

2. The people able to afford such homes are usually those on their third-time buy. The price of semis and detached houses will be set by the gains made on their original property ladder climb. Speculative investors would also like to buy these properties as they let out easily, but are out of their reach due to the high price the properties command.

Direct interaction

Since investors are involved with only stages 1 and 2 we can say that property investment *directly interacts* with stages 1 and 2, that is, the first-time buyers: the young single person, the young couple and the young family.

Property investment used to meet the needs of people who had no interest in buying property and were happy to rent. We were in equilibrium between first-time buyers and investors, that is, both first-time buyers and investors were able to buy. Now what is happening is that investors are buying properties that are suitable for first-time buyers at a faster rate than first-time buyers are, thus forcing them to rent properties rather than to buy. What then happens is that the rental sector grows and the home ownership sector shrinks within stages 1 and 2. If the home ownership sector shrinks too much it will affect stages 3 and 4 as there will be fewer buyers moving round the lifetime property clock. This will be the *indirect interaction*.

Indirect interaction

The best way to understand this is to look at extremes. So in the extreme, if stages 1 and 2 were at a ratio of 100% rental and 0% home ownership then the prices of semis and detached would have to fall as no one would have a gain on their previous property to put down as a deposit. This will slowly drive down the prices of executive homes as there will be no one to buy them. The prices will fall to a level just above the undifferentiated terraced properties.

So the mix of investors to first-time buyers is critical to sustain the prices of stages 3 and 4. It is *not*, however, critical to prevent a crash in housing. You may read about the lack of first-time buyers entering the market and somehow this is going to trigger a crash, but this is a red herring. It will only cause ridiculously priced houses at the top end of the market to come back down to a sensible level.

PART THREE: TYPES OF PROPERTY BUSINESS

5

RESIDENTIAL OWNER (RENT A ROOM)

VITAL STATISTICS

Earning potential before tax	£2,500 to £20,000 per year per property
Capital required	£10,000 to £50,000
Skills required	None
Qualifications preferable	None
Competitiveness: low/medium/high	Low
Risk: low/medium/high	Low
The business model in a nutshell	To buy a property to live in and rent out the rooms for maximum profit
Potential gaps in the market and suggested USPs	• Monday to Friday rent a room for workers • Overseas students • Special event hire, e.g. Wimbledon • Men/women only • Luxury professional market

Rent a room: sounds simple doesn't it? Well, it is! The first ever rent cheque I got was from this method. I always wonder if I had never rented out a room would I ever have entered the world of property. This is the simplest way of making money from property.

I am going to tell you the way to make the most money you possibly can from this method. You can always tone it down to suit you.

THE FORMULA

Buy the biggest property that you can afford with the least amount of money, returning the maximum amount of profit.

Let me break down the formula for you.

Buy the biggest property – you want to get the most rooms for your money. The more rooms, the more rent you can get. The idea is to get the most rent for every pound spent on the property.

That you can afford – you will need to get a residential mortgage to buy this property. Residential mortgages are given based on affordability and it will be a multiple of your gross annual salary. It is the only way you can buy this property and live in it – unless of course, you have bundles of cash!

With the least amount of money – the less you put down the more you can buy! This ensures that you get the highest return on your investment. The more you have put aside for when things go wrong the more chance you have of success.

Returning the maximum amount of profit – rent minus expenses equals profit. You want to buy rents are a decent amount but costs are low: costs being the mortgage, council tax, insurance and other costs associated with running a home.

CHOOSING THE RIGHT PROPERTY

Location

This decision is pretty much in your court. It will take into account non-business factors, such as friends, family and work, so analysis of the numbers exclusively will not take you to the right decision.

However, I am going to ignore all those non-business factors! I am assuming that you are a mercenary individual who wants to make as much money as possible from this venture. Apply these principles to suit your own personal circumstances.

Financials

Choose a location that can return you the highest profit figure. The way you establish this is to calculate my magic number called: YIELD. Yield is calculated as follows: *annual rent divided by purchase price*. So first calculate the annual rent. This is quite simply 52 weeks × weekly rent × (number of bedrooms minus one). You take away one from the total number of bedrooms as this is where you live!

So if you have found a property with six rooms and you can get on average £50 per room then the annual rent will be: 52 × £50 × (6 − 1) = £13,000.

If you wanted to be more accurate then you could split the rooms into single and double rooms and allocate a respective rent to each one. So if this six-bedroomed house had two double and four single rooms and you were going to reside in one of the double rooms then the annual rent would be:

```
52 × £40 × 4 =   £8,320
52 × £60 × 1 =   £3,120
TOTAL            £11,440
```

Now let's assume that the total rent you can get from the property is £13,000. Is that profitable? Is it worth it?

The key question is: how much do I have to pay to get this £13,000 income?

This is where the calculation of yield is so great. It tells you in neat percentage terms how much rent you get relative to the purchase price. If you buy this property that can return £13,000 for £130,000 then the yield is: £13,000 divided by £130,000 = 10%.

If you found another property that would deliver £13,000 rent every year and you can buy it for £260,000 then the yield for this property is: £13,000 divided by £260,000 = 5%.

It is quite obvious to you that the higher-yielding property is superior.

Now I have made a big assumption here: that there is equal demand for these rooms. In a city centre demand for these rooms will be pretty much solid but if you are comparing a city centre house with a suburban house, demand might vary.

Before I buy I always perform this little trick to assess demand. I place an advert in the local press (which costs about £25) and I see how many calls come in. You have to be as specific as possible in the advert, stating the road the property is in. If you are swamped you will be able to rent the rooms out. If you do not want your phone bombarded then consider using www.gumtree.com and putting your email address as the main point of contact.

Remember to do this all *before* you buy. This small action can save you making some very expensive mistakes.

Tip

A good yield for rent a room is 12%. It ensures that there is enough profit for you after all costs and expected interest rate rises. The easiest way to calculate this is to take the advertised price then knock off two zeros. If you can rent it for at least that amount then it is a good buy!

Or do it the other way round. If a property that can be rented for £1,000 per month add two zeros and if it can be bought for £100,000 or less, then it is a good buy.

Size

Generally the more rooms you have the more money you can make. You will find that houses with additional bedrooms beyond three go up in price by a smaller amount. On a housing estate with a selection of two, three four and five-bedroom houses prices are usually as follows:

Number of bedrooms	Price	Cost per room
2	£120,000	£60,000
3	£150,000	£50,000
4	£175,000	£43,750
5	£195,000	£39,000

The more rooms the property has, the cost per room goes down. This helps your yield massively. But remember that more rooms means more management on your part.

From research conducted in January 2010 we can see that from Scotland down to Essex there are potential rent-a-room properties exceeding a 12% yield.

For example:

Town	Price	Number of rentable bedrooms	Rent	Yield
Northampton	£90,000	6	£1,558	20.7%
Cumbernauld, Scotland	£70,000	5	£1,299	18.5%
Harlow, Essex	£170,000	5	£1,732	12.2%

FINANCING THE PROPERTY

Unless you have bundles of cash you will have to get a mortgage to buy your chosen property. The right mortgage is the one that suits you. I can tell you what suits me: the cheapest! The cheapest should be what suits you too. If we look at this venture as a business we can apply some basic rules.

A brief lesson on mortgages

Residential vs buy to let

You will need to get a **residential** mortgage. Do not confuse it with a **buy-to-let** mortgage. You are buying a property you want to live in, which means you need a residential mortgage.

Deposit levels

Residential mortgages require the least amount of deposit out of all mortgages. You used to be able to borrow more than the value of the property itself in the days before the credit crunch. Now the most you can get is 95% of the purchase price. So deposit levels start at just 5% of the purchase price.

Affordability

The amount you can borrow will be based on your **salary** and your partner's if you are buying together, your **outgoings**, and your **current liabilities** (loans, credit cards, HP agreements, etc.).

Lenders look to multiply your gross salary less your annual payments to your current liabilities, by around 4 to calculate the amount they will lend to you. There is some flexibility: they can take into account extra payments such as overtime and bonuses, and at the security of your job. I recommend you see a broker to help you get an exact figure of how much they will lend.

A new breed of 'rent-a-room' mortgages that will add the rent you will get from the rooms to your income, so you can borrow more, may be available. Ask your broker about these as they may let you borrow just that little bit more to make properties you thought out of reach now possible.

Interest only vs repayment

The monthly mortgage payment you make can either pay the **interest charge** only, or pay the **interest and the capital**.

Paying off the interest only results in a lower monthly payment, which means a lower cost base and thus an overall higher monthly cash flow. I would highly recommend you adopt this type of payment if you get the option.

However, it means that the capital never gets paid off. This is not a problem, no matter what anyone tells you. It is unlikely that you will own this property for 25 years, so you won't need to come up with the amount you borrowed at the end of the 25-year period.

What usually happens is that you sell the property (and buy somewhere else) once the market has risen, therefore there was no need to pay off any debt in the first place. By not paying off the capital every month this saving can be used to fund other eventualities like repairs, non-payment of rent or even further business ideas!

Fixed, tracker or variable

These terms relate to interest rates. These are the main types of rates you can get:

☐ **Fixed**. The rate is fixed for a period of time, so you do not need to worry about interest rate rises as these will not affect you during the period it is fixed. Outside the period is another story! If you are really risk averse go for a long period. The maximum you can get is 25 years.

- ☐ **Tracker**. Tracker rates track an official rate, which can be the Bank of England's rate, LIBOR, or the lender's Standard Variable Rate (SVR). This is not an exhaustive list as lenders can be very sneaky. Make sure you find out what the tracker rate tracks. The rate moves in line with this official rate. I would always try to get a tracker rate.

- ☐ **Variable**. This is a rate set by the lender, who has full freedom to increase or decrease this as and when they like (although most do not do this). In the environment we are in I would avoid these if you can.

I hope from my little education in mortgages you can see that you should be going for:

- ☐ a 95% residential mortgage;
- ☐ interest only;
- ☐ tracker or fixed (whichever is lower).

This will ensure that you have to put the least amount of money into the venture and you will get the lowest monthly payment possible.

GETTING THE PROPERTY READY

So you have just picked up the keys to your new multi-roomed property. What is next? The mortgage payment is due next month so you have to get your act together and prepare the house for occupation!

Amenities

I am going to assume that the normal utilities are connected to the house. So each room has heating, the house has running hot water and there are also basic cooking facilities and refrigerators at the property. Extra amenities you could consider are:

Satellite/digital TV

Your tenants will really appreciate having more than just the five channels. You do not have to pay out for a multi-room Sky package contract. Upgrade your aerial and install freeview boxes in each room. Do your sums. If a more expensive package costs £10 per week extra per room and you can get £15 extra rent then it is worth it.

Wireless broadband

For both students and workers having broadband will be a great selling point. You could put your own WiFi sign up and be just like Starbucks!

Additional cooking facilities

This depends on how many people you have in your house. I reckon one cooker and microwave per three people is sufficient. Also a big chunky American-style fridge-freezer can fend off a lot of future arguments.

Washing facilities

Have a washing machine and tumble dryer for tenants' use. They will certainly appreciate it and you can charge more rent for this privilege. Washing machines and tumble dryers cost around 10p an hour to run plus there will be additional maintenance costs due to heavy usage. Make sure you factor this into your costings.

Showering facilities

Most people prefer showers to baths if they lead busy lives. And as showers are cheaper than baths, this will keep your bills down.

Decorating

If the property is not already decorated then please follow this really easy step: **keep it neutral**. That is:

- ☐ walls to be magnolia or white;
- ☐ flooring to be beige or brown or wooden flooring;
- ☐ bathrooms to be white;
- ☐ kitchens to be modern.

No one can argue with neutral. It is completely inoffensive. Just as stated on every property programme out there.

Furnishing

You will probably furnish the common rooms such as the kitchen, living room, dining room and bathrooms as you want. Just make sure they are hard-wearing. As for each room, I suggest as a minimum:

- ☐ one bed – a single bed in a single room and a double bed in a double room;
- ☐ one bedside table – you only need one regardless of whether it is a single or a double;
- ☐ curtains – they need to be able to get some sleep!

That's it. The less the better. Less for the lodger to break and it leaves them able to put their own stamp on the room so they can make it their home.

Do not buy duvets or duvet covers, or towels, or furniture such as desks, as they will take them with them when they leave. These are easily bought cheaply by the tenant. They won't ask you to buy them as it will seem too cheeky.

Optional purchases might include a wardrobe and/or chest-of-drawers. Supply these only if tenants ask you to.

This should keep your upfront costs right down, vital from the beginning. You need to control costs from the start.

House rules

This is very important. You want to put up a friendly sign, 'House Rules', which can be seen when you open the front door, so no one misses it. Number each rule. Things to consider are:

1. Visitors – when they are allowed in and until what time. Also the procedure of requesting an overnight visitor.
2. Noise – what time music can be played until and at what volume.
3. Rubbish – when to empty bins in the room and kitchen.
4. Food – rules about communal food.
5. Payment – when to pay rent and by which method.
6. Chores – state any communal chores to be done and how they are allocated.

Cleaning services

You might want to consider taking on a cleaner. You need to keep the house clean and tidy if you are going to charge rent for it. You do not want tenants leaving due to poor hygiene. It just takes one messy or dirty tenant to spoil it for the rest. If you have an effective cleaning strategy (like Doris the cleaner!) it might prevent the mass exodus because of stinky Joe.

Now that you have done all of the above, you are in a position to fling open your doors to whoever will pay the rent... Well, sort of!

FINDING AND CHOOSING THE RIGHT TENANTS

Demand for rooms to rent is currently high. There is a shortage of properties to let, hence they are expensive. Plenty of people simply cannot afford, or refuse to pay rent for a self-contained flat or house.

A long time ago there was a stigma associated with sharing a house, but now it is quite normal. I have heard of headteachers and senior doctors sharing a house so it is a far cry from the old days.

So where do all these quality tenants look for a place to live? Read on! I have isolated the best seven ways of finding nice, friendly and credit-worthy lodgers for your multi-roomed house.

1. **In your window**. Your ground floor window may be an excellent way to get passersby. Completely free and very effective.

2. **Local press**. Adverts cost anywhere from £5 to £50.

3. **Large employers**. Employers in the area may be willing to add your property to their intranet advertising for free. Ask for their HR department.

4. **Shop window cards**. They cost about £1 per week. Try Tesco, off licences, corner shops, etc.

5. **Universities, colleges and schools**. A little poster in the right place can work wonders. You could also speak to the accommodation officer and list your room with them.

6. **Word of mouth**. Ask your current lodgers if they know anyone and offer them a trip down the pub as a reward. It will work wonders for lodger relations!

7. **Internet**. There are plenty of sites where you can advertise. Just type in 'rent a room' or 'find lodger' in Google and they will all come up.

What type of lodger?

You need to be able to picture how you want the house share to be. It makes it easier to spot the right lodger when they walk through the door. Various general themes include:

- □ **Monday to Friday workers**. These tenants are rarely in the house, expect heat and hot water between 7 a.m. and 9 a.m. and 5 p.m. and 10 p.m. and live their own lives. They go home on Friday and you do not see them till Sunday night sometimes even Monday night.

- □ **Students**. In a student house most people will be young, and perhaps around during the day. It may be a less formally run house with fewer rules.

- □ **Events**. Being located in certain areas may mean particular types of people will be want to rent your rooms (like tennis fans near Wimbledon or construction workers near development sites).

- □ **Luxury**. You could just go for lodgers of a certain income bracket so they may be of the same class, profession or earning potential. Only the best will do for these people!

□ **Men/women only**. If you want to be gender specific then that's OK! If a woman wants only women tenants then so be it.

□ **Age**. There is quite a demand for over-50 type of accommodation. So you could tap into that sort of market especially if you are of that age. You may have similar interests and habits. Or you might want a young house, which could be fun and relaxed.

So once you have decided on your theme (and it is very important that you do) then you can start short-listing your prospects.

The selection process

Enquiries will come in quite quickly after you have placed your ad, I am quite sure of that. Now always be open-minded. Let *anyone* view, even if you do not like the sound of them. You can never tell from just a phone conversation. Unless they drop real clangers like admitting they're being evicted for non-payment of rent, for example.

The idea is first to get people interested. Once you have interested parties, you can start filtering them out. I suggest that you do the following in this order:

1. Check that they have the required cash. Explain that the deposit is four weeks' rent and the rent is payable once a week. So they need five weeks' worth of rent to pay *upfront* before they can move in. If they do not flinch then you are getting warm. If they state they can pay this then on to stage 2.

2. Do a credit check. This is worth doing if you want to be safe. They are very cheap (about £10) and you can even get the lodger to pay for it. It will give you a snapshot of how they conduct their finances.

3. Get a reference. A verbal reference from their employer should be enough. Check the number they give you corresponds to their place of work. If you want it in writing then write to their employer.

4. Use your instincts. If you get a funny vibe about a prospective lodger and you can hold out for someone else then do so. Your instinct is a powerful thing. Remember that this is your home and you want to feel comfortable. You also don't want to upset your other lodgers.

So if you go through those four steps you should be OK. The worst case scenario is you ask have to ask a lodger to leave. A lodger has no rights to occupy your property and you can literally give an hour's notice for them to leave. So it is quite difficult to get this business very wrong. Many people do this just to supplement their income.

Others have 12-bed properties in bedsit cities and live off the proceeds very nicely income indeed.

A word of warning: do not get the idea of moving out and renting your room and think that your rights will stay the same. As soon as you move out, the property becomes a 'house in multiple occupation' (HMO) which has a whole different set of rules regarding eviction and licensing.

PROFIT FORECASTING

Fill in the figures in the profit forecaster table to work out how much you can expect to make from renting out your rooms. You can get an electronic version of this by joining my newsletter at wwww.ahuja.co.uk.

Profit forecaster table

Income	Enter rent per week below	Multiply by	Annual	Income
Room 1		52		
Room 2		52		
Room 3		52		
Room 4		52		
Room 5		52		
Total				(A)
Expenses	Enter amount below	Multiply by	Annual	cost
Monthly mortgage		12		
Monthly council tax bill (10 instalments)		10		
Monthly gas bill		12		
Monthly electricity bill		12		
Monthly water bill		12		
Monthly Sky/cable bill		12		
Monthly telephone		12		
Monthly broadband bill		12		
Sundry/other				
Total				
				(B)
Anticipated annual profit				(A−B)

LODGER AGREEMENT

This is an example of the type of agreement you need your tenants to sign. You can get an electronic version of this by joining my newsletter at www.ahuja.co.uk.

HOUSE/FLAT SHARE AGREEMENT
for a room in a furnished house or flat – resident owner

Dated_____
(Insert date of agreement)

The Property_____
(Hereinafter "the Property")

_____

The Room Being the room at the Property that has been nominated by the Owner
(Hereinafter and agreed to by the Sharer: "the Room")

_____

(Identify the Room, e.g. by number/location)

The Owner_____
(Hereinafter "the Owner")

_____

(whose address is the Property above)

The Sharer_____
(Hereinafter "the Sharer")

_____

The Period _____ weeks/months* beginning on_____
(Hereinafter "the Period") (*Delete as appropriate)

Early Termination
Either party may at any time end this Agreement earlier than the end of the Period by
giving to the other written notice of ____ weeks / months*

The Payment £_____(_____)
(State amount in figures and words) per week/ calendar month* payable in advance on the
_____ of each week/month*

Important:

(1) The Payment is INCLUSIVE of/DOES NOT INCLUDE* utility bills [e.g. electricity/gas].

(2) The Payment is INCLUSIVE of/DOES NOT INCLUDE* water bills.

(3) The Payment is INCLUSIVE of/DOES NOT INCLUDE* Council Tax.

(4) The use of telephone is NOT included in the Payment.

The Deposit £_____(_____)

(State amount in figures and words)

The Inventory Being the list of the Owner's possessions at the Property, which has been signed by the Owner and the Sharer

Signed by the Owner:

_____

Signed by the Sharer:

_____

THIS HOUSE/FLAT SHARE AGREEMENT comprises the particulars detailed above and the terms and conditions printed overleaf whereby the Property is licensed by the Owner and taken by the Sharer for occupation during the Period upon making the Payment.

IMPORTANT NOTICE:

(1) This form of Agreement is for use in those cases where the Room is part of a House or Flat which the Owner occupies as his/her only or principal home so that an Assured Tenancy is not created.

(2) This form of Agreement does not require either party to give any form of notice to the other at the end of the fixed Period, but if either party wishes to end this Agreement early, then written notice should be served for the period as stated in the Early Termination clause.

Terms and Conditions

1. The Sharer will:

1.1 in conjunction with the occupation of the Room only be allowed to share with the other occupiers of the Property the use and facilities of the common parts of the Property (including such bathroom, toilet, kitchen and sitting room facilities as may be at the Property).

1.2 pay the Payment at the times and in the manner aforesaid without any deduction abatement or set-off whatsoever.

1.3 make a proportionate contribution to the cost of all charges in respect of any electricity, gas, water and telephonic or televisual services used at or supplied to the Property and

Council Tax or any similar tax that might be charged in addition to or replacement of it during the Period

[**NB** STRIKE THIS CLAUSE if the Payment is inclusive of all household bills as referred to in definition of the Payment overleaf.]

1.4 keep the Room and share with the other occupiers of the Property the obligation to keep the interior of the Property in a good, clean and tenantable state and condition and not damage or injure the Property or any part of it and if at the end of the Period any item on the Inventory requires repair, replacing, cleaning or laundering the Sharer will pay for the same (reasonable wear and tear and damage by an insured risk excepted)

1.5 yield up the Room at the end of the Period in the same clean state and condition it was in at the beginning of the Period

1.6 share with the other occupiers of the Property the obligation to maintain at the Property and keep in a good and clean condition all the items listed in the Inventory

1.7 not make any alteration or addition to the Property nor without the Owner's prior written consent do any redecoration or painting of the Property

1.8 not do or omit to do anything on or at the Property which may be or become a nuisance or annoyance to the Owner or any other occupiers of the Property or owners or occupiers of adjoining or nearby premises or which may in any way prejudice the insurance of the Property or cause an increase in the premium payable therefor

1.9 not without the Owner's prior consent allow or keep any pet or any kind of animal at the Property

1.10 not use or occupy the Property in any way whatsoever other than as a private residence

1.11 not assign, sublet, charge or part with or share possession or occupation of the Room or the Property or any part thereof

1.12 pay interest at the rate of 4% above the Bank of England base rate from time to time prevailing on any payment or other money due from the Sharer under this Agreement which remains unpaid for more than 14 days, interest to be paid from the date the payment fell due until payment

2. In the event of the Payment being unpaid for more than 21 days after it is due (whether formally demanded or not) or there being a breach of any other of the Sharer's obligations under this Agreement, or in the event of the Sharer ceasing to reside at the Property, or in the event of the Sharer's death, this Agreement shall thereupon determine absolutely but without prejudice to any of the Owner's other rights and remedies in respect of any outstanding obligations on the part of the Sharer

3. The Deposit has been paid by the Sharer and is held by the Owner to secure compliance with the Sharer's obligations under this Agreement (without prejudice to the Owner's other rights and remedies) and if, at any time during the Period, the Owner is obliged to draw upon it to satisfy any outstanding breaches of such obligations then the Sharer shall forthwith make such additional payment as is necessary to restore the full amount of the Deposit held by the Owner. As soon as reasonably practicable following termination of this Agreement the Owner shall return to the Sharer the Deposit or the balance thereof after any deductions properly made. No interest will be payable to the Sharer in respect of the Deposit

4. The Owner will insure the Property and the items listed on the Inventory

5. The Owner hereby notifies the Sharer that any notices (including notices in proceedings) should be served upon the Owner at the address stated with the name of the Owner overleaf

6. In the event of damage to or destruction of the Property by any of the risks insured against by the Owner the Sharer shall be relieved from making the Payment to the extent that the Sharer's use and enjoyment of the Property is thereby prevented and from performance of its obligations as to the state and condition of the Property to the extent of and whilst there prevails any such damage or destruction (except to the extent that the insurance is prejudiced by any act or default of the Sharer) the amount in case of dispute to be settled by arbitration

7. As long as the reference to a notice of early termination in the definition of the "Period" overleaf (the "Early Termination Notice) has not been deleted then either party may at any time during the Period terminate this Agreement by giving to the other prior written notice to that effect, the length of such notice to be that stated in the Early Termination Notice, and upon the expiry of said notice this Agreement shall end with no further liability for either party save for liability for any antecedent breach

8. The Owner may at any time nominate for the Sharer another Room in the Property in replacement of the Room occupied by the Sharer until that point ('the replacement Room') and all reference in this Agreement to the 'Room' shall thenceforth be deemed to refer to the replacement Room and this process may be repeated by the Owner any number of times during the Period PROVIDED THAT the Sharer may after such a nomination give to the Owner an Early Termination Notice as referred to in clause 7 above and be allowed to remain in the Room occupied prior to the said nomination until the expiry of the said Early Termination Notice

9. The Sharer shall not have exclusive possession of the Room and the identity of the other occupiers of the Property shall be in the absolute discretion of the Owner

10. Where the context so admits:

10.1 the "Property" includes all of the Owner's fixtures and fittings at or upon the Property and all of the items listed in the Inventory and (for the avoidance of doubt) the Room

10.2 the "Period" shall mean the period stated in the particulars overleaf or any shorter or longer period in the event of an earlier termination or an extension or holding over respectively

11. All reference to the singular shall include the plural and vice versa and any obligations or liabilities of more than one person shall be joint and several and an obligation on the part of a party shall include an obligation not to allow or permit the breach of that obligation

source: www.limecastle.co.uk

6

RESIDENTIAL OWNER (BED AND BREAKFAST)

VITAL STATISTICS

Earning potential before tax	£7,500 to £50,000 per guest house per year
Capital required	£20,000 to £75,000
Skills required	Food, hospitality
Qualifications preferable	Hospitality, travel and tourism
Competitiveness: low/medium/high	High
Risk: low/medium/high	Low
The business model in a nutshell	To buy a property to live in and rent out the rooms on a per night basis
Potential gaps in the market and suggested USPs	• Various modern-day themes and niches • Boutique-type B&Bs

This is like rent a room but on steroids. That is to say you can earn many times the amount you make simply renting out rooms to lodgers. Why get £50 a week rent when you can get £50 a night! Now before you get pound signs in your eyes I have got news for you: *Running a B&B is a job*!

So the rewards are higher but so is the effort. It is not simply a case of flinging a resident a key and telling them to get on with it. When you run a B&B you have a very high turnover of residents and you are at their beck and call. Also the guests will need feeding!

However, if you are good at it the income can be very respectable. If you get really good at it you can scale up and own many properties, as some big players do.

There are high advertising costs, regulations to conform to and long hours. But the rewards are there and if you like people then this could be the business for you.

THE FORMULA

Buy a well-located multi-roomed property, theme the property to stand out and price discriminate to maximize profit.

Let me break this down:

Well-located – you need to have a fairly decent occupancy rate for this to work. There has to be demand for the rooms in order to cover certain fixed costs over and above the mortgage, such as advertising, food preparation, higher rates, and this can only be achieved by being well located.

Multi-roomed – you need a minimum of three rooms to make the numbers work. Below I show you what thresholds need to be met.

Theme – the B&B needs an edge. It is a saturated market so there needs to be a reason why potential customers would choose you over others.

Price discriminate – this is so important. You must alter your room rates depending on the season of the year and also on the time of day. This is sometimes the difference between profit and loss.

Maximize profit – you must chase profit, not turnover. To do this you chase revenue and control costs. It is easy to overspend, and very difficult to keep costs down while also delivering a great service and making a profit.

THE NUMBERS

So what makes a good B&B? Well, in my opinion it is one that can deliver a 33% yield. That is, the anticipated annual revenue from the B&B should equal approximately one-third of what you can buy the property for.

You have to be careful here. It is not a simple case of multiplying the number of rooms by the nightly rate and then multiplying it by 365 to give you the annual revenue! So, a four-roomed B&B which has advertised rates of £60 per night the anticipated annual revenue would *not* be: $4 \times £60 \times 365 = £87,600$. The reason for this is because it assumes (a) full occupancy, and (b) no price discrimination.

Full occupancy rates

No property has a 100% occupancy – that is, the rooms are full every day of the year. It would be crazy to assume this. What needs to be calculated is the occupancy rate. Occupancy rates are available for all sectors of the hotel market including the B&B and they analyse down to geographical towns and cities.

Now this data can only be as good as what is input and its validity is down to you to decide. However, occupancy rates can be used as a guide to what to expect when it comes to occupation.

Price discrimination

Most of the time your published prices will remain static, but at certain times they need to change.

- ☐ Prices should go up at times of increased demand: school holidays, or special events nearby.
- ☐ Prices should go down when lack of demand is low.

If you do not push your prices up in high demand periods and lower them in low demand periods you will:

- ☐ miss out on additional revenue over and above the published room rates in the high demand periods;
- ☐ lose out on the room rate altogether in the low demand periods.

So the idea is to base your anticipated revenue on these fluctuations to get a more accurate figure.

BUILDING THE ANTICIPATED REVENUE FIGURE

It is so important to build an accurate revenue figure. If you get this figure right then the rest is simple mathematics. If you can build the anticipated revenue figure more precisely than others then you may be able to spot opportunities to your advantage.

If you do not know how to use Excel now is the time to learn. Search on the internet and you will find hundreds of guides. Excel is a piece of software that assists you in creating forecasting spreadsheets which you can use time and time again. If you join my newsletter at www.ahuja.co.uk I will send you one for free! Your sheet for a four-roomed B&B needs to look like this:

	Room 1	Room 2	Room 3	Room 4	Total
Week 1					
Week 2					
Week 3					
….Week 52					
Total					

And then you fill in the gaps. So the first box is for Room 1 in Week 1 and the figure that goes in here is what you can achieve as a room rate for the first week of the year in that room.

You would isolate the weeks where there is high demand and low demand and adjust the room rates accordingly. If you were considering a B&B in Clacton you would isolate the school holidays as high demand weeks and the winter months as the low demand weeks.

You may find that some of this work will have been done for you. Potential competitors' websites may have a room rate table so you can see when their rates change.

The actual room rates you charge will have to be an estimate. Again, look at what your competitors of similar quality are charging. Look at the diamond/star ratings for comparable properties.

Now assume full occupancy for all the weeks. Occupancy levels are dealt with below. So if the room rate is £50 per night for Week 1 for Room 1 then the figure that goes in the first box is: 7 × £50 = £350.

If there is more demand at the weekend, and the room rate on Friday and Saturday may be £70, and then the figure would be: (5 × £50) + (2 × £70) = £390.

Now do this for every week. A lot of the weeks will be the same; the only time you have to tweak it is in the high and low demand weeks. So your spreadsheet might look like this.

	Room 1	Room 2	Room 3	Room 4	Total
Week 1	£350	£390	£350	£420	£1,510
Week 2	£350	£390	£350	£420	£1,510
Week 3	£350	£390	£350	£420	£1,510
Week 4	£350	£390	£350	£420	£1,510
Week 5	£350	£390	£350	£420	£1,510
Week 6	£350	£390	£350	£420	£1,510
Week 7	£350	£390	£350	£420	£1,510
Week 8	£350	£390	£350	£420	£1,510
Week 9	£350	£390	£350	£420	£1,510
Week 10	£300	£320	£300	£350	£1,270
Week 11	£350	£390	£350	£420	£1,510
Week 12	£350	£390	£350	£420	£1,510
Week 13	£350	£390	£350	£420	£1,510
Week 14	£350	£390	£350	£420	£1,510
Week 15	£350	£390	£350	£420	£1,510
Week 16	£350	£390	£350	£420	£1,510
Week 17	£350	£390	£350	£420	£1,510
Week 18	£350	£390	£350	£420	£1,510
Week 19	£350	£390	£350	£420	£1,510
Week 20	£350	£390	£350	£420	£1,510

Week 21	£350	£390	£350	£420	£1,510
Week 22	£350	£390	£350	£420	£1,510
Week 23	£350	£390	£350	£420	£1,510
Week 24	£350	£390	£350	£420	£1,510
Week 26	£500	£550	£600	£650	£2,300
Week 27	£500	£550	£600	£650	£2,300
Week 28	£500	£550	£600	£650	£2,300
Week 29	£500	£550	£600	£650	£2,300
Week 30	£500	£550	£600	£650	£2,300
Week 31	£500	£550	£600	£650	£2,300
Week 32	£600	£650	£700	£750	£2,700
Week 33	£350	£390	£350	£420	£1,510
Week 34	£350	£390	£350	£420	£1,510
Week 35	£350	£390	£350	£420	£1,510
Week 36	£350	£390	£350	£420	£1,510
Week 37	£350	£390	£350	£420	£1,510
Week 38	£350	£390	£350	£420	£1,510
Week 39	£350	£390	£350	£420	£1,510
Week 40	£350	£390	£350	£420	£1,510
Week 41	£350	£390	£350	£420	£1,510
Week 42	£350	£390	£350	£420	£1,510
Week 43	£350	£390	£350	£420	£1,510
Week 44	£350	£390	£350	£420	£1,510
Week 45	£350	£390	£350	£420	£1,510
Week 46	£350	£390	£350	£420	£1,510
Week 47	£350	£390	£350	£420	£1,510
Week 48	£350	£390	£350	£420	£1,510
Week 49	£350	£390	£350	£420	£1,510
Week 50	£350	£390	£350	£420	£1,510
Week 51	£350	£390	£350	£420	£1,510
Week 52	£350	£390	£350	£420	£1,510
Total	£19,200	£21,330	£19,900	£23,380	**£84,210**

So the total anticipated revenue if the B&B is 100% occupied is £84,210. However, as mentioned earlier, you have to apply an occupancy rate multiplier to this figure. Let's say the occupancy rate for the particular area is 72%. We get the following calculation: £84,210 × 72% = £60,631. So the anticipated revenue is £60,631. We use this rental figure to calculate the yield. Yield is: *Anticipated revenue divided by purchase price.*

So if you could purchase the property for £200,000 then the yield would be: £60,631 divided by £200,000 = 30.3%.

So this B&B would fall short of the 33% yield threshold. It would not be worth buying unless the price went down to: £60,631 divided by 33% = £183,730.

So the B&B needs to be priced at £183,730 for it to be worth buying.

Why use yield as the threshold?

You may have noticed I have ignored the other costs involved. Why have I not included costs such as rates, food costs, mortgage costs and utilities?

There is one good reason why. Yield takes care of all that. The threshold yield is set at a rate that allows for all other costs. If you can get a 33% yield then it will take some serious mismanagement of other costs before you lose. A 33% yield means that you can make mistakes and still survive.

If you accepted a lower threshold (and you may do this in the future) then there is no margin for error. So when interest rates go up, electricity bills rise, unexpected repairs need doing and occupancy rates drop, your anticipated profit could soon be a real loss.

But you have a chance with a 33% yield. As a rule of thumb you have 27% of the purchase price to run the B&B (33% – 6% = the 6% being the borrowing costs).

If the purchase price was £183,730, as above, you would have 27% × £183,730 = £49,607 to play with. Let's call it £50,000. So if you can provide a B&B service for less than approximately £50k the difference will be your profit.

How do you run a B&B efficiently so you make a profit? Well, that is largely down to you. Hard work yourself rather than paying someone else will hold you in good stead. However, I will give you some pointers later in the book (see Part Four) but next the question is where to find the right B&B.

FINDING THE RIGHT PROPERTY

You have two choices. The hard way is converting a residential property into a B&B. The easy way is to buy an existing B&B. Let's look at the first way just to see how hard it is.

Converting a residential property into a B&B

Converting your home into a B&B is possible in some areas without planning permission if you will have no more than three rooms. In all other circumstances you will need planning permission, and it is best to run any ideas through the planning department just to make sure.

You will need to obtain a change of use licence, from residential to commercial. How easy that will be depends on the effect your B&B will have on your neighbours. Parking, potential noise and the impact of having commercial premises in the area will be taken into account.

I suggest that you use the skills of a planning consultant. They may save you valuable time and effort trying to gain planning permission that they know will not get approved.

You may have to move a few walls in order to make your living quarters fully self-contained. Any alterations will have to comply with building regulations. It's advisable to use an architect.

Now my advice is, unless there is a specific reason to buy this residential property and convert it (such as the location, or you got it really cheap) I would avoid going down this route. Aim for an existing B&B that is up for sale. There will be no change of use application nor any major building works.

Buying an existing B&B

The existing B&B is all set up for you, complete with immediate cash flow as it's already operating. But it will come as no surprise to you that most are not worth buying. They will be too expensive as they will fail the 33% yield test, based on the declared income from their business accounts and your anticipated revenue calculation.

However, you may be able to spot opportunities where you can get a higher revenue, thus a higher yield. You will need a belief in your abilities to turn a B&B around.

Consider the following when looking at potential B&Bs to buy.

Reason for sale

If a B&B is selling because the business does not work, that is a big clue that it won't work for you. You can quickly establish this by looking at the accounts. If it's not working, try to see the reason for failure: a simple case of bad management, or loss of trade to the large Travelodge erected next to it last year!

Retirement, ill health, relocation, alternative investment, or anything that does not seem related to the actual business are reasons that should not alarm you. You have to read between the lines. If a major attraction close by is shutting down next month then this will directly affect your revenue. The owners will not volunteer this information.

View the accounts

The accounts will be sole trader or partnership accounts. They will not be audited and are prepared from the information and statements provided by the owner. Some owners do not declare all their income, perhaps if they receive some amounts in cash. So the figures may be understated.

To verify the revenue you could ask to see copies of (1) the **signed VAT returns**, or even better, official documentation from HMRC showing their turnover levels; and (2) their **tax return**, or their SA302 from HMRC, which will show their tax computation based on their profit for the last tax year.

Watch the property

Spend an evening opposite the B&B and see how many people arrive to check in. If the owner has told you they are fully booked every night, check that the footflow matches that claim. If there are five rooms you should expect to see five different residents coming or going during the course of the evening.

Size

B&Bs fall into two sizes.

- **Fewer than five rooms**. This size can be operated by you and you only, without the need for any staff. The breakfast, laundry and cleaning can be managed by you and/or your spouse, and the business will not take over your life.

- **More than five rooms**. This size requires a bit more effort. You will need to take on a cleaner and/or cook as a couple will not be able to do all the work. You will need a decent-sized kitchen to cater for the number of guests, and sufficient car parking. However, a bigger size means you can benefit from economies of scale and take on group bookings.

If you look at average B&B prices you find that the higher the number of rooms, the cheaper the cost of the room. So five-bedroom B&Bs may go for £200,000 and ten-bedroom B&Bs for £300,000. So the smaller B&B room purchase price is £200k/5 = £40k, but the larger B&B room purchase price is £300k/10 = £30k.

So there are good reasons to go for it big style as it will be easier to break the 33% yield threshold.

CHOOSING THE USP/THEME/NICHE

You need to have a theme for the B&B. You can expand this idea to one of the following: **USP**, **theme**, or **niche**.

USP stands for unique selling proposition. There should be a reason why people come to your B&B that is unique to your business.

Your theme could be shown by the décor you use. It could be to do with the local area, an attraction, or even a famous person.

If you aim for a niche market you will focus on certain groups of people with a common interest.

- ☐ **Price**. You can be the cheapest or the most expensive. Either way will be a reason for people to come.

- ☐ **Quality**. Five star or unclassified? Positioning yourself as the highest quality is a common way to stand out. Think Hilton Hotels and you'll get the idea.

- ☐ **Location**. Is your B&B right in the centre of where it is all happening? People will pay a premium to be in the heart of it.

- ☐ **Food**. Do you do a mean English breakfast? Let your sausage be the talk of the town and watch them pile in.

- ☐ **Age**. You could run a really funky young B&B, or one that focuses on families, or single parents.

- ☐ **Outdoors**. Focus on specific outdoor activities such as rock-climbing, or birdwatching.

- ☐ **Sports**. Focus on local sporting activities such as surfing or snow-boarding.

- ☐ **Sexuality**. Gay B&Bs are quite common in Blackpool and Brighton. Does your area lack a gay B&B?

Nothing I have said is ground-breaking, just common sense. But do not be caught out and get what is technically called 'stuck in the middle'. Differentiation is key – there must be a reason for people to come to you.

MAXIMIZING REVENUE

Customers will come from a number of sources. The following shows you how to maximize this.

Customer source and how to increase it

Footflow

Make sure your B&B has kerb appeal. A nice, clean exterior with an attractive sign will catch the attention of passersby.

Make sure your 'No Vacancies' sign is turned round the right way!

Website

You definitely need a web presence. Include clear pictures of the outside, the rooms and communal areas. Include a capture form for emails and telephone numbers so you can get back to people when they enquire.

Consider emailing/sending a newsletter once a quarter to anyone who does enquire, including your latest offers. A 24-hour answering service will mean you never miss a call.

If you are brave enough, include customer feedback rating, but make sure you monitor it. A negative response could kill enquiries.

Use Google Adwords to promote your site. See my book *How To Make A Fortune On The Internet* for advice on how to create an online presence.

Online networks

Networks such as www.laterooms.co.uk can give you an excellent amount of leads. Some only charge per lead or even per booking.

Offline ads

Write articles or pay for adverts in magazines and newspapers that specialize in your niche or theme.

Tourist board

Listing with tourist guides or tourist boards can generate enquiries and the great thing is it's completely free!

Word of mouth

The best form of advertising. If you provide a great service you can be sure you will get repeat bookings.

Additional streams of revenue

Here are some other ideas on how to get your turnover up.

- ☐ **Sell memorabilia/goods**. Depending on your theme or location you could benefit from selling goods you think your customers might be interested in.

☐ **Offer food and/or alcohol**. You could expand the kitchen to offer lunch or dinner and even a glass of wine to go with it. Margins are very high on food if you keep an eye on wastage. The margins on alcohol are even better!

☐ **Install broadband**. You would offer metered access to broadband. Some hotels charge £10 for 24 hours, so there is nothing stopping you doing the same.

COMPLYING WITH REGULATIONS

Running a B&B requires compliance with certain regulations and guidelines. They fall into three main categories: **fire**, **food and hygiene**, and **health and safety**.

Fire

A fire officer needs to come and assess the fire risk. You will need to do the following.

☐ Install fire doors as the internal doors.
☐ Have emergency lighting.
☐ Have protected fire escape routes.
☐ Put up signage in case of fire in all rooms.
☐ Have a fire blanket at high fire risk locations like the kitchen.
☐ Install fire extinguishers in the hallway.
☐ Have a mains-wired fire alarm system with smoke detectors.

Food and hygiene

You will have to comply with the many regulations regarding cooking and food, which include:

☐ storage of food;
☐ preparation of food;
☐ hygiene (both personal and of equipment);
☐ waste disposal;
☐ cleanliness of water supply.

Health and safety

All areas where the guests can enter – the rooms, communal areas and hall, landing and stairs – need to be free from trip hazards. You need a full electricity safety certificate, and electrical goods must undergo a five-year electrical test. Put anti-slip mats in all bathrooms.

Consult an H&S professional to do an assessment on the property to make sure you have covered all bases.

Having someone available who can perform first aid is advisable though not a legal requirement.

Complying with regulations is essential and costs money. It is important you comply but cost-effectively. I set the 33% threshold yield suitably high to take into account compliance costs.

7

PROPERTY TRADER (TRADITIONAL)

VITAL STATISTICS

Earning potential before tax	£5,000 to unlimited per property
Capital required	£nil to £50,000
Skills required	Ability to act quickly
Qualifications preferable	None
Competitiveness: low/medium/high	High
Risk: low/medium/high	High
The business model in a nutshell	Buy extremely cheap and sell cheap B2B trader
Potential gaps in the market and suggested USPs	• Auction to auction sales • Portfolio break-up

You will like to hear what I have to say about this business model: *a LOT of money can be made if you know what you are doing.*

The reason is that trading properties is just that. You do absolutely nothing to the property. You simply buy and then sell. There is no need to pander to the whims of an owner-occupier as you will be dealing with property businesses.

The success of this business is all in the buying. If you buy right then the rest is all taken care of. So what is buying right? Buying right is *buying cheap*!

You must buy cheap so you can sell cheap. You make small margins on each property and you focus on volume. That is to say, you are better off selling ten properties to make a quick 10% on each one rather than holding out for 100% profit on one property and realizing none.

This business can work even in a credit crunch. As long as you have bought well enough to factor in a further decline in prices then you will make money.

I know of property traders who are able to buy properties at 15% of market value. Yes, 15%. When they get a whiff of a bargain property and the vendor perceives their options are limited, they show no mercy! They will pay the least they can.

THE FORMULA

☐ Buy at maximum 50% of market value.
☐ Sell at minimum 60% of market value.
☐ Do it in the quickest time possible.

If you can achieve this then you will become wealthy. Plenty of property traders do just this. They never get their hands dirty, just shuffle bits of paper between solicitors and lenders and cream off 10% to 20% gross profit each time they trade.

And remember, we are not talking 10% of a small figure. Assuming an average transaction value of £100k then each trade can make you £10k and sometimes a lot more. Let me explain the formula in a bit more detail.

Buy at maximum 50% of market value

This game is all about buying right. For me, that's 50% of market value, basically half what a property is worth. Take the following properties available in a property auction:

Fire damaged three-bed semi in Grimsby – Guide £5,000
City centre apartment in Glasgow two-bed – Guide £50,000
Two-bed house in Hull rented for £300 per month – Guide £25,000

Do you think those guide prices are reasonable? Do you have any idea or would you be just guessing?

Now you have to work out what each property is worth in its current condition in today's market to spot whether it is a bargain. This involves getting inside the mind of an investor. It is these investors who will buy from you so you need to know what makes them tick.

You may wonder why an investor will not buy a property before you. Well, the property market is a very imperfect market. True market prices are hard to realize.

The property market exists as a mass of mini platforms: property auctions, estate agents, private sales. All are littered with arbitrary possibilities. You can buy from one mini platform and sell to another and make a profit in doing so.

So as long as these mini platforms exist then there will be opportunities to make money simply by buying and selling properties. This is a B2B trader game. Nice and clean and plenty to make.

Sell at minimum 60% market value

I deem 60% market value to be good for two reasons.

1. It guarantees you at least 10% profit on your deal. 10% will net you at least 5% profit after fees on an average purchase price of £100k. This equates to £5k per deal, which really is the minimum you should expect from each property transaction.

2. 60% of market value is a bargain to an investor. There should be no reason why you accept anything less. If the investor is the end user, i.e. they are buying it to hold on to it, then they will be more than happy to pay 60% of market value. If they want more of a discount they are simply being greedy. If you are not brave enough to tell them so say I said so!

A price of 60% of market value should result in a swift sale, which is what any property trader wants.

Do it in the quickest possible time

A trader makes their money by selling, cheaply and quickly. Don't be greedy. A trader who bought correctly at 50% of market value but wanted to sell at 100% of market value could wait a very long time. During this time the trader would make no money as no sale has taken place. In the meantime the following could and/or will happen.

1. The property market in general may drop. As a result you will have to revise your asking price downwards, or will not be able to sell until the market recovers which could be ages away.

2. The property itself degenerates. The longer you hold the more likely something will go wrong. It's your property, so you assume all the risks of ownership. Even with insurance, repairs can be costly.

3. The longer you hold the more interest costs you pay. This directly eats into your margin. So if your interest costs are £1,000 per month and you think it will take you six months to get £3,000 more on the selling price, then is it really worth it? You should always look to minimize your holdings costs and opt for a swift sale.

4. Exposure – that is, whether or not a trader is in the market. If you are holding £1m worth of property that is up for sale then you are in the market. You are exposed. Let's say the credit crunch hits at that point. Depending on how quickly you can sell, by slashing prices and cutting your losses, you could find yourself in the bankruptcy courts. As a trader you want to keep your exposure to the minimum. Sales at 60% of market value during a credit crunch would probably still go through. Buyers would appreciate that it is still a bargain. At 60% of market value there is enough of a safety buffer zone for everyone.

So, what is cheap? You need to be able to work out what market value is with a certain degree of accuracy, in order to establish what cheap is.

DETERMINING MARKET VALUE

So what is market value? A B2B trader deems market value to be what market value is to an investor. An investor deems market value to be what sort of return they want to get from an investment.

Returns wanted by investors

The minimum return on average an investor wants from an investment is 12%. There will be variations to this in different areas. Where I invest in Hull I would want 15%; in Harlow a 10% return would do. But on average a 12% return is pretty good.

In pre-credit crunch days a 5% return was touted as good. All change. Sanity has returned. I would never buy at such a low return and nor did any professional investor back then.

Market value of rentable properties

So with a 15% return being universally acceptable to a professional investor you can then work out what market value is. Simply fill in the missing numbers to this equation: market value = (monthly rent × 12) divided by 12%.

If there is a property that commands a monthly rent of £500 then its market value would be calculated as: (£500 × 12) divided by 0.12 = £50,000.

The price to pay for this property is 50% of this market value. So the buy price is: 50% × £50,000 = £25,000.

So if you see the property for sale at anything below £25,000 then grab it. You will then find an investor willing to pay at least 60% of market value, being £30,000.

This assumes that it is in rentable condition. Properties that require work need to be calculated in a different way.

Market value of properties requiring work

Let's say the same property that commands a rent of £500 a month has now been seriously fire damaged. The cost to repair it is £20,000. Then the price to pay is the buy price minus the cost of refurbishment, which works out as: £25,000 – £20,000 = £5,000.

If the refurbishment cost was £30,000 then the buy price of the property requiring work would be: £25,000 – £30,000 = –£5,000.

That's a minus figure. Hence the property is worthless and you would have to be paid £5,000 to take it on. This explains why there are plenty of properties that just sit empty. They will never find a buyer. The only way these properties can come back to life is if the council provides grants to would-be purchasers. If there are no grants then the bulldozers are brought in.

You have to be able to estimate the cost of the repair works. This is where the skill comes in. If you over-estimate you will put the buy price too low. If you under-estimate you will put it too high and end up buying something you cannot sell.

There is plenty of information around that can help you estimate the costs, but as a rule I use this scale.

- ☐ Full decoration of a property – £10k.
- ☐ Repairing fire damage – £20k.
- ☐ Re-kitting out a shell of a property – £40k.

These are very rough prices and I have ignored size. I just attribute a general figure to any property that comes my way. So for a two-bed flat with old décor I would guesstimate the cost of the refurb as £10,000. I know I could do it for less than that but it allows for any unexpected problems.

Now these refurb estimates assume a basic finish. Do not expect a Versace bathroom from these budgets! If you are thinking of trading anything over a purchase price of £125k, adjust the refurb costs to match the intended rental market. If a fire-damaged flat in Mayfair comes up, expect to spend a little more than £20k!

FINDING THE PROPERTIES

It will come as no surprise to you that the UK is not overflowing with properties at 50% market value! There are two sources of bargain properties: **auctions** and **desperate sellers**.

Auctions

Bargain properties can be grabbed here because reserve prices can be low and there is not much competition.

A property ends up in auction as a last resort. Auctions are great for sellers as exchange of contracts happens at the fall of the hammer. The buyer is then financially committed to the purchase.

Someone entering a property for auction is thus already primed to accept a lower price. This may be their only chance of realizing some cash quickly.

Sellers in auctions are, however, often banks. Banks only really care about getting back the amount they lent, plus fees. This could mean that only £25,000 is needed on a property worth £200,000. So a property could be entered worth £200k with a reserve of only £25k. This property will be sold to the highest bidder. If there aren't many bidders, then BINGO!

This results in some properties having very low reserves. It is these properties that can be had as bargains. But it is not enough to find properties with low reserves. If there are many bidders then the property may sell for well in excess of the reserve.

You want to find auctions where there are not only low reserve properties but few buyers.

Imagine an empty auction hall and you have the perfect auction hall. You will be the highest bidder in every scenario and all you need to do is name your price! As long as your named price is in excess of the reserve, then you have a match!

I have described an imaginary situation, but there can be times when there are few buyers for specific properties, or few buyers in general. You want to look for environments where these situations can occur.

There are three types of auctions: **national**, **regional**, and **local**.

National auctions

These are usually in London. Properties from all over the UK get auctioned off at one event. Big sellers are present, such as the well-known banks and large investors.

You may find a property in a little-known town being auctioned off sandwiched in between a mansion in Hampstead and a block of apartments in Birmingham city centre. This little property may have low interest levels and Mr Local Landlord from this little town is simply not there to bid. So this property will either get no bids (which is very common) or your bid!

So don't ignore these large national auctions. You may be able to benefit from the situation of having few buyers for one or two specific properties. If you are patient you might just grab a bargain that everyone else misses.

Regional auctions

Typical regional auctions cover such areas as Scotland, the North West, the South East and London.

They can be as large as national auctions, and they can throw up bargains if there are few bidders. Again you may benefit from the situation of having few buyers for one or two specific properties. During the summer months and either side of Christmas bargains may be had – while others are on holiday you can be buying!

Local auctions

Some auctions sell local properties only, and will be specific to the town or city. These auction halls can sometimes be deserted. There can be as few as ten people in the room, and a couple of them will buy nearly everything. They will only stop buying because they run out of cash, or really do not favour the property. Here you can benefit from the situation of having few buyers in general.

So remember you want to find properties with low reserves within a room of few buyers. Then the bargains can be had.

Desperate sellers

Desperate sellers are private individuals who have defaulted (or are about to) on their mortgage commitment. They may have lost their job or have over-borrowed and can no longer afford to pay their mortgage.

These sellers want out quick. They do not have the money for a HIP, or the time to wait for prospective buyers or the patience to deal with estate agents. They want a buyer who will give them the best price in order to clear their mortgage and even give them a little bit on top.

Your only competitors at this game are other buyers like you. To beat the competition you need to be fast.

First you need to find the desperate sellers. Advertising is one option, on the **internet**, in the **national and local press**, and by **leafleting**.

Advertising on the internet

Just Google 'sell home fast' or 'sell home quick' and plenty of websites will come up offering to buy your home. Study these to see what wording you should use. Include things like:

- ☐ No HIPS.
- ☐ We will complete in 7 days.
- ☐ Up to 90% of market value paid.
- ☐ We pay all fees.

There will be an easy to fill out form prominent on the site to capture the desperate seller's details. It is these details that will make you the money. Once you have these you need to follow up with a phone call as soon as possible.

Advertising in the national and local press

Towards the back of any newspaper you will see adverts such as 'Sell Home Fast'. To advertise here costs around £200–£500 per day. You can specialize by region to get a cheaper price.

You could start off gently with local advertising. Your local paper will probably have a 'Properties Wanted' section among the classified pages. Use a catchy title that will attract a desperate seller to pick up the phone and call.

Display advertising is the logical next step once you have made the classified advertising work. Remember that this is expensive. You have to have your business model down to a T if you are going to do this, and be quite clear how many leads you expect to get for every pound of advertising.

Leafleting

Get leaflets printed and deliver them to your chosen area. Make the leaflet clear and attractive: 'Sell Your Home Fast!'. The phone number you use could be an 0800 number which costs the homeowner nothing. If you use a call centre they will send on messages via email to you.

Always include an alternative number, such as a mobile. If the homeowner has had the phone cut off and is reliant on their mobile, a call to an '08' number can cost quite a bit.

If you delegate the delivery to someone else, make sure they are trustworthy. You do not want to find your leaflets in a litter bin or spread across the playground. Some people offer the person dropping the leaflets a £100 bonus for every deal they find as a result of their leafleting. Not a bad idea!

FINANCING THE DEAL

Cash is the best method to buy these deals, but I am going to assume you have very little. Even if you do have cash, it is always best to think that you are using other people's money in order to aim for the best return.

You can buy properties using other people's money in these ways: **buy-to-let mortgage**, **commercial finance**, **bridging finance**, and **venture capital**.

Buy-to-let mortgage

To say that the buy-to-let mortgage market has shrunk over the years would be an understatement! We had 4,000 buy-to-let mortgages back in 2007; at the time of writing we have exactly 59. The good thing is, the only way is *up*.

The mortgages I want to talk about here are the refurbishment buy-to-let mortgages. These are currently offered by two lenders – Northern Rock and The Mortgage Works – but I suspect more will follow.

Refurbishment mortgages allow you to buy properties that are unlettable by putting down only a 30% deposit. The mortgages remove the risk of a valuer knocking back a property because of its condition. When you are trying to buy at 50% of market value it is likely that some refurbishment is required, even if only light. This includes tenanted properties. I have had many properties that have been tenanted and perfectly habitable (as proved by the tenant) knocked back by a surveyor as unmortgageable.

Refurbishment mortgages enable you to buy without this worry. Since you are trying to buy and then sell you want a mortgage lender that is not going to baulk at the sight of a damp patch on the living-room wall.

They also give you a back-up strategy if you are unable to sell. These lenders will lend you 70% of the value of the property post-refurbishment. Sometimes this valuation is given at the same time and you may get the absurd happening when the property is valued a fair bit higher than what you paid for it.

So, you could find a property to buy at £50k and they say post-refurbishment it will be worth £100k. It may take only £5k to refurb. Then you have the following figures:

Purchase price = £50k
Mortgage lender lends 70% × £50k = £35k
Post-refurbishment loan from same lender: 70% × £100k = £70k

Cashback of £70k − £50k − £5k = £15k

If the opportunity arises where the valuer gives a generous valuation post-refurb, then please be clever enough to spot it and change the strategy (like buy, refurb and sell to first-time buyer etc.) to get a better return.

Now, you still need to come up with the 30% deposit, but that is better than coming up with the full amount. The great thing is that it is easy to rack up a big credit limit with these lenders. They will probably lend 70% to every 30% you can find. If you could get your hands on £3m I would not be surprised if they lent you £7m.

Commercial finance

Commercial finance is where lending is conducted outside of the CML (Council of Mortgage Lenders) rules. All buy-to-let and residential mortgages follow these rules. But there are some mortgages that do not have to follow these rules, and this is where commercial finance comes in.

Commercial lenders include: RBS, NatWest, Lloyds, Barclays, HSBC, Bank of Scotland, Clydesdale Bank, Bank of Ireland and Allied Irish. I am sure there are more.

Any bank that has a high street presence and is not a building society seems to have a commercial division and can grant commercial mortgages, which can be struck based on commercial terms rather than CML terms. Now here are the three really cool things about commercial mortgages:

1. **No minimum valuation**. This is how I built my portfolio quickly. A lot of properties fall under lenders' minimum valuations, set at £50,000, occasionally £40,000. So when a property worth £60,000 comes up for sale for £30,000, you cannot get a mortgage from a regular CML buy-to-let lender. But commercial lenders will happily lend up to 70% of *any* purchase price.

2. **No six-month rule**. This rule has caught a lot of property people out. It means that you cannot remortgage or purchase a property that has been owned for less than six months. So buying a property worth £60k for £30k one day and remortgaging it the next at a value of £60k would not be possible. You would have to wait six months to do so. With commercial lenders you do not need to wait.

3. **Tailored service**. The terms agreed are set by you and the lender, for example the rate, loan to value (LTV), arrangement fees. It is up to you to strike a good deal. They often offer as a margin over base and you can actually get deals that are much better than your standard buy-to-let lenders.

Before you rush to contact your nearest branch to obtain some commercial mortgages, here is the bad news.

□ You need to have an existing minimum borrowing level of at least £250k, usually £500k. They like to deal with full-time property people. A certain level of borrowing usually indicates whether you are serious about investing or just playing. If you are currently doing property as a hobby but aim to be full time, I suggest you reread Chapter 2. It can be well worth it just to get access to commercial finance.

□ These lenders offer repayment mortgages. They hate interest only. The best you can get is a couple of years' interest only but then it reverts to capital and repayment.

□ The maximum term is 20 years. My commercial mortgages are 15 years repayment, which results in hefty monthly payments even though the rate is at a sensible 3%. I am simply paying back the capital over a short period of time. So make sure you sell the property quick!

□ Loan to values (LTV) are usually around 60%. In some circumstances you can get 70% (and 80% is very, very rare).

□ You may need to open a bank account with them. Depending on how pushy they are they may want you to switch your business account to them so they can charge you banking fees. Do your sums. If it is your only option then you just have to do it. Having a commercial lender is *very* beneficial in the property world.

So weigh up the pros and cons of commercial mortgages. If you decide it is right for you, contact a high street branch and they will point you to the right department.

Bridging finance

This is short-term finance that people use to buy at auctions. The money is advanced fast to ensure that you adhere to the tight completion deadlines set by the auctions.

Bridging finance is fast but not cheap! They will charge you, for example:

□ valuation fees: £500;
□ legal fees: £1,000;
□ arrangement fees: 3%;
□ exit fees: 1%;
□ interest: 1.5% per month.

You can see how the costs can add up. So why I am recommending bridging finance? The best thing about bridging is that some lenders offer *70% of the valuation of the property*.

So if you had got a property worth £100k for £70k, the bridging company would lend you 70% × £100k = £70k. This is 100% finance. A bridging lender will lend 100% of the purchase price if the valuation is significantly in excess of the purchase price.

Traditional lenders would only lend you 70% × £70k = £49k. You would need to find £70k − £49k = £21k as a deposit. If you do not have £21k then no deal, unless of course you have access to bridging finance!

So, as long as you can find the deals then there is nothing stopping you buying. The only real limit is the total credit limits set by all the bridging finance companies that will work with you.

Do your maths very carefully on this one. As mentioned above, you want to sell quickly in this game. If you get bridging finance then you have to sell doubly quick as you are paying 1% to 2% a month. On a £100,000 loan that is £1,000 to £2,000 per month holding cost – ouch! So try to buy *really* cheap to factor in a hold of six months. 40% of market value would be a good threshold – but ultimately it's your call.

Venture capital

You may have heard of this type of financing. The Dragons on the BBC programme *Dragons' Den* offer venture capital. They venture their capital on your idea. And guess what your idea is? Buying and selling property.

Before you reach for the business plan software I will say that most venture capitalists do not invest in property trading. It could be due to the climate we are in, or the fact that most business plans require additional borrowing, which scares them as it changes the risk profile massively.

However, you may be able to find less formal venture capitalists, such as the Bank of Mum or Dad, early inheritance from grandparents, friends, and people you meet at networking events.

There may be many people around you who want to make money but cannot be bothered to work for it. They may have cash tucked away and want to put it to work. So a venture capitalist could be closer than you think!

I do not have to explain the delicate nature of going into business with friends or family. Just remember to be clear from the start and *put everything in writing*.

SELLING THE PROPERTY

Now as explained earlier, you need to sell the property quickly. You may not necessarily get the highest price, but you can still make a very healthy living.

Use every avenue

My strategy to get a quick sale is not to put all your eggs in one basket. I recommend you use every selling avenue at your disposal.

1. Estate agents

No sales commission is payable with an estate agent until you sell. So you can list your property with many estate agents in one area. Explain that you want a quick sale and don't take the property off the market until exchange of contracts.

You will have to pay for a Home Information Report (HIP) which costs about £250.

Set the price at around 75% of market value and let the prospective purchasers bid you down.

2. Auction

You may have found your bargain at auction; you can sell at auction also. You simply need to do the opposite of when you are buying: place your property where there will be many bidders for it. For example, you could put the property from a local auction into a regional auction where there will be more buyers. Or keep the property in the same auction but avoid August and December.

Note that with auctions *you do not need to wait for the sale date*. You will get plenty of bids prior to the auction.

Property sourcers

Property sourcers (like me!) have plenty of hungry clients who will take your property if the figures stack up. I know I can sell any property within two hours that yields 7.5% and is at 70% of market value. This is because that kind of property is attractive to around 80% of the investors out there! So price it right and you can get rid of a deal in a few hours.

Advertising

It can be worth advertising in local papers and websites. For ads that cost less than £25 you could get a profit of £10k. It's a no-brainer, isn't it?

All the activities in this chapter should give you the best chance of getting a sale. And remember what I have said all the way through: *Don't be greedy!*

8

PROPERTY TRADER (ENHANCE)

VITAL STATISTICS

Earning potential before tax	£5,000 to unlimited per property
Capital required	£nil to £50,000
Skills required	Project management
Qualifications preferable	Building trade, surveyor, architect
Competitiveness: low/medium/high	Medium
Risk: low/medium/high	High
The business model in a nutshell	Buy property needing work, refurbish and sell to first/second-time buyer or investor.
Potential gaps in the market and suggested USPs	Sell to DSS landlords Package deal so no money in by purchaser

The property enhancement market has changed since mortgage lenders introduced the six-month rule. It is usually the case that the majority of refurbished properties are sold to the end user (i.e. they will live in it!) and the majority of these will require a mortgage, so the six-month rule has to be taken very seriously. Otherwise you may end up holding a property far longer than you expected.

There are three strategies you can adopt to make money in the property.

1. **Refurbishment** – otherwise known as 'a lick of paint'. All you do is a cosmetic refurbishment, smarten up the kitchen, change the bathroom, paint the walls, put in new floor coverings and nice shiny paint on the front door. It can be done this very quickly and cheaply and add many times your investment in refurbishment as profit.

2. **Conversion** – you convert part or all of the property (a loft conversion or split it into flats) to realize a profit due to the conversion you apply.

3. **Extension** – add floor space area to a property, realizing your profit in the enhanced value you give the property.

All exciting stuff! Those of you who like to see a finished product will love this game. There will be plenty of ups and downs but those who persevere and know what they are doing can make some serious money.

THE FORMULA

Determine which enhancement method you want to follow (refurbishment, conversion or extension). Work out the buy price, enhancement cost and sell price. Enhance. Sell.

So after you've decided what type of enhancement you want to do the rest is just following through.

REFURBISHMENT, CONVERSION OR EXTENSION?

Each method has its attractions. However, the increasing levels of enhancement result in increasing levels of risk, which are compensated by increasing levels of profit!

Refurbishment

The attractive thing about refurbishment is that no planning permission is required. You can buy, refurbish and then sell. It is the lowest risk way of adding value to a property and is how property developers usually start off. If you have an eye for interior design then you can make decent profits. Refurbishment can involve:

1. Painting and decorating
2. Plumbing
3. New bathroom and kitchen
4. Flooring
5. Basic electrics
6. Installation of gas central heating
7. New windows
8. Basic exterior work

You can manage the various subcontractors yourself or you can instruct a building company to do the whole project. If you are new to the enhancement concept I suggest you choose the latter method. Also, try to stick to properties that require only numbers 1–5, above. It is best to break yourself in gently.

Once you have done a few refurbs, and you want to get top dollar for your property then numbers 6–8 can be worthwhile.

To be good at enhancement requires project managing. If you feel you have this skill then enhancing properties could be for you. Paperwork is minimal and you can just crack on with the project as soon as you get the keys.

Conversion

Conversion is the next natural step after you have mastered refurbishment. If you are looking for a bigger return then conversion can deliver the goods. It can involve:

1. Knocking down and erecting walls
2. Creating bathrooms and kitchens out of empty rooms and spaces
3. Seeking planning permission from the council
4. Dealing with the land registry with creating titles

You might now see why most people do not do conversions. It is not a simple process. You need to have not only project managing skills but also the following:

- **Paperwork skills**. There will be a lot of paperwork being shuffled between architects, solicitors, land registry, and planning departments. You have to be organized.

- **Good negotiating and people skills**. You will have to deal not only with subcontractors such as builders and plumbers but also with white collar professionals such as architects, council officers, fire officers. Persuasion rather than instruction is necessary here in order to get what you want.

- **Persistence**. Conversion projects can be fraught with problems. Procedures need to be followed and each section of work needs to be signed off before the next stage can begin. Also, creating rather than replacing can mean that a lot of other problems emerge. So a fair degree of persistence is required to see the project through. There are plenty of abandoned projects for sale at auctions.

Extensions

Extensions require all of the above plus:

1. The building of foundations
2. The building of walls
3. Construction of roofs

This is serious stuff. So again you need all of the above skills but you'll have a greater number of contractors to do this extra work. Projects are lengthier and more costly but the rewards are naturally higher if you get it right.

So which one?

Refurbishment, conversion or extension? Only you can decide. It is common to start off with refurbishment and then progress to the others. The next stage beyond that is property development – building flats and houses – but that is another book!

HOW TO MAKE MONEY FROM REFURBISHMENT

The enhancement game is all margin led. You have to know what you want to make as a profit before you start.

The best way to express what you want is as a percentage of the eventual selling price. This eliminates the obvious mistake many novice refurbishers make by chasing absolute figures. You see non-businesspeople developing a £1m property to make £10,000. That is chasing a 1% return. The slightest problem will bring the project out of budget and into loss. Setting your margin as a percentage is a rule set in stone. Please do not deviate from this.

Your margin is best based on the selling price, as this is market led. Focus on the selling price as this is the only figure really out of your control. If you invest time in determining what it will be then this should reduce the margin of error.

The margin you should aim for is 25% of the selling price. So if a property has an estimated selling price of £100,000, you should expect to make £25,000 profit before tax but after all direct expenses. The 25% allows for:

- ☐ you estimating the selling price to be wrong;
- ☐ a fall in the market during refurbishment;
- ☐ you over spending on the project.

So, if you were 5% out on the estimated selling price, there was a 5% fall in the property market during refurbishment and you overspent on the refurbishment by 5%, based on the estimated selling price you would still make: 24% — 5% — 5% — 5% = 10%.

If you estimated the selling price to be £100,000 you would still make: 10% × £100,000 = £10,000.

Let's look at all the costs. I have created something for you that you are going to love. It will take all the hard work out for you. It is a cheat sheet and you just need to fill in the blanks. Once you have done this you will derive the price that starts the whole thing off: the **buy price**.

If you buy right then even if you make a pig's ear of the refurbishment you can still make money. I have filled in the cheat sheet as an example.

Calculating the buy price: refurbishment

	Income and expenditure	Amount £	% of selling price
	INCOME		
What you think you can sell the property for.	Estimated selling price (A)	100,000	100
Estimated cost of the HIP needed when you come to sell the property.	HIP (B)	300	
Your estimate of what your solicitor charges for selling a property for you.	Legal fees (C)	600	
Estimated as 2.5% of the estimated selling price.	Selling commission (D)	2500	2.5
An amount for unforeseen expenses.	Sundry (E)	500	
25% of the estimated selling price.	Margin (F)	25,000	25
What you can spend on the whole project.	Contribution to project (G) $(A - B - C - D - E - F)$	**71,100**	
	EXPENDITURE		
The legal fees to purchase the property.	Legal fees (H)	600	
Stamp duty payable to buy the property: 0% <£125k 1% >£125k 3% >£250k 4% >£500k	Stamp duty (I)	1,500	
Estimated refurbishment costs. This cost is directly linked to the estimated sales price. So if you have planned a luxury bathroom in order to get the estimated selling price then make sure it is budgeted for here. For a basic refurbishment: • Decorate and carpet bedroom/reception room, HSL (hall, stairs, landing): £1,000 per room • Kitchen or bathroom: £2,000 • Install gas central heating: £2,500 • New windows: £2,500	Refurbishment cost (J)	10,000	
An amount for unforeseen costs.	Sundry (K)	500	
Financing costs of holding the property for a minimum of six months. I would budget for nine months.	Interest costs (L)	2,000	
A percentage of the amount borrowed, usually between 1% and 3%.	Mortgage arrangement fees (M)	1,000	
Estimated survey cost.	Valuation costs (N)	500	
Estimate mortgage broker cost.	Broker fees (O)	500	
Sum of the costs.	Total purchasing and refurbishment costs (P) $(H + I + J + K + L + M + N + O)$	**16,600**	
Derive the buy price of the property.	Buy price: Amount left over to purchase property $(G - P)$	**54,500**	

Looking at the figures in the table the following should be noted:

1. A buy price of anything less than £54,500 is a good buy price.
2. You would need to achieve at least £71,100 to not lose any money.

Visit my website www.ahuja.co.uk and join my newsletter and you can get this cheat sheet for free, which will perform the calculations automatically.

Be prudent with all your estimates. You may see opportunities go by but it is better to let ten opportunities go than buy a dud. It is a patience game. That deal will come along. Remember that there are literally millions of properties for sale. Take your time and hold out for the property that can give you an estimated 25% return. As I said before, if you buy right *everything* is taken care of.

HOW TO MAKE MONEY FROM CONVERSION

Conversions simply use the current space of the property in a commercially better way. This game is all about seeing the value of space in a given location. You need to take the value per sq ft and calculate whether by enhancing the current space you can achieve the value per sq ft *and* make a profit.

The cost of conversion is your only cost, as you already own the space. So it is a simple calculation of: *value created by conversion – cost of conversion = profit.*

The profit has to be worthwhile. Much depends on where the property is located. I have a neat way of determining whether or not a property is worth converting. You have to find out if the property sits on desired land. To do this you need to work out the market value relative to the rebuild cost.

The calculation you need to perform is: *current market value divided by the rebuild cost.*

You can establish the current market value by visiting land registry websites such as www.houseprices.co.uk. The rebuild cost is approximately £100 per sq ft. If the ratio is greater than 1, then the property sits on desired land and is potentially worth converting.

For example, a four-bed property worth £300,000 is for sale. It has a large loft area totalling 1,000 sq ft. The property living space is 1,500 sq ft. You would then do the following calculation: £300,000 divided by (1,500 sq ft × £100) = £300,000/ £150,000 = 2.

So on the face of it it appears that it is worth developing the loft. For every £1 spent you will get back £2.

The higher the number, the more reason to convert. Let's say a London flat is worth £1m and is 1,000 sq ft with a loft space of 1,000 sq ft. The ratio is then: £1m divided by (£100 × 1,000) = 10.

I have assumed a £100 per sq ft rebuild cost, which is an average figure. It will be cheaper for a loft or garage conversion and more expensive for a house into flats conversion.

I would set a threshold of 2. This will cover you quite safely. So if market value divided by the rebuild cost is greater than 2, then it is worth buying in this area.

Generally the more desirable areas are worth developing in. It is kind of obvious, but I do see some strange conversions going on, such as terraced properties being converted into two and one-bed flats. The only real gain is a bit of extra rent, which will take ages to pay back the cost of conversion.

What is your target return?

The target return to go for is a 30% profit margin on the selling price. This is higher than the refurbishment threshold as there are more things that can go wrong with a conversion. You may not get the planning permission you require or the conversion may be restricted. This will affect your selling price. So in the worst case scenario that planning is refused you can just refurbish and aim to at least get your money back.

I have created a cheat sheet (page 130) so that you can just fill in the blanks. This will calculate the maximum price you should pay to get the target return.

Again, do not forget to be prudent! It is better to underestimate the selling price and overestimate the costs. This way you will ensure your chances of success.

This cheat sheet is available for free by joining my newsletter at www.ahuja.co.uk.

HOW TO MAKE MONEY FROM EXTENSION

This is similar to conversion, except you are adding space to the property. The same rules apply regarding desired land. You need to calculate the ratio of market value to rebuild value.

Since the costs are higher for extensions I would set the threshold to 2.5. That is to say, the ratio of market value to rebuild cost should be greater than 2.5. So for a property with a market value of £400,000, and a rebuild cost of £200,000, then the ratio is £400k/£200k = 2.

Calculating the buy price: conversion

	Income and expenditure	Amount £	% of selling price
	INCOME		
What you think you can sell the converted property for. If you have converted a three-bed one-bath to a four-bed two-bath property or a four-bed house into two one-bed flats then it should be easy to get comparables.	Estimated selling price (A)	100,000	100
Estimated cost of the HIP you will need when you come to sell the property.	HIP (B)	300	
Your estimate of what your solicitor charges for selling a property for you.	Legal fees (C)	600	
Estimated as 2.5% of the estimated selling price.	Selling commission (D)	2,500	2.5
An amount for unforeseen expenses.	Sundry (E)	500	
30% of the estimated selling price.	Margin (F)	30,000	30
What you can spend on the whole project.	Contribution to project (G) (A − B − C − D − E − F)	**66,100**	
	EXPENDITURE		
The legal fees to purchase the property.	Legal fees (H)	600	
Stamp duty payable to buy the property: 0% ‹ £125k 1% › £125k 3% › £250k 4% › £500k	Stamp duty (I)	1,500	
Estimated conversion costs include: • Architect fees • Legal fees to get planning • Planning application fees • Building works Use these costs per sq ft: £40 per sq ft for loft conversions £50 per sq ft for garage conversions £65 per sq ft for conversion into flats Assumes at least one bathroom is being installed	Conversion cost (J)	20,000	
An amount for unforeseen costs.	Sundry (K)	500	
Financing costs of holding the property for a minimum of six months. I would budget for nine months.	Interest costs (L)	2,000	
A percentage of the amount borrowed, usually between 1% and 3%.	Mortgage arrangements fees (M)	1,000	
Estimate of the survey cost.	Valuation costs (N)	500	
Estimate mortgage broker cost.	Broker fees (O)	500	
Sum of the costs.	Total purchasing and conversion costs (P) (H + I + J + K + L + M + N + O)	26,600	
Derive the buy price of the property.	Buy price: Amount left over to purchase property (G − P)	**£39,500**	

So while the property is on desired land, an extension would not be worthwhile. For all the extra effort of effectively developing a property you want a safe return. These projects can sometimes take more than a year so you want a comfortable margin.

Fewer areas will be suitable than for refurbishment and conversion. The more desirable areas will be those that have ratios greater than 2.5.

The properties you should aim for will be small properties. You can effectively make a small house into a large family house, doubling the value of the property without spending too much.

The extensions that really add value are bedrooms and bathrooms. Have a flick through www.Rightmove.co.uk and do a little research.

Ascertain the average price of different property types, then compare the price differentials to give you the potential value you could add by adding bedrooms and bathrooms. For example, let's say you want to buy and extend a two-bed one-bath property and the average property values in the area are as follows:

2 bed 1 bath – £100,000
2 bed 2 bath – £125,000
3 bed 1 bath – £135,000
3 bed 2 bath – £160,000
4 bed 1 bath – £160,000
4 bed 2 bath – £185,000

Then calculate what the extra bedrooms and bathroom add to the value of the property.

	+ 1 bath	+ 1 bed	+ 1 bed +1 bath	+ 2 beds	+ 2 beds + 1 bath
2 bed, 1 bath	£25,000	£35,000	£60,000	£60,000	£85,000

Then compare this with your estimate for doing the works. For example, the costs to do the above might be:

	+ 1 bath	+ 1 bed	+ 1 bed + 1 bath	+ 2 beds	+ 2 beds + 1 bath
Cost	£10,000	£20,000	£40,000	£30,000	£60,000

The respective profits from the proposed extensions would be:

	+ I bath	+ I bed	+ I bed + I bath	+2 beds	+2 beds + I bath
Profit	£15,000	£15,000	£20,000	£30,000	£25,000

The profit is the value added less the cost. It can be seen that the optimum extension to do is to add two bedrooms only, as this will deliver the highest profit, assuming you have done your research properly.

What is your target return?

I believe you should aim to get 33% of the selling price as your profit. Again I have created a cheat sheet (opposite) so that you just fill in the blanks.

So if you can acquire the property for less than £31,500 it would be worth extending.

All this is a lot to digest but try to understand the numbers. I do not want you appearing on the next *Property Ladder* episode hoping for a property boom to rescue you from underestimating the building costs and overestimating the selling price!

FINANCING THE PROJECT

I spoke about refurbishment mortgages in the previous chapter (see page 118). The main thing that will slow you down is the fact that the capital you use for deposits and refurbishment will take at least six months to come back to you.

So you need to raise as much cash as you can and then see if the figures still work. If you can raise £100k and you estimate you need £50k per project then you can only do two projects at a time. If each project has an anticipated profit of £25k then the most you can earn is £50k every six months. Will this be enough? If not, you either need to raise some more cash or consider other types of financing – bridging finance, commercial mortgage or venture capital route described in the previous chapter.

- ☐ **Bridging finance**. Great for this type of buying and selling, but remember, bridging is not expensive – it is damn expensive. Speed is everything. You want to have that property finished and marketed so it can be sold just after the six-month rule expires. Every month you hold could cost you 2% per month! You can get your refurbishment costs and fees paid if you buy significantly under value as some lenders offer 70% of the valuation of the property not purchase price.

- ☐ **Commercial finance**. Commercial lenders are happy to lend on properties requiring work or mini projects, but they like to know what your plans are. Otherwise they will just knock back a mortgage on any property that needs work.

Calculating the buy price: extension

	Income and Expenditure	Amount £	% of selling price
	INCOME		
What you think you can sell the extended property for. If you have converted a three-bed one- bath to a four-bed two- bath property or a four- bed house in to two one-bed flats then it should be easy to get comparables.	Estimated selling price (A)	100,000	100
Your estimated cost of the HIP which you will need when you come to sell the property.	HIP (B)	300	
Your estimate of what your solicitor charges for selling a property for you.	Legal fees (C)	600	
Estimated as 2.5% of the estimated selling price.	Selling commission (D)	2500	2.5
An amount for unforeseen expenses.	Sundry (E)	500	
33% of the estimated selling price.	Margin (F)	33,000	33
What you can spend on the whole project.	Contribution to project (G) (A − B − C − D − E − F)	**63,100**	
	EXPENDITURE		
The legal fees to purchase the property.	Legal fees (H)	600	
Stamp duty payable to buy the property: 0% ‹ £125k 1% › £125k 3% › £250k 4% › £500k	Stamp duty (I)	1,500	
Estimated extension costs. Include: • Architect fees • Legal fees to get planning • Planning application fees • Building works Use these costs per sq ft: £100 per sq ft	Extension cost (J)	25,000	
An amount for unforeseen costs	Sundry (K)	500	
Financing costs of holding the property for minimum of six months. I would budget for nine months.	Interest costs (L)	2,000	
A percentage of the amount borrowed usually between 1% and 3%.	Mortgage arrangement fees (M)	1,000	
An estimated survey cost.	Valuation costs (N)	500	
Estimated mortgage broker cost.	Broker fees (O)	500	
Sum of the costs	Total purchasing and extension costs (P) (H + I + J + K + L + M + N + O)	31,600	
Derive the buy price of the property.	Buy price: Amount left over to purchase property (G − P)	**£31,500**	

HOW TO MAKE MONEY FROM PROPERTY

□ **Venture capital**. You need to convince the investor that you know what you are doing. Make sure you have pictures and figures for any previous projects. They will want to see that you handled the job and made a profit.

GETTING PLANNING PERMISSION

Planning permission is *not* required if:

□ The extension or conversion does not add more than 10% to the building if terraced or 15% if semi-detached or detached if the property is not in a conservation area.
□ There is no change of use.

However, my advice is always to seek permission just in case. I am sure you have heard horror stories of town planners demanding the demolition of someone's beautiful extension because the roof was one inch too high.

For a planning application I would use the skills of a planning consultant. They will have direct access to the planning department, and will know what type of applications will succeed or will get knocked back.

Also instruct a good architect, who will design a layout that will (a) be friendly to the planners, (b) add the most value to your property, and (c) comply with building regulations.

If these three conditions are met then you can say hello to making lots of money. It all starts with the architect – a good one will make your ideas become reality.

SELLING THE PROPERTY

You will get the best price by selling to an end user, who will usually be found by an estate agent.

Choosing the right agent

There are no right agents. Choose them all! For the reasons outlined in the previous chapter it is important to cover all bases, and not put all your eggs in one basket.

You are more likely to find a buyer using all the estate agents in the area and get a 1% higher price, than using one agent in the area and get a 1% discount on the selling fee. So if the multi-agent fee is 2.5% and sole agent is 1.5% then you are better off listing it with all agents and putting 1% more on your asking price. This means the net price you receive is exactly the same.

The reason for this is that each estate agent has their own set of skills.

☐ Some spend more on internet marketing than others. So they will be not only on Rightmove but also other portals which interface with other sites. I use www.propertyfinder.co.uk to advertise, which interfaces with MSN.co.uk. This means that when I advertise on propertyfinder you will find my property on MSN.

☐ Some concentrate on traditional advertising such as local press, brochure mailouts.

☐ Some have large client databases. So as soon as your property comes on to their books it is immediately fired out to matching prospective buyers.

☐ Some agents are part of a bigger network, such as a chain. Your property will get increased exposure by being marketed in neighbouring branches.

☐ Some agents have a more visible high street presence than others, with a better location and hence higher footflow. This means more people will see your property.

There are plenty of reasons why you should use multiple agents. I always end up getting a better deal this way. And the agent you think is least likely to sell your property usually ends up selling it.

Setting the price

It's simple: HIGH!

You are constrained by the six-month rule so the earliest you can sell is six months from when your name was registered in the land registry (make sure your solicitor registers it promptly – as some leave this to well after completion).

I hope you have realized that you can, and should, market a property even if you have not finished the work. You can sometimes sell a property before the work has even started! So you have time to fish out a buyer who can pay top money. The worst thing you want to do is undersell the property, and that will happen if you price the property too low.

Go in high and skim the price down. That is how every self-respecting business operates. You do not see brand new cars or properties going cheaply and selling out overnight. The sale comes later, if ever.

If one agent knocks you back, refusing to list your property at that price, do not worry. There are plenty of other agents who will take it on. Sometimes estate agents are poor visionaries. They cannot see what you can see. That is why they are an estate agent and you are a property trader!

9

PROPERTY TRADER (OPTIONS)

VITAL STATISTICS

Earning potential before tax	£5,000 to unlimited per option
Capital required	£2,000 to £20,000
Skills required	Communication
Qualifications preferable	None
Competitiveness: low/medium/high	Low
Risk: low/medium/high	Low
The business model in a nutshell	To acquire long-term options on properties that will rise in value quickly.
Potential gaps in the market and suggested USPs	• Education then acquire

Options, lease options, sandwich options and management agreements. They are the answer to all your dreams... well, kind of, anyway. If used properly you can make money, a lot of it. Especially if we see a boom in prices over the next five years or so.

First I will define what options are. I start in this chapter with options and deal with lease options and later in the book.

OPTIONS EXPLAINED

An option is exactly that. It gives you the option to buy a property at a set price within a set period of time. It is a legal agreement between you and the owner of the property. It specifies the **price** you have agreed, called the exercise price, and the **period** which can be a date or a set amount of time from the date of signing. For example:

5 London Road	You can buy this property for £250,000 if you complete by 1 January 2011.
12 Acacia Avenue	You can buy this property for £200,000 if you complete by 12 December 2015.
4 Jones Street	You can buy this property for £55,000 if you complete by 30 June 2020.

Please note that you never have to buy the property. It gives you the *right* to buy (but not the obligation) within the time period.

So there should be two key parts to the option: the price and the period. Think of these as the 2Ps of options. You have to look at both together to determine whether or not you have a valuable option.

VALUING OPTIONS

A valuable option has a good price and a good period. You need to remember this:

☐ a good price is a *cheap* one;
☐ a good period is a *long* one.

You want the property price to be as *cheap* as possible (no surprise there!) and the period to be as long as possible. That is where the negotiation comes in.

For example: a property has a market value today of £100k. You find a seller who will grant you an option to buy this property in five years' time for £110k. You now have to decide whether or not you think that the property's price will rise in excess of £110k over the next five years.

This is the key question. If you say, 'I don't know', that is a good answer! No one knows. But if you think that the property could be worth £150k in five years then the option could generate you a profit before fees of: £150k − £110k = £40k.

So the option could make you a good return. You need to keep the exercise price as low as possible and the period as long as possible.

To increase the value of this option of £110k over five years you could decrease the exercise price to £108k or increase the period to seven years. Or decrease the exercise price and increase the period to six years.

The key point to note is that the option may still be worthless. No one knows what property prices will be like next year, the year after or the year after that!

So if after the five-year period property prices have declined and your property is now worth £90k, then the option to buy at £110k is worthless. You would simply offer market value of £90k.

From this you will see that valuing an option is not easy. It largely depends on what you think property prices are going to do. The longer the period, the more certainty you have that prices will rise, as property prices rise in the long term.

A typical property cycle lasts around 10–15 years. So if you had an option for 15 years and property prices were currently on the line of the long-term average you would be assured the long term average rate (2.9% pa) of property price inflation.

The big question now is, what would you *pay* for an option to buy a property that is currently worth £100k for £110k within a five-year period? Let me tell you, the owner of the property is going to want something off you. You do not get the option for free!

The four steps to valuing an option

To value an option properly you have to:

1. Come up with what you think the minimum price will be for this property in five years.
2. Calculate this profit element after fees.
3. Discount the profit based on inflation.
4. Incorporate a risk multiplier.

And you will get the value of an option! Sounds tough, doesn't it? Let me remind you that the options game is very risky. All you own is the option. You do not own the property. If the period expires and you haven't exercised your option then anything you paid for the option is lost. An option is a bit of paper and it only comes to value when you exercise it – assuming that it is worthwhile.

So bear with me. If you want to get good at this you have to apply the four steps above. Take the example of the option of £110k in five years on a property worth £100k today. Let's say that I think the property will be worth £150k in five years. Then the profit is: £150k − £110k = £40k.

Then deduct fees of buying and selling the property: say £5k. So the profit is: £40k − £5k = £35k.

Then you have to discount that £35k profit in the future in today's terms. I am going to assume an inflation rate of 3%. To do this you need a scientific calculator. The calculation is $(1-0.03)^5 = 0.85873$.

So a £35k profit in five years' time is actually worth: $0.85873 \times$ £35k = £30,055.

Now you apply a risk multiplier to this. This £30,055 is not money in the bank and is in no way guaranteed. So you have to multiply this by a suitable percentage.

If you are looking to me for this percentage then you are mistaken! This is your call. But let's just say you were 100% sure of this profit, then an asking price of anything less than £30,055 would mean that you would profit.

If you were less than 100% sure, you would just have to decide what to pay for it. Whatever you paid for it, you would deduct this from the £30,055 and this would give you the profit from the option.

Now I advise you to be extremely pessimistic. Only pay for an option what you are prepared to lose. It is a form of gambling unless you get a really long period where market volatility is evened out and the price is within the long-term average.

If you paid 10% of the expected profit for an option that could not be said to be an unfair bid. So in the above example, a fee of £3,005 (10% of £30,055) for the option would be a fair price, if I thought the property would be worth £150k in five years' time.

The good thing is you can exercise your option at any time within those five years. So if there was a mini boom after only one year you could make around £35k, less the price paid for the option. Not bad for shuffling a few bits of paper about.

FINDING PROPERTY OPTION DEALS

Generate your own leads

- **Advertise online**. Websites can be cheap to set up but need to be done well to fit the purpose. See my book *How to Make a Fortune on the Internet* which will teach you how to create and promote a website for maximum profit.

- **Advertise offline**. Newspaper advertising (local and national) can be expensive, but can be very rewarding if you get it right. Some traders spend £50,000 per month on advertising, but they know it is worth their while.

- **Leaflet dropping**. You can get 5,000 leaflets printed for £50. So if you can be bothered to deliver them or trust someone to do it for you, and it is well targeted, you could generate some good leads.

Qualify other people's leads

There are businesses that do all of the above and generate their own leads. Now they may end up with leads that they do not want, that do not meet their strict pricing criteria or are simply out of the region where they buy.

Approach these businesses and ask for their unwanted leads. Offer a kind of a joint venture. You can suggest that they get a fixed fee or a percentage of purchase price of any deals you do. I am relying on your business savvy here, so do your best!

Buy leads

There are companies out there whose sole business is to generate leads for people like *you*. They will want anywhere between £25 up to £200, depending on the lead quality. This could be an excellent way to get into options without investing too much time. If you then find that you have the knack for it you could start generating your own leads.

Estate agents

Approach estate agents to see if they would be interested in putting offers in on your behalf. If an option sale is agreed you pay their estate agency fees and an option fee to the owner. As long as you set the price and the period right then covering the estate agency fees should not be a problem.

NEGOTIATING THE BEST DEAL

Apart from stating the obvious about negotiation techniques, the following can help you specifically when negotiating property options.

Cash is king!

From the vendor's point of view, when an option deal is struck, the document is signed and cash is put into the vendor's pocket. That's it. This is all that could happen during the duration of the option. For the vendor it could really be 'money for nothing'!

So highlighting this point to the vendor may be quite persuasive to get the deal signed. If they are in financial difficulty, you could be the person who has saved them from repossession.

Education

Options are a new thing. Most investors are not aware of how they work, and very few owners of properties know about them. Spend some time with the vendor explaining how options work. They are naturally going to be sceptical.

You could suggest that they seek legal advice that you will pay for if they go forward with the deal. Then there is no risk on their part. Just make sure you send them to a solicitor who understands options!

No survey required – it's a done deal

The deal can be done quickly, as there are no surveyors, lenders or solicitors (if you choose) involved. Just a few simple searches (title and environmental), registering the option with the land registry and a signature and the deal is done.

Buy out

The vendor may be worried that they might change their mind and not want to sell. The vendor does not have to sell. They can buy their way out of the deal at a mutually agreed price. You could agree this break clause fee and make it part of the contract.

SELLING OPTIONS

The whole strategy of making money by being an option trader is to both buy and *sell* options. The two ways of selling options are: selling to the **end user**, and selling to **another trader**.

The end user wants to live in the property and the trader wants to make money from the transaction, selling it on or exercising the option at some point in the future. The ways you find the these two buyers are very different.

When you are selling to the end user they must find you. When you are selling to a trader you must find them.

Selling to the end user

As options are relatively new, do not expect estate agents to fully understand them. Even though estate agents would be your obvious choice, it may be a while before they start selling options for you.

The most effective way to sell options is via the internet. You need to:

☐ create a website and display the properties;
☐ promote the website via Google adwords;
☐ educate the reader about options;
☐ process the leads that come in.

Advertising online can be a steep learning curve. If you are not an expert in web design consider employing a professional to build one for you.

Or you could go for the easier option (pardon the pun!): consider selling to another trader.

Selling to another trader

This avoids you having to educate people about options. A trader may simply buy your option straight off, making you a nice profit, or they might ask to market your option to their database of clients and charge the client a sourcing fee.

EXERCISING OPTIONS

If you are unable to sell the option, then assuming you cannot go back to the owner and vary the option you have two choices: **letting the period lapse**, or **exercising the option**.

Letting the period lapse

This is a do-nothing strategy. If the value of the property is not in excess of the option price then the option is worthless. You will struggle to sell it as people who buy options are not mugs!

If you did not pay a lot for the option then it's no big deal. You have to put it down to experience. You got the market wrong. Next time try to make the period longer or the price lower. And remember what I said earlier, about getting value from an option. You have to make the price low and the period long.

Exercising the option

If the option price is lower than the value of the property then you should consider exercising the option. You can buy the property and then sell it to realize your profit (being the value less the option price less fees).

To exercise the option you must serve notice to the owner and complete within 28 days. I suggest you get your mortgage in place before you serve notice so you can complete as agreed.

You then become the owner, there is no clock ticking away. You own the property, and all the liabilities that come with it!

POWER OF ATTORNEY

Occasionally the owner of the property may disappear, which means that you cannot exercise your option. The way round this is to make sure that you appoint someone to be power of attorney. This involves a legal document called 'A Lasting Power Of Attorney' which needs to be registered with the Office of the Public Guardian (OPG).

Try to get someone who is on your side to assume power of attorney. If the owner goes astray you can utilize this document to exercise the option.

If there is more than one owner of the property then each owner needs a power of attorney individually. I recommend you use a solicitor for this as it is important you get it exactly right.

SUMMARY

Trading in options is an excellent way to make a lot of money fast. If you are confident about which way the market is going (and you are right) then the only limiting factor is the amount of option fees you can pay.

It is possible to have options on properties worth hundreds of thousands of pounds for fees of a few thousand pounds. If you see a modest 25% growth in the next five years you could see astronomical returns on the small money you have outlaid.

10

PROPERTY INVESTOR (SERVICED APARTMENTS)

VITAL STATISTICS

Earning potential before tax	£5,000 to £25,000 per property per year
Capital required	£10,000 to £50,000
Skills required	Interior design
Qualifications preferable	Hospitality, travel and tourism
Competitiveness: low/medium/high	Medium
Risk: low/medium/high	Medium
The business model in a nutshell	To buy a centrally located property and rent to business people as an alternative to a hotel.
Potential gaps in the market and suggested USPs	• Cities other than London and Edinburgh • Houses in the suburbs

A serviced apartment is one that is available for hire for a short time from as little as one night. It provides an alternative to staying in a hotel and offers the resident:

☐ A home from home experience – avoids the sterile environment of a hotel.

☐ Lower cost – serviced apartments can often be cheaper than a hotel room of equivalent quality.

☐ More privacy – you can come and go as if you were at home.

☐ More space – not just a bedroom with a bathroom, but a living room and kitchen.

☐ Cooking facilities – you can cook for yourself in your fully equipped kitchen.

☐ More entertainment – usually an apartment will have broadband, Sky TV and DVD collections.

Serviced apartments are the way forward. This growing market, pioneered by the Americans, has been here for at least ten years but I think this industry will take off as advantages of serviced apartments are realized.

So if you want to grab a piece of this market then read on. This is not a passive investment, though. This is a business. Expect it to disrupt your life. If you are willing to put in the hard work, take the emotional ups and downs and have thick skin, then there will be a pot of gold for you in the end.

CHOOSING THE RIGHT PROPERTY

Hotel users fall into one of two categories: **business** and **leisure**. Both these markets are worth chasing. It will come as no surprise that the business bookings are in the week (Monday–Friday) and leisure bookings are usually at the weekend (Friday–Sunday).

If you choose the right location you can be booked all week! And if one market were to suffer you would still have the other market to fall back on.

Location

Obvious locations with a market for both business and leisure residents include, for example, London, Brighton and Edinburgh. Others might be near national event centres or with a thriving business sector as well as nightlife, such as: Cardiff (Millennium Stadium), Birmingham (NEC Centre), South London/Kent (O2 Centre), Liverpool (business/nightlife), Manchester (business/nightlife), Glasgow (business/nightlife).

Size

Most serviced apartments are studios or one-bedroomed. A studio flat sleeps two, but if there's a sofa bed in the living room of your one-bed flat it can sleep four.

So a one-bed apartment will be attractive to a wider audience than a studio. They don't cost that much more than a studio and can be easier to sell if you need to realize your asset.

But before you start searching on Rightmove for all the one-bed flats in the city of your choice I am going to force you to number crunch. It has to be done if you are going to make a success of it.

Return

You need to go for a property that will give you a gross 25% return on the purchase price of the property. The income should be at least 25% of the purchase price of the property. So if you bought a place for £100,000 then you would want an income of £25,000.

This is a very strict threshold. For a property in Mayfair priced at £500,000, the rental income you would need to make it work is: £500,000 × 25% = £125,000.

Expressing this as a daily amount it would be: £125,000/365 = £342 per day.

Now if you can book a hotel room next door for £170 a night then your Mayfair serviced apartment is not going to do very well no matter how attractive it is.

Remember that hotel rates fluctuate daily, based on demand. In order to compete with hotels and maximize your profit you will need to flex your prices to meet demand.

To get a better picture of what you can expect to get as an income, compile an Expected Income table.

Expected income table

		Room rate	Multiplied by	Income
Week 1	Sun–Thurs		5	
	Fri–Sat		2	
Week 2	Sun–Thurs		5	
	Fri–Sat		2	
Week 52	Sun–Thurs		5	
	Fri–Sat		2	
			TOTAL	

Fill out the room rate for the Sun–Thurs room rate and Fri–Sat room rate for each week, so that you can derive the total income expected for the five weekdays and the weekend.

You can get this table for free by visiting www.ahuja.co.uk and joining my newsletter.

The total income for the year will then be a true representation of what you can expect to earn from the prospective property.

Find out room rates by looking at rival competitor sites, or simply ring them up. They may even have a rate card for all the different dates. Periods that get above average demand and thus higher rates are:

- □ school holidays;
- □ bank holidays;
- □ event days (like the FA Cup);
- □ New Year's Eve.

Make sure you do not miss out on these. The internet should be able to throw up most dates that correspond to your location. Consult the events diary of local venues. Popular attractions will really push the rates up.

Once the Expected Income table is complete you should be able to derive an expected income. Divide the expected income by the purchase price and you will come up with the expected return, which should be in excess of 25%.

EQUIPPING THE PROPERTY

If you will enjoy creating a home from home experience for your customers then you will love this business. You need to equip the home with the following as minimum:

- □ beds, bedding, soft furnishings, curtains, etc.;
- □ kitchen with hob, oven, microwave, pots and pans;
- □ small dining table and two chairs;
- □ TV/DVD;
- □ cutlery and crockery.

You can include the following extras to get a higher rate and encourage repeat custom:

- □ WiFi;
- □ desktop PC;
- □ full Sky package with sports and movies;
- □ plasma screen;
- □ TV in bedroom;
- □ basic food such as coffee, tea, milk, biscuits;
- □ welcome pack;
- □ parking.

And if you want to go the whole hog you could offer the following services for a fee:

- □ pick up and drop off service;
- □ babysitting;
- □ food (breakfast, lunch and dinner) of various cuisines;
- □ laundry.

For these services it is best to do deals with local taxi, restaurant and cleaning companies. Simply add their numbers to the welcome pack and the customer can deal direct with the contractor.

Choose your contractors *very* carefully. If they do a bad job the customer will hold you responsible. Test them out yourself for quality and reliability. Shop around for the best deal.

The serviced apartments industry is quite competitive. Book yourself into one on an off-peak time. Check how others do such things as:

- □ where they source their goods, and what brands they use;
- □ the level of equipping;
- □ what methods they use to discourage theft, to increase the customer's comfort with little cost, to increase revenue or to save cost;
- □ ensuring everything runs smoothly. Chat to your competitors. As they will not know who you are, ask them quite detailed questions.

The great thing about this business is that it is not rocket science. It can suit a couple where one partner does the booking, paperwork and finances and the other does the practical side and customer service. I will let you decide who does what!

FINDING CUSTOMERS

Among your business and leisure customers, you will aim for two types: **new customers**, and **repeat customers**.

The idea is to get as much repeat custom as possible. This is basic business sense. Once you have an established clientele you can cut back on advertising costs and the business can almost run on autopilot. The best repeat customers are corporate clients. Corporate customers might book your apartment not just one night a month but for whole months or even years at a time!

So the idea is to:

1. attract new customers;
2. encourage repeat custom;
3. establish longer-term relations with corporate customers.

Attract new customers

Think of yourself as both a hotel operator and a holiday home owner in your marketing. Establish your presence with both **online** and **offline** advertising.

Online

- □ **Website**. Include plenty of pictures, a list of the services you offer and, most importantly, a booking form. If there may be international interest then consider having a translation of your site for target countries. A feedback system and rating facility might be beneficial, as long as you police it. A 24-hour call centre could take your calls so you never miss a lead. Linking your website with Google Adwords will boost enquiries. My book *How to Make a Fortune on the Internet* shows you how to set up a site and start making money straight away.

☐ **Networks**. These provide customers with a one-stop shop to search and compare hotel rooms, holiday homes and serviced apartments. Sites such as laterooms.co.uk, holidayrentals.co.uk and ownersdirect.co.uk may be worth getting on to.

Offline

☐ **Mailshots**. HR departments of prospective corporate customers need to know about you. Your letter should include details about your apartment and its USP, and what you offer. Most will throw your mailshot in the bin but some will give you a call.

☐ **Cold calling**. Choose large employers, relocation agents and travel companies, and try to make your proposition interesting for them (such as a kickback commission for every booking they make). They just might be willing to give you a go.

☐ **Magazines and papers**. *Dalton's Weekly* and many other papers will advertise your apartment in the holiday sections. This can be expensive. A trial and error process is necessary to find which publications deliver you customers.

Encouraging repeat custom

Sometimes the advertising described above eats up all your profit. This business model is so competitive, this is to be expected. Where your profit lies is in repeat custom.

This involves no major advertising cost apart from a bit of printing and postage. As a minimum you must:

☐ Capture the contact details of anyone who has used your services, including email. Then you can remarket to them with special offers to entice them back. You could extend this to anyone who shows interest in your apartment – they may not be a customer now but will be further down the line.

☐ Provide a welcome information pack outlining what you offer, any special promotions and how to book again as an existing customer. Email this as a pdf when a booking is made, and have a hard copy in the flat for customers can take away with them.

☐ Follow up corporate customers with a phone call to ask for feedback. These are your most important clients. Address any negative feedback, offering some kind of compensation such as a free stay or refund. Get in their good books and it will be well worth it.

Establish longer-term relationships

Treat your corporate customer like royalty. They have the power to make your life very comfortable. Once you have a corporate customer, consider the following:

☐ Visit them in person. See how you can further meet their expectations on price and quality.

☐ Offer them a longer term contract at a reduced price, which should help even out your cash flows over the year.

☐ Offer to buy more flats. If the demand is there, you could offer them more accommodation.

☐ Offer additional services. These could be services available *only* to your corporate customers.

☐ Don't be shy of corporate hospitality. At Christmas send the HR staff a few bottles of champagne.

☐ Offer bigger kickbacks in commission if certain sales targets are met.

It's all pretty much common business sense. Remember this is a business, not a passive property investment. Which brings me nicely to the next section.

RUNNING THE BUSINESS

A good business will **maximize income** and **minimize expenditure**. And make sure that income exceeds expenditure. That is being successful in business in a nutshell.

Maximize income

☐ Keep abreast of the rates you can charge. Check what your competitors are charging. Can you put additional items in the flat that would result in achieving higher rates? Everyone is looking for that edge to make their apartment stand out from the rest. Look at other apartments outside your area to get ideas of how to get that higher rate.

☐ Something is better than nothing. Flex your rates so they are reduced later in the day. Set a minimum low amount. You don't want to go too low and attract the wrong sort of customer.

☐ Accept multiple payment methods: cash, cheque, credit card, Paypal. The more methods, the more likely it is to get a sale.

☐ Have a choice of methods for leads to come in. Give out a booking form online, your direct email address, telephone, mobile, fax and even Skype! The more methods you offer for potential customers to get in contact the more you get.

☐ Suggest they subscribe to your newsletter/social networking tag. Use Twitter, Facebook, LinkedIn, and communicate with them regularly with your latest offers.

☐ Try new marketing methods. If a new network springs up online offering a free trial, use it! What is the worst that can happen?

☐ Get kickback commission from contractors you recommend, such as taxi firms, laundry companies, restaurants.

I hope that these suggestions act as a catalyst to inspire you to get creative so that your income is maximized at all times.

Minimizing expenditure

Apart from the obvious costs such as cleaning, mortgage payments and insurance the major cost under your control is the maintenance of the contents of the flat. You really want to prevent: **theft**, **damage**, **excessive wear and tear**, and **complaints**.

☐ **Theft**. Expensive items such as TVs and PCs can be screwed down, but subtly so it does not look like a school or library. Expect to lose the odd towel, glass or plate every now and again.

☐ **Damage**. One way to reduce this is to avoid single-sex groups, such as a group of lads out for a night on the town. Your risks are lowered if you go for couples and families. If you do the check-in and check-out (and the customer knows that this will happen) most wrongdoing can be prevented. And many people are honest enough to come clean about breakages. Take credit card details at check-in to cover any damage that may occur.

☐ **Excessive wear and tear**. It is not rude to ask about the purpose of a customer's visit. If you are not happy with how the flat may be used, the customer may not be worth taking on. Avoiding single-sex groups should means this doesn't happen, however.

☐ **Complaints**. If you provide poor quality items the customer will be calling you up all the time reporting faults. Going for cheap fixtures and fittings does you no good in the long run. Stick to brand names and middle of the range goods.

General advice

☐ **Maintain standards**. The apartment needs to be tip-top clean. The customer will expect this. If you outsource the cleaning then make sure you perform periodic spot checks.

☐ **Rapid response**. You ideally want to be no further than 15 minutes away from the flat, or have a representative on hand. You want any problems to be sorted out fast.

☐ **Keep the neighbours happy**. Even though I mention this last, it is *so* important. Neighbours can cause a lot of problems for you if they are not happy. Apologize for any disturbance, and perhaps send a box of chocolates. Neighbours can be your eyes and ears and so be very valuable to you.

11

PROPERTY INVESTOR (BUY TO LET)

VITAL STATISTICS

Earning potential before tax	£1,000 to £7,500 per property per year
Capital required	£nil to £10,000
Skills required	None
Qualifications preferable	None
Competitiveness: low/medium/high	Low
Risk: low/medium/high	High
The business model in a nutshell	To buy properties with little money down that return a monthly profit after all expenses
Potential gaps in the market and suggested USPs	• DSS let only

This method netted me a cool £15m. I bought, bought and kept on buying until my portfolio hit 200 properties worth £15m. I started with only £500. If you want a guarantee that you'll be rich and can play the long-term game (greater than ten years) then this model comes highly recommended from yours truly.

Property prices were rising when I bought, but this does not mean that you cannot do the same on the way down. The whole industry of Below Market Value (BMV) properties emerged in 2006/07 and purchasing property with sophisticated legal 'no money down' techniques has now become the norm for those people in the know.

Some of you may be thinking I am encouraging mortgage fraud, as there are no such things as 100% mortgages. However, the opposite is true. These techniques are disclosed to the lender and are CML compliant. The transaction of purchasing a property has to go through two solicitors, one for the buyer and one for the seller, and solicitors do not like to get involved in fraud. These are acceptable techniques at the time of going to print. Unless these loopholes get closed down large portfolios can be built in short periods of time.

THE FORMULA

It's simple:

- ☐ decide what you want;
- ☐ maximise your starting capital;
- ☐ invest wisely;
- ☐ remortgage and reinvest aggressively.

There are key aspects in each of the steps that need emphasis so I'll deal with one part at a time.

DECIDING WHAT YOU WANT

It amazes me that many people do not know what they want. They pay for a consultation and I ask them what they want from investing in property. They look at me as if it is a stupid question and they answer: 'Money!'

Now, it is taken as a given that money is the goal. The two key questions you should be asking yourself are: **how much**, and **by when**?

How much?

So how much do you want? Loads? A little bit more than you have already? More than your parents or other family member?

All the answers above are *wrong*. Why? There are no figures attached to them. You cannot be driven to succeed if you do not know where you are driving to! Here are some ideas on putting a number to your target:

- ☐ **Lump sum**. Do you want one specific amount of money? For example, £1m. Is there something out there (like a dream house to live in) that you want, of which you can quantify the value and set this as a target?

- ☐ **Equity**. This is the value of the property portfolio less debt. So if you had a portfolio worth £1m and mortgages totalling £500,000 then the equity is £1m–£500,000 = £500,000. Equity can be a good target as it sets your net worth. If you sell up you receive the value of equity in your portfolio.

- ☐ **Monthly income**. One of my first targets was a monthly income, to match my salary when I used to work. A monthly income is a real income, which can be a great motivator as you can spend everything you make! So what is the monthly income you would like to make?

☐ **Number of properties**. My current target is to own 1,000 properties. This number has no particular relevance – but it inspires the hell out of me. What is your target number? 10, 100, 1000, or even 10,000?

☐ **Portfolio value**. A lot of property investment clubs have used this target to lure people in, with catchy headlines like 'Become a property millionaire' or 'Build a million-pound property empire'. They were all talking about portfolio values. I have to admit a big driver for me was to break the £10m portfolio value.

☐ **Rental income**. Rental income can be another good target. It's the revenue you can earn from the portfolio. It works quite nicely if all your mortgages are on repayment. You know that after the term of the mortgage you can expect to earn that income as pure profit. And remember that rent is inflation proof so the rental income will be a real amount in the future.

By when?

So once you have established what it is you want you have to put a timescale to it. Do you want it

☐ next month (!)?
☐ next year?
☐ in five years?
☐ when you turn 50?
☐ by the year 2015?

There are many milestones you can use, but a date needs to be set. A target means nothing if there is no date attached to it. Before you set the date, I want you to consider one more thing, your attitude to risk.

Your attitude to risk

If you want to go from having nothing to having £1m in six months then you should appreciate that you are going to have to take some large risks. Many people have made £1m in six months but they have taken a fair few chances along the way.

Think about your attitude to risk. The fact that you are considering investing in property means that you accept a certain degree of risk, but how much? I would categorize your risk profile as:

☐ **low**, if you do not wish to borrow to purchase a property (0% borrowing of purchase price);

- **medium**, if you are willing to take out a mortgage to purchase a property (75% borrowing of purchase price);

- **high**, if you are willing to borrow the deposit to put down on a mortgage to purchase a property (100% borrowing of purchase price).

If you have a low attitude to risk then make sure you put a long timescale on your target. If you are the opposite you can (only if you want to) put a short timescale to your target. Or you can pitch it somewhere in between!

The target

You have created a target with a timescale. Now stand back, think about it some more, then revise it. Your target is going to be with you all the way, so you want it to be a real friend. Examples of targets might be:

- £1m portfolio by age 40;
- £5,000 per month income by the year 2014;
- £2m equity by 30 June 2012;
- £30,000 monthly rental income in five years.

If you still need help with refining your target into a true friend then follow these golden rules of target setting.

Golden rule No.1: Achievable

If you are unemployed, have no money, bad credit, a low attitude to risk and want a £10m property portfolio in six months then you have to admit this might not be achievable. Your target must be achievable. There is no point daydreaming or waiting for a miracle.

If it is not achievable you will quite soon lose interest in it. This has happened to me many a time. I put an ambitious target in place, then find myself revising the target downwards, to the point where the target doesn't look that exciting any more!

Factor in all that is mentioned above. Look at your attitude to risk and your current situation. If you have £50,000 in the bank, have a medium attitude to risk and want to make £10,000 per month in the next five years then your target just might become reality if you stick to it.

Golden rule No. 2: Motivational

The target has to motivate and inspire you. It has to be something you don't just want but really, really, *really* want. A well-constructed target will motivate you. As I said earlier, one of my first targets was to earn exactly my net take home pay from my previous employment. I wanted to prove that I could do just as well being self-employed as employed.

This target had meaning. Not only could I earn the same amount from self-employment, but I was my own boss, and the money came from my own initiative and shrewdness. If that target was not motivating I do not know what would be!

So choose a target you can get emotional about. Perhaps someone has said to you that you could never make £1m and this touched you where it hurts. Use the negative energy and let it drive you to your target.

Golden rule No. 3: Understandable

You need to understand your target easily. If you have to pump a whole load of figures into a spreadsheet to see if you are getting anywhere near, your target may be too complicated. As they say: Keep It Simple Stupid (KISS).

The simple ones are the best. One of my best targets was getting my portfolio to 100 properties. There was no financial benefit for the portfolio to be that size, but it was a nice simple target. As you can imagine, once I had broken the 90 barrier there was no stopping me getting to the 100.

So make sure your target is understandable to you. Make it something which does not require you reaching for your laptop to track.

Golden rule No. 4: Memorable

It has to stick in your brain. Your target is going to be your best friend, so you don't want to forget their name! A target yield of 11.45% may not be the best idea, but a target of 40 properties by age 40 has a nice ring to it. £50m by age 50 is also quite memorable. This was the target of Jim Moore, the founder of Inside Track.

Golden rule No. 5: Measurable

You need to know if you are on track. If your target is 40 properties by 40, and at age 30 you have five properties then this target is measurable and trackable. So if you have 30 properties at age 35 you are on track to reach your target. If you only have six properties then you know you will have to play catch up.

You can split the target down and plot its route. If you needed to acquire 30 properties over the next ten years then three properties per year would be the annual target if you chose to grow your portfolio at a steady pace.

MAXIMIZING STARTING CAPITAL

The more money you have, the more money you can make. No one can argue with that concept. As long as you know what you are doing then the only thing that stops you from making it is lack of starting capital. People call this starting capital 'seed capital' as it is this 'seed' that can grow into a giant oak tree.

I have got around 500% return on my money every year. A few calculations will show how your seed capital can dramatically affect your wealth. Imagine you were able to get the same return as I did, of 500%. If you started off with £1,000 then your return at the end of years 1–5 would be:

Year 1	£5,000
Year 2	£25,000
Year 3	£125,000
Year 4	£625,000
Year 5	£3,125,000

But if you started off with £3,000 then the figures look like this:

Year 1	£15,000
Year 2	£75,000
Year 3	£375,000
Year 4	£1,875,000
Year 5	£9,375,000

So simply by having a couple of grand more at the start, after five years you have an extra: £9,375,000 − £3,125,000 = £6,250,000. That's over £6m! If you are convinced about what you are doing then you should plough *all* your money into it.

Chapter 3 of this book is all about how to raise starting capital. Please reread this, armed with what I have just told you, and go out there and raise some cash. You have to do it. It is the only thing that sets you apart from a daydreamer. Those with no money simply get left behind. To get involved in property you need some cash behind you. Then you can enter the arena of investing.

INVESTING WISELY

It is an easy comment to make. Invest wisely. But what is wise? Well, a property has to meet two criteria:

1. The yield is in excess of 10%.
2. The total money input is less than 10% of the purchase price.

I call this my 'ten ten' rule. You've heard of 20/20 vision, now it's time for ten ten vision!

Now I hope you understand what yield is. To recap, yield is annual rent divided by purchase price. So a 10% yielding property would rent out for 10% of the purchase price. A property bought for £75,000 should rent for at least £7,500.

As for cash input, if a property is being sold for £75,000 then you should aim to put no more than £7,500 in to the deal to cover deposit, legal fees, arrangement fees and any other fee associated with buying the property.

Before you ask where you get 90% Loan To Value buy-to-let mortgages, wonder no more. You can structure the purchase so that you put hardly any money in, if any. I have six ways (Types A–F) of buying property with very little cash (see table overleaf).

These methods are out there and being used by investors all the time. These techniques have helped people build large portfolios that could not have been achieved through the traditional method of putting down a 25% deposit plus fees.

So remember my rule of minimum 10% yield and maximum 10% cash input. By the way, this applies to British properties only. The ten ten rule should not be applied overseas. If you are going to invest abroad you should be looking for a higher yield than 10% to take into account the higher risk you are taking on due to different laws, management risk, political risk, etc. I would avoid buying properties overseas, unless you have a high attitude to risk – but please start off slowly! I have heard the USA is good...

Remember use *all* your starting capital to invest. Do not leave anything other than working capital in your bank. You will then get the greatest exposure to the property market possible, which is what you want. High exposure means that you will benefit from the boom that will come at some point in the future.

A high exposure means that you are exposed to the downfalls as well, but if you have bought high-yielding properties it really won't make that much difference. Your portfolio value will go down, but on a monthly basis you will not notice anything as the rent will keep on coming and the costs will be the same.

Once all your cash is invested it is just a waiting game. How long that wait is no one knows, but eventually you will start to hit your targets, and can move on to the final part of the strategy.

Six ways of buying property

Type	Informal name	How it works	Example	Time to get money back	Pros and cons
Type A	Six-month bridge, open bridge, traditional bridge.	1. Get property valued up in excess of purchase price. 2. Buy property using bridging funds at 100% of purchase price, as bridger lends based on valuation. 3. Hold property with bridging funds for six months. 4. Remortgage with traditional lender.	1. Valuation of property £100k. 2. Purchase price £70k. 3. Bridging Funds released (70% of valuation) = £70k Total money in: Nil. Six months later a remortgage is done: 1. Valuation £100k. 2. Remortgage at 75% of valuation = £75k 3. £75k is used to clear bridging funds of £70k and bridging interest of £5k Total money in: Nil.	Six months	Pros: • Easy to purchase as requires no collaboration with vendor. • Can choose any lender after six months. Cons: • Have to wait six months to get your money. • Bridging is expensive (typically 1.25% per month) so need to get high BMV. • Property might have declined in value after six months.
Type B	Bridge and remortgage, same day bridge, daylight bridge.	1. Purchaser gets a valuation in excess of purchase price. 2 Purchaser buys property with bridging funds at purchase price. 3. On the same day purchaser remortgages the property at the higher valuation.	1. Valuation of property £100k. 2. Purchase price £70k. 3. Buy property with bridging funds £70k Total money in: Nil On the same day or 1 day later: 1. Remortgage at 70% of value (70% × £100k) = £70k. 2. Clear bridging funds of £70k. Total money in: Nil	1 day	Pros: • Simple. • No need to state purchase price at valuation. Cons: • Limited lenders.
Type C	Purchase and further advance.	1. Purchaser gets a valuation in excess of purchase price. 2. Buys property at purchase price and puts deposit down. 3. Immediately goes in for a further advance once first mortgage payment has come out and gets deposit monies back from further advance.	1. Valuation of property £100k. 2. Purchase price at £70k. 3. Buy property with 30% deposit (30% × £70k) = £21k Total money in: £21k Within two months: 1. Apply for a further advance based on valuation of £100k. 2. Further advance is 70% of value less outstanding mortgage which is £70k − 49k = £21k 3. This £21k replenishes the £21k you used to buy the property with. Total money in: Nil	Two months	Pros: • Simple. • No need to state purchase price at valuation. Cons: • Limited lenders.

	Method	Steps	Time	Pros/Cons
Type D	Back to back, assignable contracts, option agreements.	1. Middle person buys property from vendor at below market value. 2. Middle person sells on property to investor at full market value and lends them the deposit. 3. Mortgage funds raised using this borrowed deposit. 4. Deposit comes back on completion to the middle person and the rest of the funds go to the vendor.	1. Valuation of property £100k. 2. Middle person gets the right to buy the property for £70k by using an option agreement. 3. Middle person sells on the property for £100k and lends the deposit of £30k to the buyer. 4. Sale goes through at £100k and the vendor gets their £70k and the £30k comes back to the middle person. Total money in by buyer: Nil	One day	Pros: • Higher purchase price great for mitigating capital gains tax. Cons: • Restricted number of lenders.
Type E	Bridged deposit, loan rebate scheme.	1. Purchaser gets valuation in excess of agreed purchase price. 2. Purchase price set at valuation figure. 3. Purchaser borrows deposit from loan company. 4. Vendor agrees to pay loan company a finders fee equal to amount of deposit borrowed by purchaser.	1. Valuation of property £100k. 2. Purchase price £100k. 3. Buyer borrows £30k deposit off loan company. 4. Lender lends 70% of £100k = £70k. 5. £100k goes to vendor and £30k comes back to the loan company. Total money in: Nil	One day	Pros: • Can use all lenders. Cons: • Vendor needs to use your solicitor.
Type F	Borrow deposit.	1. Purchaser borrows deposit via remortgaging of current home or portfolio, off credit cards, overdraft, unsecured loan or from family. 2. Uses these funds as a deposit to raise mortgage. 3. Remortgage at higher value when property prices rise to clear loan taken out for deposit.	1. Valuation of property £100k. 2. Buyer borrows £30k from family, credit cards, remortgaging, etc. 3. Lender lends £70k based on 70% of £100k valuation. 4. Buyer purchases property. Total money in: Nil Six months plus later, whenever prices have risen to £150k: 5. Go in for a remortgage at 70% of value i.e. = £150k × 70% = £105k. 6. Redeem current mortgage of £70k and £30k additional borrowing from credit cards etc. Surplus £5k. Total money in: Nil	Six months plus	Pros: • Can use all lenders. • Simple! • Great in a rising market. Cons: • Deposit fund borrowings will have to be paid over a shorter period of time, thus pushing up the monthly payments overall.

161

REMORTGAGING AND REINVESTING AGGRESSIVELY

This is a very key stage in the process. Many investors who could have made fortunes got cold feet, cashed in, spent the money and are now trying to get back in the game. True investors hate selling, and will do so when the offer is so good they can't turn it down. You need to hang onto your properties and do the following:

1. Remortgage the properties to get more seed capital to invest.
2. Reinvest as before, following the ten ten rule.
3. Do it aggressively!

Now, say you have invested all your cash in ten properties worth £75,000 each, which you bought for £50,000 and have £50,000 outstanding on in mortgages. They are rented for £5,000 per year and the mortgage cost is £2,500 per year. Your portfolio value will look like this: 10 properties × £75,000 = £750,000. Your annual profit is: 10 × (£5,000 − £2,500) = £25,000.

Now you have to wait for the portfolio to grow in value so that you can get some cash out. One thing is guaranteed: property price growth will happen. Property prices rise in line with general price rises, so as long as you have wage increases you will have property prices moving upwards.

The long-term growth rate is the same as the long-term wage growth rate of 2.9%. However, property prices like to yo-yo around the long-term growth line. Now how and why these yo-yos occur is not your concern. Your concern is to pounce when the market rises by remortgaging.

Say the market rises by 25%. Then your portfolio grows to: £750,000 × 25% = £937,500.

If you can get a 75% Loan To Value buy-to-let mortgage then the new borrowing amount you can get is: £937,500 × 75% = £703,125.

The current mortgages are £500,000 so the amount you can release is: £703,125 − £500,000 = £203,125. Or £200,000, to keep the figures simple.

Can you imagine how many properties you can buy with that? Your portfolio can now grow by five times. If with each property you are putting in £5,000 then you will be able to buy: £200,000 divided by £5,000 = 40 properties.

Each of these properties will return perhaps £2,500 profit per year. The additional profit you have just added to your personal bank account is 40 × £2,500 = £100,000 per year.

Let's say the £200,000 extra borrowing costs you £1,000 per month, £12,000 per year on an interest-only mortgage. Then you have a net benefit of: £100,000 − £12,000 = £88,000.

Not bad for a bit of remortgaging and reinvesting. This is how I became wealthy. I would just keep on raising seed capital from the equity that builds up in the property. And the great thing is, lenders will lend. This is because each one of the original properties you buy for £50,000 will still be cash flow positive after the remortgaging. If you add £20,000 loan to each property, which costs another £1,200 per year on top of the £2,500 annual mortgage payment, because the rent is £5,000 per year they are still happy to lend as the rent is in excess of the mortgage payment (£5,000 − £2,500 − £1,200 = £1,300).

So you can just keep going and going until you hit your target. Isn't that wonderful? Your future really is in your hands if you are willing to commit to a ten-year plan. It may take only four years, it may take longer, but you can be reasonably sure that it will happen. And you can do it with just one wave of property price increases. It all depends on your targets but if you buy well and remortgage to the maximum at the right times then you can increase your portfolio by up to ten times.

12

PROPERTY INVESTOR (STUDENT/HMO LETS)

VITAL STATISTICS

Earning potential before tax	£3,000 to £20,000 per house per year
Capital required	£10,000 to £60,000
Skills required	None
Qualifications preferable	None
Competitiveness: low/medium/high	Med
Risk: low/medium/high	Med
The business model in a nutshell	To buy high-yielding properties in an area where there is demand for room-only rentals.
Potential gaps in the market and suggested USPs	• Hi tech broadband • Mature students (over 25) • DSS HMOs

While the buy-to-let market is seemingly oversaturated, a steady and buoyant student buy-to-let market is one that still offers the potential of good returns.

There are multiple reasons as to why the student buy-to-let is a worthwhile investment. UCAS, the university applications agency, has seen a year-by-year increase in applications. Increased student numbers are fuelling a rush to build.

It is a well-known fact that universities are struggling financially, which is having knock-on effects. Increased numbers of students, massive student housing shortages and a lack of investment in new housing initiatives by the universities means that the benefits of private investment have never been better.

In some student cities in the UK private developers have latched onto this investment opportunity and are building high-rise student apartment blocks.

UNIVERSITY TOWNS = STUDENTS = £££!!

Well, not necessarily. There are roughly 200 institutions of higher education in the UK. Some are placed in cities where the number of students exceeds the number of local residents. Some, however, do not have enough students to make the investment worthwhile or sustainable.

Students typically reduce costs by sharing and minimizing personal expenditure. Consequently, student houses can improve higher than average yields by maximizing the available space. However, you should also take into consideration the responsibilities of renting to students, such as higher maintenance, furnishing costs, increased wear and tear, when compared with renting a professional couple, for example.

The location of the property will be a deciding factor in your purchase, particularly on a local level which will be dictated by the campus location, access to local amenities, nearness to bus stops, etc.

FINDING THE RIGHT PROPERTY

Like any property investment, I always apply a rule of thumb. Here, I call it the rule of 10. Simply calculate the annual rent and multiply it by 10 – this gives you the purchase price. So if you see a three-bed two reception house (one reception room could be bedroom 4) and you know the room rate is £60 per week then the calculation is: $4 \times £60 \times 52 \times 10 = £124,800$.

So if you see the house advertised for £110,000 then go for it, but if it's £150,000 then forget it. Speak to letting agents or look in the local press for typical rental values in the area you are looking at. This yield is also stated as a payback period – the length of time it would take to own the property if you reinvested all the income earned to replenish your savings. You calculate it like this:

$$\frac{1}{\text{Gross yield}/100} = \text{payback period}$$

This equates to ten years. Ten per cent is a like-for-like comparison with a bank or building society rate. So if your bank is offering 4% you know that you can earn 2.5 times as much from investing in property. But this assumes that you have funded the whole property purchase out of your own funds. Usually this is not the case. When you borrow to finance the purchase the returns are significantly higher.

There are many areas that offer you a return of 10% or greater and student properties can do the same.

Sometimes for student rental, the *average* gross yield per year is calculated as:

$$\frac{(42 \text{ weeks} \times \text{room rate}) + (10 \text{ weeks} \times (\text{room rate}/2)) \times \text{ number of bedrooms})}{\text{Property purchase price}}$$

As you can see, the average has been calculated by charging half-rent during the summer period. The landlord charges 50% rent (or retainer) during the summer so as to reserve the property for the next academic year. During this agreed period the property is not let to anyone else.

The VarsityLets scheme offered by Bradford and Bingley guarantees full rent for the year, and so in this situation the yields are increased. How much in demand or desirable your property is will have a considerable effect on this average. If my house has all the latest mod cons, full speed internet access, large bedrooms, newly fitted bathroom and so on, then I would feel extremely confident in charging full rent 52 weeks of the year and adjust profit and yield figures by +1% or 2%. A less desirable property would only be attractive if rent was charged for termtimes only.

Take a three-bedroom house (with the front reception converted into a bedroom, equalling four bedrooms) at a purchase price of £145,000. If the standard room rate is £52 a week, then the figures are as follows.

Median room rate	£52
Average yield 1	6.7%
Estimated annual profit 1	£1,296
Average yield 2	7.5%
Estimated annual profit 2	£2,128

Average yield 1 includes half-rent for non-term time and average yield 2 is full 52 weeks' rent.

In general, when looking through the university listings, the yield and profit given are considered as a calculated minimum/average and should be weighted roughly +1% or 2% if the landlord decides, and has the capability to charge full rent for 52 weeks.

The example shows that the average expected yield range for a three-bedroomed house is between 6.7% and 7.5% if 52 weeks' full rent is charged. Personally, I would choose not to invest in this example.

Capital appreciation

Capital appreciation is the amount the property rises in value over time. I never include the gains by capital appreciation in my calculation of yields because it is an unknown figure at the point you make the investment. If there was any certainty of the capital appreciation of a property then the purchase price of the property would include this gain. As there is a lot of uncertainty over capital appreciation because of the numerous variables involved it is very difficult to predict when house prices will rise. And remember the gain is only realized when you sell the property and the difficult thing with any investment is knowing when to get out and sell.

I see capital appreciation as a bonus. I focus on the investment as it stands. If it makes money now it will almost certainly make you money in the future. If the property prices crash – who cares! You are still making money as the rent rises with inflation and the mortgage payment is still the same. If property prices increase again – great! You can realize that equity by remortgaging or by selling and buying further properties! This way there is no downside risk and only upside potential.

Admittedly there is a lot of money to be made in capital appreciation speculation but this speculation should be left to the professional property investors. They have the time to research the market and can stomach the loss if there is a property price crash.

What's so good about student properties?

Well, the good thing is that the market will always be there! And, if you play things right you can achieve higher yields than if you were to let a property as normal. For example, if you were to let out a three-bed terraced house to a couple with two children then your average gross income would be, say, £433 per contract month. However, if you were to let it out to four students, with a ground-floor room converted to a bedroom, for an average rent of £50 a room, this might almost double what you receive, over £800 per month. This increased yield can be achieved with the commitment and correct attitude required to attract the right student for the right property.

What to look for when viewing a property

Do not believe the myth that a property is only worth buying if you could see yourself living there. The fact is you aren't going to live there. You should ask 'Would *students* live here?'

Matching the right property with your target group is of crucial importance. How can a potential student buy-to-let purchase be made as competitive as possible within its local setting? For example, if you know that the latest student developments offered by the university will have full access to high-speed or broadband internet in every room, then you must provide at least the same.

You can find out the demand and suitability of property from talking to the students' union and the university student housing office. It's good to get both perspectives.

When viewing a property check for the following.

- ☐ **Carpets**. You have a legal duty to provide floor coverings. If there are no carpets then you will have to pay for new ones.

- ☐ **Kitchen**. Is the kitchen big enough to accommodate a small dining table? This is attractive if there is only one reception room and it turns the kitchen into a kitchen diner.

- ☐ **Smallest bedroom**. If the smallest bedroom is smaller than 6 foot 6 inches in any direction then it cannot be described as an adult's bedroom! You need to consider this when deciding what type of tenant you want. If you are looking for two professional people to share a two-bed flat then the second bedroom must be bigger than this.

- ☐ **Bathroom**. Is there a fitted shower? A bathroom is a lot more desirable if there is a power shower. More than one bathroom makes the property very desirable, even if the second one is only a shower room.

- ☐ **Heating**. How old is the heating system? This can be costly to replace. If possible get it checked prior to purchase. It is your legal duty to provide heating and to issue a gas safety record.

- ☐ **Electrics**. Are the electric sockets old? If so, this will tell you that at some point the whole electric system will require rewiring.

- ☐ **Service charges**. For a flat you will have to pay service charges. Ask the agent for details of the service charges. Some are exorbitant, and may render the whole investment unprofitable. Avoid listed buildings as they have frequent redecoration policies that can be expensive.

If the property is in a reasonable condition then buy it. If demand is high there should be no problem letting it out.

Furnished or not?

In addition to the location and price a key factor in attracting the right student for your property is how you furnish your house. The answer to the furnished or not question is almost definitely, a big yes!

More appropriately what furnishings are required to attract the right student? For students this will probably be their first time searching for a house or room to rent and they will be attracted or otherwise by the furnishings and fittings. The higher the quality of the property and its entities, the better chance you have of finding responsible students to look after your property.

What items does the student expect to find in the house? Some key furnishings related to student accommodation include the following.

1. Kitchen appliances

In general, a fridge freezer and cooker are always basic requirements. Often microwaves, washing machines and dryers and to a lesser extent dishwashers are provided.

It's important to match the appliance to the desired student tenant. For example, a washing machine should be durable and long-lasting, intended for heavy usage. It's no good buying one that, despite being very cheap, could start breaking down five months down the line.

Microwaves tend to be a good buy as they add to the aesthetic appeal of the kitchen and can cost as little as £30 for a decent one.

Don't forget that often neglected aspect: availability of workspace in the kitchen. You could have a new hob or dishwasher, yet no space to butter a slice of bread.

2. Sofas, couches and beds

With student properties, it could be that the front room reception gets converted into an extra bedroom, so that the remaining room becomes a living-cum-dining room. A good sofa that looks appealing to the eye and is fairly comfortable will suffice. If bedrooms are large enough then get double beds if your budget allows.

3. Television, Sky, digital

TV sets are really cheap these days and if you feel that the prospective tenants you are looking for will look after the set, then this will add to the attractiveness of your home. However, I'm a bit wary of installing Sky in student properties, although I know of others who have done so with little problem about the bill being paid. You should consider that you might not always have a tenant from July to September, so you may have to bear the brunt of the costs.

Internet

Internet access will undeniably make your house appealing to all students, as computer and internet usage has become a mandatory part of university studying. Even better if you can incorporate a way of accessing the internet from every bedroom in the house.

Location

As the market swells with buy-to-let investors, you must choose the best area within your budget to ensure that the profitability of the location is worth spending your money, time and dedication. For example, very few spots in London would generate enough yields to compensate for the huge initial investment for a student buy-to-let.

Not so profitable areas include Bristol, Cambridge, Liverpool and Oxford, due to low yields. Some areas in Liverpool, buoyant as the student market is, are plagued with buy-to-lets. Rent prices cannot keep up with increased house prices and this has resulted in a standstill or general reduction of rents due to this saturation, producing relatively low yields. Despite this, you can still pick up a bargain in a student area. If it means that with your purchase you can offer competitive rental rates and still make a profit, then it's worth a look.

Contrastingly, other universities such as Brighton and Bournemouth have a lack of student housing. The universities encourage landlords to register with them in order to let out to students. High house prices will deter those who cannot afford the huge initial outlay, but there are some good returns on the right property, if it is within your reach.

When considering the location of the property, don't go for something cheap straight away due to the low prices of properties in a certain area. If that area is not in demand by the students, then it's not worth the effort. Studies have shown that 20% of the 700,000 student lettings offered by the traditional landlord sector in the UK are unfit for letting. You don't want to add your property to that list by buying a block of houses in a run-down area or an area that is renowned not to be student friendly.

The best areas are, not surprisingly, immediately next to or near the campus or university lecture halls, followed by properties on or near bus routes leading to the university and town centre. These houses also tend to have better capital appreciation.

FINDING THE RIGHT STUDENT TENANT

Finding and attracting the right student tenants for your house depend primarily on two factors: **the property** and **you**.

The property

Getting the right tenants will be significantly determined by the type of property you have. A two-bed city apartment may do the trick in attracting affluent students but could, depending on your financial constraints and mobility, have limitations on the competitiveness of the property in the student market.

The properties I have found to be most adaptable and suitable are two-bed, three-bed and four-bed houses. The reason is simple – if I can't find students to let a house to, it will just as likely appeal to a family.

The most popular, it would be safe to say, is the three-bed terrace which becomes a four-bed property once a downstairs living room has been converted into a bedroom.

You

If you are targeting the student market, then you must be comfortable with letting your property out to predominantly 18 to 22-year-olds. The student stereotype of beer-swilling layabouts is an out-of-date image; such pictures could be painted of different people from other walks of life!

But you should not ignore the fact that if you let out to students, you must be comfortable with the idea that three, four, five or even more students in one house will inevitably lead to more wear and tear. You may have to refit the kitchen and bathroom every three to five years, lay new carpets every two to three years and let's not forget that washing machines will be susceptible to heavy usage and may need upgrading sooner than normal.

Finally, bearing in mind that there is no longer a one-size-fits-all existence within the student market, you must have a good idea of what type of student you want as your tenant. In general, student rent fluctuations are pretty flat compared with residential and professional lettings and it is fair to assume that the standard prices of rooms vary from £40 to about £80 a week.

Advertising

The best ways of advertising your property are using online accommodation websites directed at students, liaising with and providing your information through the university housing office, contacting and advertising your property through the students' union, and in local newspapers.

More creatively, you could put up information about your property on noticeboards throughout the campus, having checked to see if this is permissible with the university authorities. The university library may have an information board or something similar where you can promote your property.

The university accommodation office helps students to find suitable privately rented accommodation. Get in contact with this office to find out how things work for your university area.

Some universities offer an affiliated landlord scheme. They will let out your property as a 'university accredited' building, which gives the students a sense of security, and is a definite plus for you in obtaining a suitable tenant. But there is a cost or fixed fee to you, and it does not necessarily mean that they will collect the rent for you, nor will they show prospective tenants around the house. For these kind of services, look at the section on letting agents below.

In addition to this, every student union has a housing officer who is equipped to deal with everything from unhappiness with the room offered to problems with rent and advice on contracts or other legal difficulties with private landlords.

Advertising in the local and university press

This is an effective way of advertising. It is best to advertise in a paper that is delivered free locally or is easily accessible to the student population. The main things you should include are:

- ☐ **Area**. You must state clearly where the property is situated. You don't want to spend time on the phone repeating the same information. Similarly, the student will probably make less effort if they don't know where the property is.

- ☐ **Furnished**. State what furnishings are included and mention important items such as washing machine, dishwasher, high-speed internet access availability.

- ☐ **Number of bedrooms**. Essential information, so that readers will know if your property can accommodate them.

- ☐ **Price**. You must include the price. I always quote a weekly rent, for example £80 per week. This way the tenant assumes that the rent is £320 per month, on the basis of four weeks to a month. However, there are actually 4.33 weeks in a month so in fact it is £346 per calendar month. Your property will appear cheaper than other properties that are quoted per calendar month. If you price your property at £79 rather than £80 the impact is even more significant. You should also make clear what is included in your rent. For instance, some landlords include water rates or electricity bills, others don't.

- ☐ **Features**. If it's got a new bathroom then say so! Anything that is not standard with a property, like a garage, separate dining room, large garden or new carpets, will attract more interest.

- ☐ **Telephone number**. Include a landline number. If you give your mobile number only you will get fewer calls, as everyone knows that a five-minute call to a mobile costs a small fortune, especially the people that you are trying to target.

To find out about the local newspaper in the area of the property visit www.newspapersoc.org.uk.

Student websites

Student websites have become very popular as places to advertise. All students these days have access to the internet and it may be their first port of call to see if anything new comes up.

In addition to this, the students' union may be able to give you a comprehensive guide of where to advertise, or may even provide information on how you can advertise through them or their website links.

Through a letting agent

This is a quite costly route to find a tenant. They usually charge one month's rent + VAT. However, they will show prospective tenants round, run credit checks, ask for references, arrange a standing order and do an inventory check on the property. I would recommend this if you work or live far away from the property.

The most prominent initiative is from Bradford and Bingley Marketplace, the VarsityLets scheme. The scheme is specifically aimed at buy-to-lets for the student market.

Find out about drop-out rates

Before you think that you've found that perfect house with potential for great returns, a factor that is amazingly overlooked by naive landlords is the drop-out rates for universities. A number of the students will not finish their courses, and you may suffer the headache of being left with an empty property for half of the year. Despite the fact that student rental yields are quite stable and prices do not vary much across the UK, you might find it impossible to find another tenant. With council tax, service charges and maintenance bills, you would end up with a negative return on your investment.

Middlesbrough, for example, has been in the headlines due to it being a property hot spot. Terraced housing in the centre of town has gained considerable value over the past few years, with buy-to-let investors capitalizing on this with a view to refurbishment and letting properties out to students. On the plus side, Middlesbrough has seen accelerated house prices and an increased number of students as potential tenants. However, the university is in the process of building new halls of residences to accommodate the projected number of students. Taking this into consideration and accounting for the fact that Teesside University suffers from a 12% drop-out rate, the shiny prospect of student lets in Middlesbrough loses some of its gloss.

The London universities also experience a high drop-out rate. At the University of North London 29% of students don't finish their courses. In contrast, Imperial College's drop-out rate is 4%. Elsewhere, the Bolton Institute of Higher Education, the University of Wales Lampeter and the University of Abertay Dundee see above average drop-out rates.

Can't find a tenant!

If things turn sour and the area you have purchased in does see a significant increase of drop-outs or other negative factors, the following are suggestions to tackle this:

1. Reduce the rent

If you're having problems renting it out, then maybe you're asking for too much for the student area. Look at rental prices offered by other student landlords and then review your rental demands. Think about reducing the rent; or if you are asking for a full year's rent, consider only charging a deposit for the summer weeks when the students aren't there.

2. Promote and advertise your property

If you haven't already done so, consider registering your property with a lettings agent who may have better access to students and will take up a lot of the work for a fee.

Advertise your property through the student newspapers if possible and post your property details around campus, if permissible!

3. Widen the target group

If you are having problems letting it out to students, due to a downturn of student applications/numbers, increased accommodation offered by the university or other related factors, then consider renting it out to professionals, families and other possible tenants.

4. Furnish the property

If you haven't already done this, then maybe a few basic additions will increase the marketability of your property.

Maybe look into installing high-speed internet access to the property as this is a huge pull to the student market.

Sell the property

This should be a last resort. But your property will probably be in demand as it is in a student area, so you should find it quite easy to sell.

Void periods

As you are aware, tenants come in all shapes and sizes regardless of the 'student' tag. You should try to make your property as widely appealing as possible. The best advice is to follow the usual guidelines of neutral decoration, minimize junk, invest in high demand student areas and fully promote your property by using all advertising means possible.

Should I credit check student tenants?

Let's assume everything's going well and you find yourself inundated with potential student tenants wanting to rent your property. You will naturally ask yourself whether they can keep up with rent payments so you won't end up tenantless halfway through the academic year.

You can check the credit of your tenant just as a lender credit checks a borrower. This costs between £17.50 and £94.00, depending on what service you require. But you need to face some facts here. First, it is unlikely that university students will have much work history, so credit referencing them isn't going to amount to much use and is probably a waste of time and money.

Also, it is well documented that students are experiencing some tough times these days and with the ongoing debate of additional tuition fees, and the amount of money they or their parents will invest, there are not many viable options to guarantee rent payment.

The best option is for you to get the group of student tenants to sign one tenancy agreement, whereby if one of the tenants leaves, then they will all be responsible for funding the rent shortfall or finding a new flatmate. You may also wish to ensure they provide a guarantor, someone who will be responsible for their deposit and potential dilapidations to your property.

The relationship between landlord and tenant

We've all heard horror stories about student tenants having all-night parties and trashing the place. On the flipside student tenants have their own stories of crazed landlords refusing to fix the front door despite several burglaries within a week!

The best approach is not to assume too much. Your tenant is not your friend, but nor is he or she out to make life difficult for you! Well, here's to hoping not.

Remember that you are in business with each other and that is the only reason you know each other. For the relationship to last, the following simple contract needs to hold – you are supplying a safe property for the tenant to live in and the tenant is paying you the rent on time.

University accredited lettings

You should consider using the university lettings system if you are finding it tough to channel your energies into finding the tenant. They have better access to students and with full respect to other landlords, they will be trusted a lot more. However, it is often tough in getting your property registered with the university lettings system, as there is much demand to be on it. They also have strict controls and measures on what type of property they want, so this will make it tougher.

13

PROPERTY INVESTOR (PENSION)

VITAL STATISTICS

Earning potential before tax	£10,000 to £200,000 per house
Capital required	£10,000 to £75,000
Skills required	None
Qualifications preferable	None
Competitiveness: low/medium/high	Low
Risk: low/medium/high	Low
The business model in a nutshell	To buy a property or properties to provide for you in retirement
Potential gaps in the market and suggested USPs	• Executive lets

Let me tell you the key findings of a major investment bank's survey.

- ☐ Only one in four workers are set to retire on a pension greater than half their salary.
- ☐ This means that three out of four workers will retire on half their salary or less.
- ☐ And one in two workers will retire on less than 40% of their final salary.

Can you afford to live on half your salary in today's terms? Or even 40% in today's terms?

The reason for this is that the stock market has not performed as expected. Annuity rates have declined due to people living longer and the situation is only going to get worse with the increasing quality of health care.

I initially invested in property 13 years ago at the age of 24 in order to provide me with a pension. The main reason was that I didn't trust *anyone* handling my hard-earned cash apart from myself. The funny thing is that even though my intention was to provide myself with a retirement income, I found that my property income was in excess of my salary so I retired at age 27!

When you contribute to a pension fund you are investing in a business (by way of shares) that you have no control of. Property is something you *do* have control of. It's yours! You don't own a piece of paper called a share certificate. You own something you can see, touch and do with whatever you please. But simply owning property is not your route to retirement bliss. You need to know how to exploit the opportunities that ownership brings.

The difference between property and any other investment is the ability to borrow. You can borrow to purchase the property and let the tenant pay your interest payments by way of rent, hence it's a self-funding investment. Now you can borrow to buy shares but the dividends receivable are rarely sufficient to cover the loan repayments. Also the maximum any bank will lend you will be up to 50% of the value of the shares and the interest rate is much higher than a typical mortgage because shares are riskier than property. This begs the question – if shares are riskier than property why do people invest in shares rather than property?

Well, apart from the tax breaks you get which make investing in pension funds seemingly tax efficient, we invest in shares because:

☐ We are lazy! It's easier to simply pay over some money and let someone else do the hard work.

☐ Other people do! We follow the crowd and if others are doing it we'll do it too.

☐ We are too trusting of the big pension companies. We fall for their mock caring adverts, and impressive head offices and branches.

So it's time to take up the profession of landlord and start enjoying the rewards that have been enjoyed by the middle class for centuries – it's time to build that property pension!

TRADITIONAL PENSION vs PROPERTY PENSION

Pensions are a numbers game. But it's not about how much you put away for retirement. You can heavily contribute to a pension investment fund and it can return you very little in the long term – no matter how many tax breaks, frills or top-ups you receive. There is no come-back or guarantee – it's your loss! The tax breaks, frills and top-ups are there to entice you to invest in companies that prop up our economy but have no real strategy in providing *you* with a real long-term income that is related to your lifestyle or even your contributions.

What a cynic, I hear you say. But if you understand the principles involved you may change your opinion. I will show you clearly how property is a better way to invest for your retirement than any other method. The government, pension companies and banks *cannot* deliver you a guaranteed long-term income sufficient to live a comfortable life. Property *can* deliver an income for you, *your family and your subsequent family members* that is far in excess of what any pension can do.

You may think that this is a tall order. But if you take the time to really understand how long-term income is created you will realize that pensions is indeed a numbers game, and you will laugh at what is currently offered to you as a 'pension' from a traditional pension provider.

Traditional pension providers

There are three broad categories of traditional pension providers: **the government**, **pension companies**, and **banks**. So what is so bad about these traditional providers? Let's look at what they offer.

The government

This is the state pension. You will get this whether you want it or not. You contribute via your National Insurance contributions which are deducted at source, or if you are self-employed deducted from your profits twice a year. The contribution is capped and when you come to retirement they pay a pension currently of around £300 per month. This equates to 9% to 20% of the average UK annual salary depending on where you live in the country.

Even though the government offers a debatable value on your contributions, being only £300 per month from full service it's not worth applauding it or rubbishing it – we get it and that's it.

Another incentive the government offers is a contribution to a pension fund *if* you contribute to a pension fund, by way of not paying tax on your contributions. So if you earn £2,000 per month and pay £200 to a pension company then your taxable income is £1,800 being your income less your pension contribution. If you are a basic rate tax payer, then you will save 21% × £200 = £42 on tax. This is then expressed as an additional contribution by the government as if you didn't contribute you would have only got £158 out of the £200. So it's a contribution of £158 from you and £42 from the government.

If you're a 40% tax rate payer the government contribution is even bigger! In the above example it would be a £120 contribution from you and £80 from the government – quite an incentive on the face of it.

But what are they allowing you to contribute to? They are not giving you this money to put away or to invest for your future. They are saying you can contribute to something that only the government agrees with – their economy!

This has a double effect. First, it means that there is investment in the UK economy which helps our UK-based economies grow and increase the tax collected from these UK companies.

Second, it forces people to take a risk on their retirement income rather than have the government take the risk. If the pension fund doesn't grow to the desired level then that's just your misfortune. The government has given you a big incentive to invest in a pension fund but they carry no responsibility if your pension fund is worth zero! To be fair to the government it's not a bad trade-off. They lose anywhere between 21% and 40% of your salary, being tax, to mitigate their risk of having to provide for you in the future.

2. Pension companies

So the government have given you a tax break of up to 40% – what do the pension companies offer you? Well, they offer you no guarantees, that's for sure. What they will do, however, is take your money, charge you a fee for doing so, invest it in companies they have no control over and hope to return you an amount greater than a building society would. The reality is that in the last five years you'll be lucky to get any profit at all! The stock market is very risky even if it is managed by a pension company. You'd have been better off investing in a building society or bank (see below).

Please disregard the historical growth rates of the stock market. Quite impressively, the stock market has outperformed every investment out there in the past 50 years apart from the last ten. This is why people think that it is so safe, but you must never assume that the past = the future. The stock market has changed dramatically in the way people invest, the type of companies listed, the fluidity with which the market moves and the legislation governing these companies. Dramatic gains are likely to be a thing of the past.

3. The banks

If I were to recommend a pension fund other than property then I would recommend a good old deposit account with an established bank or building society. If you want to retire with peace of mind knowing that you will have at least something to live on then this is the safest way. The problem is you have to contribute so much to even come close to an income that will match your current salary that it seems an impossible task. There are no tax advantages of following this route and the rates the banks pay are incredibly low that it doesn't even seem worth bothering.

Also if you look at any pension fund they have cash reserves. The trend has been of late to keep most of these funds in cash – and they charge you an annual management fee to do so! This results in the poor performance of the pension fund due to their charges and the lower returns to be had from cash. You have to ask yourself – why pay a pension company to put your money into a cash reserve when you can do it yourself, for free! You'll probably get a better rate than them as well.

HOW A TRADITIONAL PENSION WORKS

The only real competitor to a property pension is a pension offered by a pension company. So it makes sense to look into how both these pensions work and how they compare. The numbers can get quite complex, even though I've tried to keep it as simple as possible. Bear with me. I guess the reason why so many people have been duped by the pension companies is because of this very fact! It is easy to get blinded by the science. Let's first look at a traditional pension.

Joe is 41. He works in an office earning £30,000 per year and is a basic rate tax payer. He decides to take out a private pension. He comes across a reputable firm offering a management fee of 1%, and estimated growth of 5%.

A management fee is what a pension company charges for managing your money. This seems reasonable from their side as no one would do this for nothing. They invest your money in so-called 'safe' investments such as cash deposits, bonds and shares. Some pension fund managers are very good at what they do and are well worth their charge as they can out-perform the general market.

Estimated growth is how much the fund manager thinks he can make your money grow. If current rates offered by building societies are 2.5% then a 5% growth is very attractive. If you took into account the tax breaks then it seems even more attractive.

Let's assume that the pension company actually achieve their estimated growth target of 5% year on year. If Joe invested £100 per month, increasing his contribution by 4.25% year on year, his personal contribution, government contribution and fund value would be as shown overleaf.

So Joe's pension fund at his chosen age of retirement, 65, is £111,814. Then Joe has to purchase an annuity, which is a guaranteed annual income until his death, with his pension fund. AXA Sunlife offer £45.78 annual income for every £1,000. So Joe's annual income in retirement is: £45.78 × £111,814/1,000 = £5,118.84 p.a. (say £5,119).

Age	Personal contribution	Government contribution (tax)	Value of year's contribution at age 65
41	1,200	252	4,868
42	1,251	263	4,833
43	1,304	274	4,799
44	1,360	286	4,764
45	1,417	298	4,730
46	1,478	310	4,696
47	1,540	323	4,663
48	1,606	337	4,630
49	1,674	352	4,597
50	1,745	367	4,564
51	1,819	382	4,531
52	1,897	398	4,499
53	1,977	415	4,467
54	2,061	433	4,435
55	2,149	451	4,403
56	2,240	470	4,372
57	2,336	490	4,340
58	2,435	511	4,309
59	2,538	533	4,279
60	2,646	556	4,248
61	2,759	579	4,218
62	2,876	604	4,188
63	2,998	630	4,158
64	3,126	656	4,128
65	3,258	684	4,098
Total	**51,692**	**10,855**	**111,814**

Now let me draw your attention to two key figures – what you put in and what you get out:

- [ ] What you put in: Total pension contributions for the 25 years = £51,692.
- [ ] What you get out: Annual income from the annuity till death = £5,119 p.a. till death.

These should be the only two figures you are interested in. They are the most important figures in the whole pension equation. In fact, these two figures are the key indicators whenever a business person appraises the likely success of a potential investment. A pension fund is an investment so there should be no other way to look at the performance of it.

What you put in is totally *within* your control. Therefore this number is known. It is for you to decide how much you should put away for your retirement. You can be *advised* on how much you should contribute but no one can *guarantee* what you'll get out of it. However, you can be assured that most sane people want to put the least away for the most gain.

What you get out is totally *out of* your control. Unless you have taken out a guaranteed benefit pension (which guarantees a fraction of your final salary, usually two-thirds), which is hugely expensive and normally only available to executive directors, you will have no idea what your pension fund and thus your annual income will be. You can only ever estimate what you'll get out with the accuracy of your estimation increasing as you get closer to the maturity date.

So in the above traditional pension Joe put in £51,692 and he's got out £5,119 p.a. He may get £1,000 p.a. or he may get £10,000 p.a. depending on the performance of his pension fund. But at 5% growth rates he has got roughly *10%* of his contributions as an annual income, being £51,692 contributions and £5,119 annual income. Now we can't say that's good or bad unless we have an alternative to compare to.

Now let's look at a property pension. More importantly – what you put in and what you get out.

HOW A PROPERTY PENSION WORKS

So what's a property pension? Well, the name suggests it all! It's a fund invested in property that delivers an income from the rent derived from these properties. In other words, retirement income from rent. But why is a property pension better than a traditional pension? It has nothing to do with the past. It's to do with the present and the future. If we were to get into a game of how pension funds have outperformed property or the other way round then we would go nowhere. The reason for this is historic. Look at these figures comparing the average individual pension with return from property, based on the average UK house price. The pension figures do not include tax relief.

Return	Pensions	Property
Over 5 years	11%	92%
Over 10 years	61%	142%
Over 15 years	191%	156%
Over 20 years	441%	358%

Both have done well but it depends on which time-frame you look at. Over 15 and 20 years pension funds win, but over five and ten years property wins! The only common thing between these figures are that they all happened in the past. The only people that benefited from these are the people that made these investments. The key to understanding how you can always win with property is to understand the concept of gearing. Or in other words, having the ability to borrow.

The mortgage market has changed dramatically. It is now possible to buy a property with the lender's money based on the rental income only. So you are not expected to earn a certain salary to obtain a buy-to-let mortgage of up to £500,000. The only problem is that you need a larger deposit – at least 15%, and in some cases 30% – compared with the traditional 5% deposit for a residential mortgage. Due to the introduction of the buy-to-let mortgage house prices have risen way above wage inflation rates. This is because property prices are now determined by the rental value of the home rather than its desirability.

So let's look at the cash flows. Jane is 41. She earns £30,000 per year and is a basic rate tax payer. She decides to build a property pension. She can afford to save £100 per month to build a deposit and buy a property costing £30,000. She can rent it out for £2,400 per year which equates to 8% of the purchase price, i.e. 8% yield. She decides to buy a property every time she saves up enough for a deposit.

Now I'm going to have to hold your hand through these figures! Jane buys four properties over 25 years with property values rising 5% every year (the same growth rate as the pension fund). She rents them out and allows a 20% loss of rent due to agent's fees, void periods and repairs. Allowing for this she gets an annual profit rising every time she buys a property and allowing for rent inflation (applied every five years). So the annual profits after tax (basic rate 21% – average used) can be calculated (see table opposite).

Now having calculated these figures, we can derive the key figures in building a comparison with a traditional pension (see table on page 186). The key figures are:

- deposit and fees put down to acquire the properties;
- the profits from these properties;
- the purchase price of these properties;
- the value of these properties at retirement;
- the debt outstanding on these properties at retirement.

Annual profits for Jane's property investments

Property	1 Years 6–10	2 Years 11–15	3 Years 16–20	4 Years 21–25	Years 26 onwards
Purchase price	30,000				
Deposit (15% of purchase price)	4,500				
Debt	25,500				
Rent (8% yield)	2,400	3,063	3,909	4,989	6,368
Interest (5% APR)	1,275	1,275	1,275	1,275	1,275
Other costs (20% of rent)	480	613	782	998	1,274
Net inflow before tax	645	1,175	1,852	2,717	3,819
After tax (21% basic rate)	510	929	1,463	2,146	3,017
Fees	1,500				
Total deposit and fees	6,000				
Purchase price		38,288			
Deposit (15% of purchase price)		5,743			
Debt		32,545			
Rent (8% yield)		3,063	3,909	4,989	6,368
Interest (5% APR)		1,627	1,627	1,627	1,627
Other costs (20% of rent)		613	782	998	1,274
Net inflow before tax		823	1,500	2,364	3,467
After tax (21% basic rate)		650	1,185	1,868	2,739
Fees		2,000			
Total deposit and fees		7,743			
Purchase price			48,867		
Deposit (15% of purchase price)			7,330		
Debt			41,537		
Rent (8% yield)			3,909	4,989	6,368
Interest (5% APR)			2,077	2,077	2,078
Other costs (20% of rent)			782	998	1,274
Net inflow before tax			1,051	1,915	3,016
After tax (21% basic rate)			830	1,512	2,383
Fees			2,500		
Total deposit and fees			9,830		
Purchase price				62,368	
Deposit (15% of purchase price)				9,355	
Debt				53,013	
Rent (8% yield)				4,989	6,368
Interest (5% APR)				2,651	2,651
Other costs (20% of rent)				998	1,274
Net inflow before tax				1,341	2,443
After tax (21% basic rate)				1,059	1,930
Fees				3,000	
Total deposit and fees				12,355	
Annual profit					10,070
Inflow	510	1,579	3,479	6,586	

Calculating Jane's property pension fund

Property	Age	Deposit and fees (outflow)	Profit (inflow)	Net outflow	Purchase price 5% growth p.a.	Property value at age 65	Debt mortgage	Net value
	41							
	42							
	43							
	44							
1	45	6,000			30,000	83,579	25,500	58,079
	46		510					
	47	0	510					
	48	0	510					
	49	0	510					
2	50	7,743	510		38,288	83,579	32,545	51,034
	51	0	1,579					
	52	0	1,579					
	53	0	1,579					
	54	0	1,579					
3	55	9,830	1,579		48,867	83,579	41,537	42,042
	56	0	3,479					
	57	0	3,479					
	58	0	3,479					
	59	0	3,479					
4	60	12,355	3,479		62,368	83,579	53,013	30,566
	61	0	6,586					
	62	0	6,586					
	63	0	6,586					
	64	0	6,586					
	65	0	6,586					
		35,928	60,764	−24,836	179,523	334,316	152,595	181,721

So Jane's property pension fund is £181,721, being the value of the properties less the mortgage debt. But just like the traditional pension fund we have assumed a 5% growth in property prices, whereas I have no idea what the growth rate will be averaged out over the next 25 years. Even though a property pension fund is *greater* than a traditional pension after tax at the same growth rates (£181,721 vs £111,814), the great thing is, *it doesn't matter*!

Why doesn't it matter? The 5% growth is nice and probably realistic but it doesn't provide us with an income. What we're interested in is the rental income. The two key figures you should be looking at are the ones I talked about earlier – what you put in and what you get out! So here's what we've put in and what these figures are:

☐ **What you put in**: deposit and fees less profits from the properties over the 25 years = − £24,836

☐ **What you get out**: profits for years 26 onwards = £10,070 p.a. for ever.

So with a property pension you actually get money back! What you put in is a negative amount. Your investment in property by way of deposits and fees are replenished by the profits made in property and more. Being prudent, let's assume that the profit just covers the deposit and fees only. This means that over the 25 years what you have put in is still only NIL!

What have you got out of it? Well, a nice income of over £10,000 p.a. which is twice as much as what a traditional pension can offer. And this income is not just for your life but for your beneficiaries after your death.

However, if you do want a risk-free pension and want to purchase an annuity, then the net value of the properties does matter because you have to sell the properties. The beauty of property is that you can sell when you want to. So you can sell when the market is high or hold when the market is low. The market could be high enough to sell within 15 years of you making the first property purchase or you may have to wait 30 years. Assuming the property portfolio performs at 5% growth p.a., then the net fund after tax will be:

Proceeds of property sales	£334,316
Purchase prices	£179,523
Profit	£154,793
Tax relief	(£61,917)
Chargeable gain	£92,876
@ 40%	£37,150

So net proceeds will be:

Proceeds of property sales	£334,316
Tax bill	(£37,150)
Net proceeds before mortgage debt	£297,166
Mortgage debt	(£152,595)
Net proceeds	**£144,571**

Using the same annuity rates as above, of £45.78 per £1,000, the risk-free pension till death is: £144,571 × £45.78/1,000 = £6,618.44 p.a.

COMPARISONS BETWEEN TRADITIONAL AND PROPERTY PENSIONS

Let's look at a proper comparison of the figures:

	Traditional pension	Property pension (buy and hold)	Property pension (buy and sell)
What you put in	£51,692	Nil	Nil
What you get out	£5,119 p.a. until death	£10,070 p.a. forever	£6,618.44 p.a. until death

You can clearly see that property pensions out-perform traditional pensions quite astronomically even with all the tax breaks. This is because you essentially put no money in and get more out! Even if the traditional fund did return you a higher income the property pension would win as you haven't put anything in! This is why traditional pensions are a joke.

Other factors to consider

But it doesn't stop there! It's not only the numbers that make a good case for a property pension. There are other factors that make a property pension superior to a traditional pension which are in part drawn out from the figures above, as outlined below.

Flexibility

Traditional

Pensions are inflexible by their very nature, as you can't get hold of your cash until you are 50. And even then it's only 25% of the fund.

Property

You can sell your property or properties when you want. So if the market is high or you need the cash then the money can be unlocked relatively quickly, whenever you want.

Longevity of income

Traditional

The income from a pension stops when you die. Now this may not be a problem for you but it could be a problem for your dependants. You can get a pension that pays out to your spouse but you have to pay for it! The annuity rates are much lower.

Property

The income streams carry on regardless of your death. Just because you die it doesn't mean your tenant has to stop paying rent. The rent will simply be paid to whoever you leave the property or properties to when you die. This is how some families have become very rich due to the inheritance of property from deceased relatives.

Income now

Traditional

There is no income stream until you purchase the annuity. This may be 40 years after you made the first payment into the pension fund.

Property

When you invest in property you will get income straight away. If you've bought the right property then you will get an income even after paying out for the expenses such as the mortgage and repairs.

Instinctive

Traditional

How do you choose a good pension fund? It's very difficult. You can use historic data but that tells you nothing about future performance. You have to take on the risk that your fund manager will do well with your money. How well he or she will do is impossible to tell. You do not even get the chance to meet them!

Property

It's easier to pick a good house than a good stock or pension company. You will have an instinctive knowledge about property as we have all lived in one! It's something you can touch and feel rather than a paper statement sent to you once a year.

Income rises with inflation

Traditional

If you purchase an annuity with a fixed income pay-out then you will receive a fixed amount till death. Your real income will diminish over time due to price inflation. The only way to counteract this is to take out an annuity that pays an income that rises with inflation. But you've guessed it – it costs! So the annuity rates are lower.

Property

Rent rises with wage inflation at the very least. However, current demographics show that property is in short supply and the situation is set to get worse. Fragmenting families, increasing population, first-time buyers being priced out and building quotas not being met will cause rents to *probably* rise above inflation.

Gearing

Traditional

You are unable to borrow to contribute to a pension fund as there will be no way you could service the loan repayments.

Property

You are able to borrow because the lender takes first charge on the property and knows you can service the debt from the rent paid by the tenant. The potential growth of your property fund is magnified due to the growth being on the whole property price rather than the actual amount invested.

Known retirement income

Traditional

You will have no idea what your retirement income will be. You can only make an estimation but that will depend heavily on the size of your fund and the annuity rates being offered at the time of retirement.

Property

It's easier to predict your retirement income if you choose properties that give you an income you desire now. For example, if you require an income equivalent to your salary of £2,000 per month then choose four properties that have a rental figure of £500 each. Then you can be assured that when you retire the rental figures would have risen roughly with inflation to provide you with a real income of £2,000 per month.

No cap on contributions

Traditional

You are capped on the contributions to a pension fund to qualify for full tax relief. You can contribute further but you do lose out on all the tax benefits.

Property

Because you have already factored in the lack of tax benefits in the whole equation then the amount you want to contribute is completely up to you.

Not relying on growth

Traditional

The fund has to grow to a desired level for you to draw an income sufficient for your retirement. This is very difficult to predict which has been shown by all the pension companies offering these types of pension.

Property

Growth is nice but you are relying on rental income. Rent does not go down – it rises with inflation so you can be assured that the income derived from your properties will be sufficient and growth will be irrelevant. (This is only applicable for a buy and hold strategy.)

Annuity rates are always inferior to property yields

Traditional

Annuity rates are very poor but will never exceed 8% for someone aged 65. This is because we live longer. In this example if they gave you 8% then they will expect you to die in 12.5 years. This is just under the average life expectancy of 79, being 77.5 years. They will give you an income based on you living till 90 and hope you die at 79! This equates to a 5% rate.

Property

8%+ yields are easily achievable – even though property prices are said to be at an all time high. Thus property will always be a better investment than an annuity.

Risk and control

Traditional

You place all the control with a fund manager. He is in full control of your money and exposes you fully to the risks that only he takes on.

Property

You take the risks that you want. You are in full control of the decisions you wish to take. You are exposed exclusively to the risks only you wish to take.

SOME ASSUMPTIONS ABOUT EACH TYPE OF PENSION

Now there have been a number of assumptions made in deriving these calculations. These are necessary, otherwise we could not build a picture of your future income. Here are a list of the assumptions I have made for each type of pension, how reasonable they are and how relevant they are to the overall performance of each.

Traditional pension

Basic rate tax payer
Reasonable?

I have chosen basic rate as most people are basic rate tax rate payers.

Relevant to performance?

Yes. A higher rate tax payer gets a higher retirement income than a basic rate tax payer in a traditional pension example but they still receive less than a property pension. So a property pension is still superior.

1% management fee
Reasonable?

There are few if any that charge less than 1% and some that charge more. 1% is the industry norm for pension funds.

Relevant to performance?

Because this is the industry standard it is a safe assumption as not to distort the figures.

5% growth of fund
Reasonable?

This is a very difficult question as we are crystal ball gazing. We cannot base it on past performance. The key fact is that it is the same growth rate as the property calculations so neither has an advantage.

Relevant to performance?

No. Both growth rates were set equal.

4.25% growth in contributions
Reasonable?

Would seem reasonable due to taking into account inflation and promotional pay increases.

Relevant to performance?

No. As we have looked at the contributions in total over the 25 years the individual contributions over the years are broadly irrelevant as in both examples the contributions were spread out.

Start age of 41

Reasonable?

The start age is not really relevant due to the fact that both pensions were being compared.

Relevance to performance?

No. Both start ages were the same.

Retirement age of 65

Reasonable?

The retirement age is not really relevant due to the fact that both pensions were being compared.

Relevant to performance?

No. Both retirement ages were the same.

Property pension

Basic rate tax payer

Reasonable?

I have chosen basic rate as most people are basic rate tax rate payers.

Relevant to performance?

Yes. A higher rate tax payer gets a lower retirement income than a basic rate tax payer based on the same contribution level under a property pension, but it is still in excess of the traditional pension.

8% yield

Reasonable?

There are many properties and areas that offer an 8%+ yield. Join my newsletter at www.ahuja.co.uk to get a full list of them.

Relevant to performance?

Yes. The higher the yield the higher the profit per year, thus reducing your overall contribution. If the yield is 6.75% then the profit over the 25 years matches your contribution to property so that your overall contribution is nil. Below 6.75% yield and you will then have to contribute out of your own pocket. Above 6.75% yield requires no overall contribution.

Over 75% of properties on the market offer a 6.75%+ yield so there is no shortage of suitable properties. 8%+ just gives you that comfort margin.

Fixed interest rate of 5% APR

Reasonable?

A fixed rate had to be used to keep the examples simple. Again we are crystal-ball gazing here. 5% APR is reasonable because we can fix interest rates to around this level for a period greater than ten years. Also, fixed rates are determined by the fixed bond market which is less volatile than the variable rate market.

Relevant to performance?

Yes. The cost of borrowing affects profits quite dramatically if we don't buy at a good yield. If you buy a property in excess of 8% then you can weather interest rate fluctuations.

You need to consider what you think the average interest rate will be over the next 25 years – and if you know the answer to that then let me know!

Interest-only mortgage taken out

Reasonable?

Interest-only monthly payments are less than repayment monthly payments, thus monthly cash inflows are higher due to the balance never being reduced. It's a reasonable assumption as all the mortgage companies offer it but it depends on whether you want the property paid in full by the time you hit retirement.

Relevant to performance?

Yes. If the example used a repayment mortgage instead of an interest-only mortgage then the profit would be the same but the cash flows would have been different. The monetary difference between repayment and interest only could be considered as a contribution. The beauty is that this contribution can be structured as a voluntary contribution if you took out an interest-only mortgage and paid the capital off as and when you wished to.

Other costs being 20% of rent

Reasonable?

20% of rent is quite a generous allowance. This equates to a one month void period, management fees of 10% of rent and 2% of rent spent on repairs.

Relevant to performance?

Yes. The amounts of voids, management charges and repairs affect profit which affects your overall contribution.

You need to consider whether 20% is enough.

Professional fees
Reasonable?

I have assumed £1,500 for year 5, increasing by £500 every five years. This is a standard charge for valuations, solicitor costs and arrangement fees. It's unlikely that you will face a charge greater than £1,500 and the £500 increase every five years is above the rate of inflation so is a prudent estimate.

Relevant to performance?

Yes. The size of your contribution is dependent on the amount of professional fees required. The less required means that you can acquire properties sooner as the requirement to purchase a property is lowered.

Deposit level of 15%
Reasonable?

At the time of writing there was only one 15% deposit level lender. However, the credit freeze is melting and I expect many more 15% deposit products to come on to the market and in the long run be the average level of deposits in the future.

Relevant to performance?

Yes. If you have to find more deposit money then this will affect performance. You could use more complicated no-money-down strategies to match if not better the performance outlined above. If you want to find out more visit www.ahuja.co.uk and join my newsletter.

Property purchase price of £30,000 rising by 5% every year
Reasonable?

I have chosen £30,000 just as a notional figure to compare like with like based on a rough £100 per month contribution. If a property can only be bought for £90,000 then a contribution of £300 per month is required.

Relevant to performance?

No. The contributions in both examples were the same. So if £90,000 had to be the purchase price then we would have to alter the contributions in the traditional pension example to £300 per month so we could compare like with like.

5% growth of property prices
Reasonable?
This is a very difficult question as we are crystal-ball gazing. We cannot base it on past performance. The key fact is that it is the same growth rate as the traditional pension calculations so neither has an advantage.

Relevant to performance?
No. Both growth rates were set equal.

Start age of 41
Reasonable?
The start age is not really relevant due to the fact that both pensions were being compared.

Relevant to performance?
No. Both start ages were the same.

Retirement age of 65
Reasonable?
The retirement age is not really relevant due to the fact that both pensions were being compared.

Relevant to performance?
No. Both retirement ages were the same.

You decide
It's up to you to decide whether these assumptions are reasonable and/or relevant. Try flexing the numbers to see what other results you get. Do whatever it takes for you to come to a decision on whether what I'm saying has some basis or is fundamentally flawed due to very relevant omissions. Until you do this you will always be wavering between traditional pension funds and property pension funds or even something else – and always kicking yourself for not making the right decision when one of them booms.

RISKS vs RETURNS

So we have established the returns to be had from a traditional pension and a property pension but what are the risks and are they worth it?

The risks involved in investing in property

A number of the fears that people have are fully justified. They are not dissimilar to what business people face when appraising a potential investment. These are called risks. The difference between the ordinary person and a business person is that a business person:

- ☐ identifies all the risks involved;
- ☐ mitigates each risk as best he or she can;
- ☐ considers the overall risk based on how well he or she can mitigate each individual risk;
- ☐ makes a decision based on the overall risk.

So to build a property pension you need to:

- ☐ identify all your fears involved in building a property pension;
- ☐ think how you can overcome each fear involved in building a property pension;
- ☐ consider the overall fear factor based on how well you can overcome each individual fear;
- ☐ decide whether or not you want to build a property pension based on the overall fear factor.

Fortunately for you I'm not going to ask you to think up all the fears involved and how to overcome them. I will tell you!

Unfortunately for you I am not going to decide for you whether or not to build a property pension. However, I will present a very strong case and recommend that you do build a property pension.

The fears and how to overcome them

For every fear I suggest a countermeasure you can take to overcome the fear. No countermeasure is foolproof, however.

There will still always be an overhang of fear, what I call **residual fear**, less than the starting fear but still present even after the countermeasure is taken. You can take further countermeasures to reduce this residual fear but there will always be some residual fear.

An example of a residual fear that cannot be eliminated is the destruction of your property if there was a war. No insurance company will take on this risk. The only way you could mitigate this risk would be to build a bombproof shell around your property – but this would be impractical and probably cost more than your property itself!

The fears, countermeasures and residual fears in buying a property are shown in the table.

Fears, countermeasures and residual fears of investing in property

Fear	Countermeasure	Residual fear	Further countermeasure
1 Can't find a tenant.	Buy a property that can be easily let out, like near a major train station or in a desirable area.	Still can't find tenant.	Reduce the rent.
2 Interest rate rises beyond affordability.	Fix the interest rate for a fixed period of time.	The interest rate rises beyond affordability after the fixed period of time.	Fix the interest rate for the whole term of the mortgage.
3 Get caught in negative equity trap.	Don't sell the property and realize your loss. Continue to rent it out. Wait for the recovery and then sell.	It never recovers and you have to sell.	Buy the property without a mortgage so that negative equity is not a possibility.
4 The tenant does not pay the rent.	Take out landlord insurance that covers you for loss of rent due to tenant default.	None.	N/A.
5 Major repair becomes due and can't afford to carry out works.	Take out a thorough and comprehensive buildings and contents insurance.	The policy doesn't capture every eventuality.	Take out specific policies for specific items, e.g. British Gas offer full insurance on your boiler from £8 per month.
6 Buying a property you can't sell.	Avoid difficult to sell properties such as studio flats, ex local authority flats, flats above shops, non-standard construction properties or any property that is difficult to get a mortgage on.	Still can't sell it.	Buy a property near a train station city or major road junction.

Overall fear

Calculate your overall fear by gathering all the residual fears that remain. To do this you:

☐ decide which fears listed (1 to 6) are fears that you actually have;

☐ decide what countermeasures you are willing to take for each fear;

☐ calculate the residual fear for each fear applicable.

For example, after taking countermeasures you have residual fears for 1, 3 and 5, your overall fear is the contents of the residual fear column (see table).

Overall fear

Fear	Countermeasures willing to take	Residual fear
I Can't find a tenant.	Buy a property that can be easily let out, like near a major train station or in a desirable area and be willing to reduce the rent.	Not being able to find a tenant for a property near a major train station or desirable area even though you are flexible on the rental price.
3 Get caught in negative equity trap.	Don't sell the property and realize your loss. Continue to rent it out. Wait for the recovery and then sell.	It never recovers and you have to sell.
5 Major repair becomes due and can't afford to carry out works.	Take out a thorough and comprehensive buildings and contents insurance, as well as specific policies for specific items.	The policies don't capture something you hadn't thought of.

So your overall fear is:

☐ not being able to find a tenant even though you have bought a desirable property and you can reduce the rental price asked;

☐ you buy a property that goes falls into negative equity and you have to sell;

☐ you get stung for a repair that you never thought you'd get.

You have to make an estimation of how likely these fears are to materialize and whether the rewards in investing in a property pension are compensatory enough. If you are happy with this overall fear then you will invest in property. If you are not then you won't, but I suggest that there are more countermeasures you could take to reduce your overall fear to a level that you are happy with so you are comfortable in investing in property.

The risks associated with a traditional pension fund

Because you transfer a lot of your control over to the pension fund manager there are only two real risks (see table).

Fears and countermeasures of a traditional pension

Fear	Countermeasure	Residual fear	Further countermeasure
I The fund is not big enough to pay your desired retirement income.	Contribute more to the fund.	Still isn't big enough.	Wait for annuity rates to rise.
2 At the time of retirement the annuity rates are poor.	Wait for the rates to improve.	Rates do not improve.	Contribute more to the fund.

You can either wait or add to your fund. These are the only two strategies you have!

So are you convinced?

I've laid out both arguments for you but it's for you to come to a decision. Do you think property is better than traditional pension funds? I really want you to study this chapter as this information is key to your motivation to build a property pension. Once you are convinced, the motivation to build a property pension will be there. This is because you understand the uniqueness of property and how property is a superior investment to virtually any other investment out there.

The illustration above is only one strategy to achieve a property pension. There are many strategies you can adopt to achieve a retirement income but this all depends on *you*. It depends on how much you are willing to contribute, how much you want and when, your attitude to risk and your level of involvement. Let's look at this in more detail.

YOUR PROFILE

Objective

If you want to build a property pension you need a strategy. A strategy is a method to achieve an objective. So in this scenario the objective is: *to have an income sufficient to meet all your needs in retirement.*

This is what a pension aims to do but often fails. So to achieve this objective you need a strategy! The first stage in constructing a strategy is to really think about the objective. The objective throws up some obvious questions you need to ask yourself.

How much do you need?

You have to know how much you need! If you don't spend time thinking about it then you face the possibility of not having enough. Setting a target income means that you have something to aim for.

On the face of it it seems a difficult question to answer. Your retirement age may be 25 years away and you will have no idea what £1 is worth in 25 years' time. The fact is, you don't need to! What you can do is ask yourself what you will need in today's value of money. Because rental income rises with inflation then all we have to do is express our desired retirement income as rental income at today's value. So if you earn £25,000 per annum now and would like to keep the lifestyle you have then you require £25,000 rental income at today's rental market value.

So how much will you need? Think about your likely monthly expenses of living and what you would like to do in your retirement. Don't forget the obvious expenses such as food, bills and clothing and don't forget to omit your mortgage expense if you plan to pay off your home by the time you hit retirement. If you wish to travel in retirement then allow for that expense. So you should be able to come up with a monthly figure.

When do you want it?

You need to know when you wish to retire so you can put a timescale to the objective. You can then set mini targets within the timescale so you can monitor how well you are doing. If mini targets are not being met you can adjust your strategy to bring you back on track.

So when do you want to retire? Answering 'Tomorrow!' is neither helpful nor practical. Consider your age now, how long you would like to work and what you want to do in your retirement. Remember, retirement can be boring for some people, as many early retirees have admitted. Set a realistic timescale which takes into account your target retirement income.

For example, an objective might be:

> Target retirement income at today's value = £25,000
> Timescale = 18 years.

What's needed from you to achieve your objective

Your objective is not going to land in your lap! It requires three things from you: **time**, **money**, and **acceptance of risk**.

These three factors are correlated. That is to say, if you don't have much money to put in then be prepared to put in more time and accept a higher degree of risk. If you increase the time you put in then you won't have to put so much money in or accept so much risk. Let's look at exactly what's expected from you.

Time

Time input required is summarized below, with ways to reduce the amount needed.

Acquisition

You need to find the properties that will deliver you an income! This involves researching suitable areas, looking through the local press, speaking and dealing with agents, visiting prospective properties, arranging finance and whatever else is needed from you to acquire a property.

You can approach a property buying company that will do all this for you based on your criteria. This costs! These companies can charge up to 5% of the purchase price so they can work out expensive.

Find a tenant

You have to advertise, do viewings, credit check and take up references of prospective tenants.

You could use a letting agent. They charge a fee of around 10% + VAT on the rent collected.

Legal documents

You need to prepare the legal documents to bind all parties or to evict tenants. A letting agent will do this for you.

Rent collection

You need to arrange for the rent to be collected. This may be face-to-face collection from the tenant's doorstep, collection from the benefits office or through your bank.

Again, a letting agent will look after this. Or set up a standing order.

Repairs

You need to either repair the problem or instruct someone to do the repair. A letting agent will look after this too.

Tax return

You need to declare what you've earned during the financial year in order to pay tax. This requires accounting for all receipts and expenditure associated with the property.

You could use an accountant. Or you can subscribe to www.propertyhotspots.net to manage your finances.

Money

You need money to buy a property! Here is why you need money and ways to minimize the amount needed:

Initial investment

You need a deposit to buy a property. At a minimum it will be 15% of the purchase price. You will also need the associated fees that come with buying a property. These are valuation fees, solicitor costs, arrangement fees, finder fees, initial void period and essential repairs required before letting the property.

You need to save for a deposit. Or you can borrow the deposit and fund the repayments to the loan from the rent achievable once the property has been bought. This increases your risk due to the increased borrowing.

You can find a property yourself, thus eliminating a finder's fee to a property agent.

Buying a property in a good state of repair will avoid any essential repair costs.

Monthly contribution

You may have to contribute over and above what is received in rent if you get hit for a large repair bill, interest rates rise, the tenant defaults or you wish to pay off the mortgage early.

Take out insurance on tenant default or any large repairs. This means the insurance company pick up the bill. The cost of this is the insurance premium.

Fix your interest rate so fluctuations are not a concern. Thus if you have chosen a property that returns a rental income in excess of the fixed mortgage payment then you are assured that you do not have to contribute.

Take out an interest-only mortgage. This keeps the mortgage payment at its lowest possible point so the margin between rent and mortgage cost is at its highest.

Go for a higher yielding property. The higher the yield the higher the profit margin. Please note – the higher the yield the higher the risk!

Acceptance of risk

There are always risks of owning an asset, but there are also benefits! You can mitigate these risks, and this costs, but there will always be a residual risk remaining. So you will always have to accept a degree of risk. You need to decide what risks you are willing to take as this will determine the strategies open to you.

How what's needed from you relates to your objective

Now these three factors – time, money and acceptance of risk – have to bear some relation to your objective.

- ☐ If your objective is to have a retirement income of £100,000 p.a. at today's value in five years and you earn £20,000 p.a., have no savings, no time and willing to accept only a very low level of risk, then it *won't* happen!

- ☐ If your objective is to have a retirement income of £100,000 p.a. at today's value in five years and you earn £20,000 p.a., have no savings, little time, are willing to contribute, and willing to accept a high level of risk, then it *might* happen!

- ☐ If you wish to earn a retirement income of £20,000 p.a. at today's value in 15 years and you earn £20,000 p.a., have no savings but the discipline to save, have a bit of time, and are willing to accept a medium level of risk, then it probably *will* happen.

So, in my professional opinion, as long as you are willing to earn a retirement income that is what you are earning now, that is 15 years away, have the time, can save and have savings, and accept a medium level of risk then it *will* happen.

Deriving your profile

You should now be able to build a profile of yourself and your aims. The following is a short summary of the questions you need to ask yourself.

Target retirement income at today's value

How much do you want based on today's value? Do you think you will have expensive tastes in retirement? Do you want a simple life in retirement? Or do you just want what you have now?

Timescale

How soon do you want to retire? Is it five years, ten years, thirty?

Time

How much time do you have available (low/medium/high)? Are you willing to be involved in the buying process, rent collection and repairs? Or do you work full-time (and overtime!) and want zero involvement?

Money

How much have you saved or are willing to contribute (low/medium/high)? Do you have a deposit? Are you good at saving? Are you willing to contribute month by month? Or do you have no savings and require a monthly profit from the properties?

Acceptance of risk

How much risk do you want (low/medium/high)? Are you willing to borrow significantly, accept fluctuations in interest rates, take interest-only mortgages and go for less desirable properties that yield highly? Or do you want minimal borrowings, fixed rate borrowings, repayment mortgages and nicer properties near your home town?

So a typical profile may be:

Target retirement income at today's value	£30,000
Timescale	24 years
Time	Low
Money	Medium
Acceptance of risk	Medium

A profile can be matched to the strategies available. What's your profile? Take your time to really think about what you want. Is it realistic? Will it be enough? Do you earn enough to save and/or contribute? Can you take a higher level of risk?

Based on your profile we can choose a strategy or a number of strategies.

THE STRATEGIES

The three core strategies

There are three core strategies to a property pension as follows.

1. Buy and then hold.
2. Buy and then sell.
3. Buy, then part hold and part sell.

There are variations, but every strategy will fall somewhere within these core three. Remember from the previous sections the definition of a pension, being the objective of a property pension: *To have an income sufficient enough to meet all your needs in retirement.*

Well, the three strategies above can meet this objective.

Buy and then hold

This involves buying a property (or properties), paying for it in full by retirement. You live off the rental income through retirement.

You rely on the property to be easily rentable so as to provide a safe income for retirement.

Buy and then sell

This involves buying a property (or properties), making the repayments during the period of ownership and then sell the property and clear the debt (if any). The balance of the monies are then used to purchase an annuity to provide retirement income.

You rely on the growth of the property to be sufficient enough to purchase an annuity to meet your target income in retirement.

Buy, then part hold and part sell

This involves a mixture of both strategies above.

Choosing the right strategy

You need to choose the strategy that's right for you based on your level of time, money and acceptance of risk. Here's how these strategies could work according to the level of time, money and risk of a potential investor.

1. Buy and then hold

Time: Low
Money: Medium
Risk: Low

Buy a desirable property with less than a 9% yield on a repayment mortgage and place with a letting agent to manage the property. The investor understands that he might have to contribute on top of the rent to cover the mortgage payment but has the assurance that the property will be paid in full. It will then provide an income for life.

2. Buy and then sell

Time: Low
Money: Medium
Risk: Low

Buy a property in a less desirable area but yielding in excess of 10% on an interest-only mortgage. The investor will manage the property himself but knows that it is unlikely that he will have to contribute on top of the rent as the property yields high and the mortgage is interest only. He hopes that the property value grows sufficiently in value in order to purchase an annuity to provide him with retirement income.

3. Buy, then part hold and part sell

Time: Low
Money: Medium
Risk: Low

He does a bit of both above. He is happy to buy more than one property and manage them himself. He uses the profits from some to fund the others but his risk is reduced due to the investor not relying on one single strategy. Overall risk is medium due to the greater exposure he has to the property market but he can capitalize in each market when the market is high.

So the questions are about whether you want to own and run the property pre- and post-retirement, how much money you want to put away for saving up for a deposit and ongoing pre-retirement, and the level of risk you want to expose yourself to. Do you want only one property or a few? Do you want repayment or interest only mortgages? Do you require a risk-free income in retirement?

Based on your own profile and personal preferences you should be able to come up with a strategy. To help you decide let's look at some examples. I ignore tax consequences to keep the figures simple.

Buy and then hold

Richard has the following profile:

Target retirement income at today's value	£24,000
Timescale	25 years
Time	Low
Money	Medium
Acceptance of risk	Low

He has decided that he wants to *buy and then hold* so he can pass the properties on to his children. But he also doesn't want to pass on any debt so he intends to own the properties outright. He works full-time so he doesn't want to manage the properties and he wants desirable properties that are easily let out. He has the ability to save and a willingness to contribute on an ongoing basis if need be.

The strategy would be to buy one or more properties that give a rental income of £24,000. As he is a low-risk investor he would buy a low-yielding property, such as 8%, on a repayment mortgage. This could be three properties costing £100,000 producing an £8,000 per year income. He will also have the property managed by a letting agent.

Using your own home to provide a retirement income

Some people use their personal home to provide for themselves in retirement. The theory is that you downsize to a smaller property, purchasing a bungalow and renting out your own property.

The key things you need to consider are as follows.

- ☐ Is the rental value of your home equivalent to your desired income in today's standards?
- ☐ Will the property be paid in full when it's time to retire?
- ☐ Will you have saved enough to buy a property for yourself to live in?

You can always sell your own home, buy two cheaper properties, live in one and rent out the other. This falls into the strategy of *buy and then sell*. But the key things you need to consider above still apply.

Buy and then sell

Susan has the following profile:

Target retirement income at today's value	£30,000
Timescale	20 years
Time	Medium
Money	Low
Acceptance of risk	Medium

Susan earns just £15,000 and cannot afford to contribute anything on a monthly basis. But she does have savings of £15,000 left to her by her late grandmother. Susan wants twice her annual income in real terms in her retirement within 20 years! Funnily enough, this is possible due to her attitude to risk.

14

PROPERTY INVESTOR (LEASE OPTIONS)

VITAL STATISTICS

Earning potential before tax	£5,000 to unlimited per option
Capital required	£nil to £10,000
Skills required	None
Qualifications preferable	None
Competitiveness: low/medium/high	High
Risk: low/medium/high	Low
The business model in a nutshell	To acquire options on property with the view to buying or selling them in the future.
Potential gaps in the market and suggested USPs	• The mere fact you are doing lease options is unique already – it is a very niche industry.

Trading options is a great way to make money quickly. However, for those of you who want to build a property portfolio and collect rent every month as a way to live then investing in lease options is the way forward.

You need to be a long-term player. If you invest rather than trade then the rewards can be much higher, depending on your timing. It is the easy way to make money. Think of a tortoise rather than a hare: a methodical approach with calculated risks will generally outperform the quick wins.

LEASE OPTIONS EXPLAINED

What are lease options? Well, the clue is in the name! It is an option but also you get control of the property by leasing it for the period of the option.

So you have an added dimension to the standard option. It is the lease element of it. This fast-forwards your ownership of the property without really owning it.

Examples of lease options are:

5 London Road   You can rent the property for £400 per month and you can buy the property for £250,000 if you complete by 1 January 2011.

12 Acacia Avenue   You can rent the property for £500 per month and you can buy the property for £200,000 if you complete by 12 December 2015.

4 Jones Street   You can rent the property for £100 per month and you can buy the property for £55,000 if you complete by 30 June 2020.

Now earlier in Chapter 9 I spoke about the two Ps in options: **price** and **period**. Well, I have another P for you: **profit**!

Profit is based on the difference between what you can rent the property from the owner for and what you can get on the open market. So look at this example:

A property has a market value today of £100k. You find a seller who will grant you an option to buy this property in five years' time for £110k. So the price is £110k. And the period is five years.

The seller will also let you rent the property from him at £300 per month. His mortgage payments are £300 and he wants rid of the property. You know that the property will rent out for £500. Then the potential profit to be made every month is: £500 − £300 = £200.

This profit is possible every month for the next five years. So the overall profit would be the total number of months in five years multiplied by the monthly profit, being: 5 years × 12 months × £200 = £12,000.

So if we were to stand back and look at the deal now, the 3Ps would be:

- price: £110k;
- period: five years;
- profit: £12k.

If we were to ignore inflation, we would have a lease option with a potential profit of £30k + £12k = £42k.

Why lease options are so exciting

The reason is that you can get on with your investing without the need of finance straight away. They fast-forward your buying as you can take control of many properties very quickly and literally build massive portfolios in months, even weeks.

I use the word invest is because as long as your options have the correct Ps – price, period, profit – then you will own that property without a doubt. It is vitally important that you understand this. *You can own the properties that you are controlling by way of lease options.*

Now there must be quite a few questions pinging into your head right now. It is a normal reaction! If you have no questions then either you do not understand it, or it is not for you.

It is essential to understand the theory before you embark on purchasing options. They are, however, only an invention from necessity. Once the mortgage market recovers then we will be back to normal. But lease options can be a true 'no money down' system without the need for finance.

BUY PROPERTIES FOR 50p

This is the real reason why you can become very wealthy with lease options. You can take *full* control of a property by paying a notional sum like 50p *and* end up buying it. This is no joke.

By way of an example, let's say that John is in the following predicament. He has lost his job. His mortgage is £100k. The value of his home is £75k.

John is trapped in negative equity. He cannot afford the mortgage and just wants rid of the property. He cannot sell as the mortgage company will not let the shortfall become an unsecured debt. This property is unsaleable. Or that is what John thinks anyway.

What he needs is someone who will pay his mortgage for him. This is where you step in. Your proposition is: *I will buy your property from you at £100k in X years and I will pay your mortgage for you up until I buy.*

From John's point of view this is as good as selling. He has no more financial liability. John is FREE!

What you have now is the liability. You have to pay John's mortgage but this is no problem as you can rent it out to cover the mortgage payments and then some.

So where does the 50p come in then? Well, if you think about it, how much do you think John needs you? He needs you more than you need him. So effectively John would *pay* you to take on his mortgage! However, John has no money and you are not willing to part with any cash so a notional amount is enough to make the contract valid.

Contracts need a thing called consideration. Consideration means that there has to be something in it for both parties to make a contract valid. So John gives you his property and you give him 50p! Sounds crazy, but houses can exchange hands for very small sums of money!

But remember, once you pay the 50p the property is yours. And there are a few steps in between handing over a 50 pence piece and getting the keys – like using a solicitor. However, you can say goodbye to quite a few people who used to be involved in buying properties.

SAY GOODBYE TO PURCHASING COSTS
When you buy a property you needed to follow this pattern or similar:

1. View property in estate agents (cost to vendor up to £5,000).
2. Instruct broker to get mortgage (cost to purchaser 1% of loan).
3. Instruct survey (cost to purchaser up to £500).
4. Mortgage application and arrangement fees (cost to purchaser up to £3,000).

Well, you can say Goodbye to all those costs. These costs do not apply as you are not actually buying the property yet. Apart from the estate agency fee these costs will only arise when you exercise your option to buy.

Not only can you say goodbye to the costs, they also lose the power they had over us investors before. The power of a surveyor to say, 'This property is not worth what you think it is', or a mortgage company's refusal to lend to you.

This is a great feeling. Here at the Lease Options Brigade we like to say YES! So you can say:

☐ Yes, I will take your property on.
☐ Yes, I will buy your property in the future at the price you want now.
☐ Yes, I can set you free.

You are no longer a greedy investor to them but a saviour. How nice are you?

So who do you need to do lease options? You need only one professional: a solicitor. I strongly recommend you use one. They will make sure that searches are done on the property, and the option is registered with the land registry. They will include all the things you have agreed with the vendor in the correct legal way.

A solicitor will register the option, which prevents the owner obtaining more finance or selling the property without your knowledge. This is *very* important, as an option without registration means that you have no protection. You are then left with court as your only remedy, which can be expensive and no guarantee of either a win or successful payment of damages.

You could be extra safe and instruct a basic survey. This will ensure that the property is mortgageable. Most properties are but something like subsidence is difficult to spot so it is best to be sure. Using a surveyor is recommended but again not essential. You need the property to be mortgageable to purchase the house in the future when you exercise the option.

YOUR AND THE VENDOR'S RESPONSIBILITIES

You now have control of the property. What happens next? If the property burned down tomorrow, are you looking at a loss?

There are many things that need to be set out so everyone is clear about who is responsible for what. This will all be taken care of by the solicitor, but remember these basic principles:

- ☐ The property is still owned legally by the person who granted the option, *not* you.

- ☐ You only have control of the property and the right to buy the property at an agreed price within a certain time period.

Your responsibilities are:

- ☐ You must pay the mortgage on the property. I would suggest you pay the mortgage company direct. This way you know the mortgage is being paid.

- ☐ Your must maintain the property. The day-to-day risks of ownership fall to you. So if a tenant reports a leaking tap then you have to fix it.

- ☐ You must be available to the owner of the property. This is a relationship you have here. The property still belongs to the owner so it is only right that they can speak to you. Circumstances can change and you need to be able to communicate and adjust if the need ever arises.

The vendor's responsibilities are:

- ☐ They have to make sure the building is insured. There must be at least buildings insurance to cover for fire, lightning, explosion & aircraft (FLEA). The cost for this should be agreed between the two of you. I would recommend you pay this, direct to the insurance company, and keep a copy of the cover note or insurance certificate.

213

☐ They need to get permission from their mortgage company in order to let the property. If the owner does not get permission and the mortgage lender finds out, they can demand full repayment of the loan. In this climate that could be disastrous.

FINDING THE RIGHT PROPERTIES

There are plenty of properties for sale out there. Most are not worth buying! If I were to estimate the percentage of properties for sale that are worth buying I would say it is about 0.7%. That is to say about one in every 140 properties on the market is worth investing in.

You determine what is worth buying by looking at the yield. To recap, yield is defined as: annual rent divided by purchase price. So a property that rents out for £5,000 per year and costs £50,000 to buy has a yield of: £5,000 divided by £50,000 = 10%.

A good yield is 10% or greater. So a property that rents out for £5,000 is worth buying if it costs £50,000 or less and not worth buying if it costs £50,001 or more.

This is the key calculation when considering a property for sale. Over my time as an investor I have found that properties priced less than £100,000 have the potential to yield over 10%.

I would aim for these sorts of properties. Properties with a 10% yield will give you good positive cash flows in the long term. You do not need to worry about interest rate rises (unless it goes beyond 10%) as the rent will more than cover the mortgage which you are now responsible for paying.

RENTING OUT THE PROPERTY

You are effectively renting out a property you do *not* own. This has implications. You cannot create a tenancy with a tenant just because you are paying the owner's mortgage. What you need to do is:

1. Position yourself as a letting agent and get a 'management agreement' in place between you and the owner. Include a clause that says you are entitled to keep the surplus of the rent over the mortgage costs as a management fee.

2. Create a tenancy between the tenant and the owner.

GROOMING YOURSELF FOR PURCHASE

The message here is simple: *stay out of trouble.*

What I mean is, do not get into conflict with any company that can affect your credit file. It is the credit file that lenders use to determine whether you are a good bet and this file records what you have been up to for the last six years.

To stay out of trouble you need to do the following.

☐ **Pay your debts on time**. This means settling your credit card payments, loan repayments and mortgages on time and in full. If you can't avoid being late, try to find out how late you have to be for it to be reported to the credit file agencies.

☐ **Stay out of court**. This is good general advice. If you have the misfortune to be on the wrong end of a CCJ (county court judgement) pay it within one month. Then you can get the judgement removed from the register and it will not show up on your file.

☐ **Do not ignore demands**. Did you know that if you fail to pay the London congestion charge or private car parking fines, you can be taken to the county court and not the magistrate? These small CCJs are enough to put a lender off. Lenders are spoilt for choice and they will look for anything that might determine the best borrowers.

A few other pointers regarding your credit file.

☐ **Electoral roll**. Lenders check to see that you are on it. If you are not on it, all you need to do is request forms from your local council.

☐ **Searches**. Try not to make too many searches if you can help it. They stay on record for a year and lenders do not like to see multiple searches.

☐ **Stick to the truth**. Do not exaggerate or change your details to fit the circumstance. These credit file agencies share information and inconsistencies show up.

The only thing that stands between you and a mortgage is your credit file. Look after your credit file and your credit file will look after you.

15

PROPERTY SOURCER (CLIENT FACING)

VITAL STATISTICS

Earning potential before tax	£5,000 to £1m per year
Capital required	£nil to £10,000
Skills required	Communication
Qualifications preferable	None
Competitiveness: low/medium/high	Medium
Risk: low/medium/high	Low
The business model in a nutshell	To assist investors building their property portfolio.
Potential gaps in the market and suggested USPs	• Specialist property like HMO • Portfolio building and sourcing • Overseas

WHAT IS A PROPERTY SOURCER?

A property sourcer is someone who finds an investment property for an investor matched to the investor's requirements. A good property sourcer will do the following.

1. Understand the level of the investor's knowledge.
2. Identify the client's needs and objectives.
3. Create a medium-term strategy for them (if required).
4. Plot the first 12 months of the working relationship between you and the investor.
5. Identify the type of investment properties the investor needs to fulfil their objectives.
6. Source these investment properties from property finders, estate agents and/or packagers.
7. See the property purchases through to completion and introduce the investor to a property manager or letting agent.

In essence you are like a marriage bureau. You are finding properties that you hope will have a long and lasting relationship with the owner!

Specialization

There are four ways you can set your business up:

1. Specialize in the type of client you have and let them dictate the properties you find for them (specialized client, non-specialized property).
2. Specialize in the type of property you find and allocate across your client base (non-specialized client, specialized property).
3. Specialize in the type of client and property (specialized client, specialized property).
4. No specialization (non-specialized client, non-specialized property).

Examples of specialized clients and specialized properties are:

- □ self-employed only;
- □ location specific (e.g. London);
- □ professional only;
- □ young;
- □ old;
- □ women only;
- □ escape rat race;
- □ wealthy.

Examples of specialized properties are:

- □ low value high yield;
- □ no money down;
- □ HMO (house in multiple occupancy);
- □ luxury;
- □ location specific (e.g. London);
- □ portfolios;
- □ overseas.

There are many others. It is key you get this bit right. You have to make sure your specialization is specific enough to attract a decent number of clients but not so specific as not to appeal to anyone other than you!

FINDING THE RIGHT CLIENTS

Who the right clients are depends on you. What type of clients do you feel you best work with? Before you say 'Anyone or everyone who is willing to pay me', think again! People will have many different needs and wants. You need to think about:

1. **Your skill set**. If you choose to work with clients who need a lot of hand-holding and education then you will need a fair degree of knowledge and be able to deliver this information in a way they will understand. Your skill set must match what is expected from your target client base.

2. **Your personality**. Some clients need someone to chat to. They need to feel that you care. Other clients have no need for small talk and are annoyed by it. Be aware of personality types and home in on the ones you know you click with.

3. **Your presentation**. Clients want varying degrees of professionalism. Some clients are fine with phone calls, and everything is done on trust and by word. Others want everything in writing, tip-top manners at all times and a professional approach. These are the extremes and there are many in between. How you present yourself will hopefully attract the right clients for you. Don't set up an image that you cannot keep up.

4. **Your peer group**. You offer a personal service. Personal services work best when empathy levels are high. If you come from similar backgrounds then a positive working relationship will probably follow.

These are not hard-and-fast rules but are worth considering. The most important thing is that you deliver to the client what they want, and you need to understand what that is.

Your clients can only be clients if they actually buy property, and in order to buy property they must possess the following qualities:

1. **They are ready to buy**. Some clients will take up all your time and not buy. Paralysis by analysis, they say. Your client base must be made up of property *buyers*.

2. **They can get a mortgage**. They must have buying power, either in the form of cash (very rare) or the ability to get a buy-to-let mortgage. You should see evidence such as a recent credit score or a buy-to-let portfolio.

3. **The right mindset**. Clients should not think that because they are using you to find the perfect investment property they will not lose any money. A property sourcer never takes on a client's risk. The client takes 100% responsibility for the risk. Your job is to present property deals to the client so they can make the decision. The right mindset is knowing that a property sourcer can provide you with deals, not ensure that you do not lose money.

You can find clients by incorporating what you have learned above and using the right wording on your marketing materials. If you want to deal with, say, self-employed clients only, you can state that. If you want to deal with only wealthy clients you can state that also. Whoever you wish to target make sure it is obvious in your marketing. This will work wonders for generating leads.

I would recommend these methods to get clients:

1. **Internet**. This is where I get most of my leads. I created a website, drive traffic to it by Google Adwords, capture their email addresses and market to them regularly.

2. **Referrals**. You set up joint venture or introducer agreements with businesses or people who might know of potential clients: mortgage brokers, solicitors, accountants, other property investors, estate agents. Whoever comes into contact with people who want to buy investment properties can refer clients to you.

3. **Your competitors**. This is quite unique to this kind of business. You will find that some potential clients will want to work with certain types of property sourcers. If you can get a competitor to refer your business for a fee then it can work both ways. This way everyone wins. I often do this with other property sourcers.

Offline advertising, such as magazines, exhibitions and newspapers, has never been successful for me. Online advertising is very effective, and brings in enough leads for my organization to deal with.

FINDING SUITABLE PROPERTIES

The following sources are listed with their respective market share.

- ☐ Estate agents (91%).
- ☐ Property finders (<1%).
- ☐ Lead providers (<1%).
- ☐ Auctions (6%).
- ☐ Private ads (<1%).
- ☐ Solicitors (<1%).

Estate agents

Rightmove has 90% of the estate agency market. Therefore roughly 80% of properties for sale can be found on this site (91% × 90%). The rest can be found on other sites, such as:

www.propertyfinder.com
www.findaproperty.com

www.primelocation.com
www.globrix.com
www.vebra.com
www.s1homes.com

In Scotland you have more localized sites such as:

www.gspc.co.uk
www.espc.co.uk
www.aspc.co.uk

A full list of estate agents by area can be found at www.ukpropertyshop.co.uk.

Some estate agents do not advertise on the internet. These can be goldmines. They are found in very small towns where one agent pretty much deals with all the transfers of property in that town and surrounding villages. These agents are often one-man bands and they keep the cream to themselves. However, you can get a look-in if you strike up a rapport with them. Keep these goldmines to yourself.

Property finders

You can find deals from people whose profession is property finding. They hunt their local area to find deals. They advertise locally (sometimes nationally), leaflet drop and buy at auctions. If you come across their marketing give them a call! They might have some deals they don't want and your clients could lap up.

Lead providers

These businesses generate leads via the internet. These leads are of varying quality and come from people who want to sell their property quickly, for whatever reason.

Apart from the normal property data such as address and postcode, the leads include data such as the likely price they are willing to take, the owner's estimated market value, and the owner's outstanding debts.

The owner usually makes multiple enquiries to other lead providing companies and it is not uncommon to see the same lead being offered by two or more lead providers.

To be successful with this method is to buy many and quickly. You want to get the first bite of the cherry so speed is everything.

Auctions

You can find plenty of cheap properties at auctions. Your type of client base will determine which auctions you go to:

- ☐ **Local auctions**. These specialize in properties that are local to the area and if you have specialized as a local property sourcer then these will be perfect. You can alert your client base to these properties and charge a fee.

- ☐ **National auctions**. These come from all over the country. There are often many repossessions as the banks use the big auction houses to sell. Bargains can be had here. Localized properties can be put in national auctions. So a little market town property finds itself listed next to a large commercial portfolio in central London. There will be very few buyers for the smaller property, hence you can get these properties at bargain prices.

To get alerts of every auction in the UK you can subscribe to www.eigroup.co.uk.

Private ads

People these days object to paying estate agents' fees. You can sell your property by simply placing an ad in a local or national newspaper or on a website, saving you thousands. Do a quick search in Google for 'sell house privately' and many sites will come up. Real bargains can be found this way. Also give www.ebay.co.uk a try. You never know!

You can find deals in any classified section. Other publications you could try include:

www.adtrader.co.uk
www.loot.com

Solicitors

Solicitors come across deals due to:

- ☐ **Aborted sales**. Sometimes sales fall out of bed and the purchaser cannot buy, but the deal is still a good deal. If the solicitor lets you know you could put in place your willing and able client.

- ☐ **Death**. Beneficiaries of a will sometimes inherit a property they do not want to own, and then want a quick sale. This is where you come in with your army of clients!

- ☐ **Entrepreneurial solicitors**. Some solicitors make as much money placing deals as they do with the conveyancing! Try and get to know these sorts of solicitors. However, do not let them act for you!

PRESENTING THE DEALS

There is no such thing as too much information when it comes to presenting a deal. As a minimum you should supply:

- ☐ a photo of the outside;
- ☐ the full address and postcode;
- ☐ the price;
- ☐ the size of property;
- ☐ the condition.

Any professional investor can make a decision based on the above. Some can decide on even less. I have bought properties knowing just the size, location and the price. Other details you can include are:

- ☐ the rental price;
- ☐ the LHA rental price;
- ☐ the calculated yield based on both rents above;
- ☐ the estimated value;
- ☐ the potential selling price in X years;
- ☐ the calculated mortgage cost;
- ☐ the monthly profit;
- ☐ the capital required to purchase;
- ☐ a description of features (double glazing, gas central heating);
- ☐ photos of the inside of the property;
- ☐ the crime stats for the area;
- ☐ a neighbourhood profile;
- ☐ recent sold prices of similar properties in the area;
- ☐ comparable properties on the market.

We do a lot of this for our clients. We try to include as much information as we can to help them make a decision. You want to give the client all the data they need to make a decision. When they make a decision, you make money.

We provide our deals on a pre-made template. This is converted to a pdf and sent to the client via email. However, there are other ways you can present a deal.

- ☐ Word document.
- ☐ Video uploaded to YouTube.
- ☐ Print it out and post it.
- ☐ Graphic images.
- ☐ SMS text message.
- ☐ Facebook, Myspace or Twitter.
- ☐ Email.

How you do this will depend on your type of client. You will quickly see what works. A well-presented deal will sell, if you have met the client's requirements.

FINDING A MATCH

There will be a point when your client says: 'I want this property! What do I do now?'

You should be prepared to put the wheels in motion as quickly as possible. Usually a good property deal does not hang around for long, so you have to act fast. Speed is everything in this business.

You need to do the following in order to secure the deal.

1. Get a commitment from your client. We do this by taking the sourcing fee upfront. Or you can ask for some of it upfront or then get them to sign or confirm something via email. It is important, however, that the client feels that they are committing to the deal.
2. Inform your source (where the property came from) as soon as you get a commitment.
3. Introduce the client to the source.
4. Introduce the client to the mortgage broker to get an application under way.
5. Introduce the client to the solicitor acting on the purchase.

You also need to see the following happen over the next four to eight weeks.

1. The client gets approved for a mortgage.
2. A surveyor gets instructed within two weeks of accepting the deal.
3. The solicitor receives all documentation from the client to cover themselves against money-laundering.
4. Contracts for exchange go out to vendor and client.
5. Survey results come back in.
6. Mortgage offer is issued.
7. Contracts are exchanged.
8. Property completes.

I employ a facilitator to do this, in order to make sure problems are ironed out and also prevent problems arising. It is quite a stressful job and takes a certain degree of persistence, but it needs to be done. It is too easy for a client to say 'Yes, I will have that' and nothing else happens afterwards. Remember, your fee is only really earned once purchase happens.

KEEPING HOLD OF YOUR CLIENT BASE

There are many property sourcing companies out there to lose business to. What will set you apart from the rest will include the following.

☐ Getting your clients the exact deals they want. Encourage the client to be as specific as possible. The more you match a deal to their requirements the more pleased they will be.

☐ Being at the end of a phone. No one likes answerphone messages, endless ringing tones or even worse a dead phone line! You have to be responsive in this game. Answer the phone and act, even if all you have to do is reassure them that the property you have found them is right for them. Clients need love!

☐ Making regular contact. A newsletter which keeps clients informed of their market will be appreciated. It lets them know you are on the pulse and aware of what is going on. They are relying on you to bring their attention to anything significant in the industry.

☐ Having good third parties. Your client base will call upon you for recommendations for services like letting agents and mortgage brokers. Make sure they are good! You may not be liable for their actions, but they will reflect heavily on you.

Master keeping hold of your client base before you think of expanding it. A very small client base can provide you with a significant income. If you have chosen to go for wealthy clients who only want portfolios and you are earning 1% of the sale price then you can effectively live off one client doing one deal a year!

16

PROPERTY SOURCER (PROPERTY FACING)

VITAL STATISTICS

Earning potential before tax	£5,000 to unlimited per property
Capital required	£nil to £50,000
Skills required	Speed
Qualifications preferable	None
Competitiveness: low/medium/high	High
Risk: low/medium/high	Medium
The business model in a nutshell	To find property deals and sell them on without ever owning the property.
Potential gaps in the market and suggested USPs	• Property specialization like HMO • Price threshold i.e. buy properties up to a certain value • Specific locations

This is the business of finding properties and selling them before you even own them. It is done by using four methods.

1. Selling the lead only.
2. Assignable contracts.
3. Sub sales.
4. Option agreements.

Each method as listed offers increasing returns but with added complexity. However, if you get this right you can make millions. This is perfect for those who love the chase, the hunt, the deal. You do not need much to get going and if you focus on territories, big returns can be had if you act fast.

You have to buy properties at below market value to be able to sell them before you own them. Properties have to be sourced at a bargain price and sold at a bargain price.

GETTING THE LEADS

Here is my list of ways to get below market value properties.

1. Estate agents

I have built an extensive portfolio and I have bought most of my properties from estate agents. Just because they are on the open market does not mean they are not cheap. If you have signed up to Rightmove alerts you will know of a deal as soon as it comes on. Some sourcers keep estate agents very sweet with bottles of champagne, boxes of chocolates and other hospitality gifts. Whatever gives you the edge so that the estate agent calls you as soon as a deal comes on.

2. Letting agents

If ever there was a source of ready-made investments then look no further than a letting agent's book! They have properties that are already tenanted and managed, it may just be a landlord who wants to sell because of ill-health or retirement. So get to know all the letting agents in your area.

3. Auctions

I talked about auctions early in Chapter 7 (page 115). Reread this section to see how you can bag a bargain by finding properties with low reserves with low bidding demand. Also sign up to EIG to get auction alerts. EIG are a one-stop shop for auction properties. They gather data from every auction house and present the information to you in real time.

4. Private ads

Some people object to paying estate agent fees., and the recent introduction of HIPs and Home Reports means paying out up to an extra £1,000 to sell your home. Private ads have seen a little surge, so check the classified sections of your local press, *Daltons Weekly*, *Loot*, Friday-Ads, eBay, www.HouseLadder.co.uk, etc. Just search for 'sell my house privately' in Google and all the sites will come up.

5. Developers

A quick sale is what developers want. They would rather have someone else manage the sale for them than having to deal with any number of different buyers all with their own different set of gripes! They will usually offer a discount of at least 15% but in the current climate 40% discounts have not been unheard of due to the lack of finance for new builds.

6. BMV lead providers

Companies that are great internet marketers are able to get leads of desperate sellers. They charge anywhere from £10 to £200 for a lead and they have all the information you need to decide whether it is worth purchasing. A word of warning, though. They do not have exclusivity on the lead. A desperate seller will have done the rounds so you could buy the lead and find out the property has already been sold. Test this by buying a number and seeing if they pay. Expect to get a one in seven hit rate: one lead you buy in every seven will result in a deal being done.

7. Solicitors

Solicitors come across properties where the owners want a quick sale, for example an unwanted property through an inheritance. This is where the solicitor should be on the phone to you! Big, big discounts can be had as all the sellers want is a quick sale with minimum hassle.

8. Internet

If you are good at internet marketing or have search engine optimization skills then building a site to capture property leads could be a good way to get property deals. It is very competitive out there. Search engine optimization is all about getting your site listed top in Google, and will take a minimum of six months. Or if you do pay per click with Google it will cost you at least £50 a day to get some decent leads. However, it can be an excellent way to obtain leads as you will be getting them fresh. It could be that they have only made an enquiry on your site so if you are serious about becoming a property sourcer then I would recommend persevering with this method. You could also sell unwanted leads for up to £200.

9. Other property sourcers

It is an incestuous business! It makes sense to do business with your competitors. Tread carefully, and protect your contacts, clients, sources, etc. However, there will be times when a property sourcer has stock he can't sell. You may be able to take on their deals and punt them out to your sources and split the fee.

10. Leaflet drops

Have some leaflets printed: 'We buy homes quick', etc. Target areas where you think you can sell. Either deliver them yourself or incentivize someone to do it for you, paying them the minimum wage plus a £500 bonus for any properties that result in a deal.

11. County court repossessions

This involves going to the county court and looking for repossession cases. You need to find cases that are listed as 'Bank v the home owner', e.g. Barclays Bank v Joe Bloggs. Go armed with a sale contract and approach Joe Bloggs saying that you will buy their property. Then Joe can go into court, present your sale contract to the judge, and repossession can be halted.

TURNING LEADS INTO DEALS

So you now know how to generate property leads – how do you turn them in to deals? Well, you need to do these three actions: **qualify**, **visit**, and **secure**.

Qualify

You need to check that the deal 'stacks'. Stack is a term used by the industry to check that the figures actually work. This means the lead is:

- below market value;
- mortgageable;
- has enough equity to be sold on.

If the lead is all these then you have a green light.

Below market value (BMV)

To establish whether the property is below market value you need to find out both the market value and the price the vendor is willing to accept.

The great thing about the internet is that market value can be determined very quickly. All you need is the postcode, the street name and the size of the property, then use www.houseprices.co.uk or Rightmove to get an idea of what properties have sold for in the area.

You can also visit all the property portal websites and see what properties in that street are going for now. You will quickly be able to establish market value from seeking information from these sources only.

You then compare this with the price the vendor will accept and to find this out you need to ask them A simple phone call or email will do. This information is key: there is no point listening to what the vendor has to say about the great area or the property until you have the price. If the price is good then you can keep on listening!

Mortgageable

If the price they want is below the market value you have established then you are getting warm. You also need to find out if it is mortgageable. This can really only be established by a surveyor but you can ask certain questions to help you establish whether it would pass a survey, such as the following.

☐ Is the property lived in currently? This would establish that it is at least on the face of it habitable.

☐ Does it suffer from subsidence? Properties with this problem are not mortgageable so it is good to get this question in early.

☐ Does it suffer from damp? Surveyors put on retentions (an amount withheld from the mortgage advance to reflect the work required) or request remedial works are carried out to make the property mortgageable due to damp issues.

☐ Does it require any work? Retentions and remedial works will be requested by the surveyor.

If the outcome to the questions above is favourable then you need to find out whether the vendor can sell it on.

Has enough equity to be sold on

A property can only be sold on as long as all debts secured on the property can be cleared. So if the mortgage is £75,000 and the vendor has agreed to sell the property for £70,000 then the vendor needs to come up with another £5,000 as there will be a shortfall. Most of the time vendors do not have this shortfall amount so the deal cannot happen.

So you need to know what debts are secured on the property. Ask about the size of the mortgage, and if they have any other debts secured on the property such as second charge loans.

If the price that you are willing to pay is greater than the total amount of debts on the property and is within the ball-park figure of what the vendor will accept then the property requires a visit.

Visit

When you see the property with your own eyes, you will quickly be able to establish whether the deal is going to work. You have to try to view it from a surveyor's point of view as they have all the power.

When you meet the vendor this is your time to start the negotiation. You need to convince them that your offer is both genuine and the best they can get.

Remember, you may not be the only person they have seen. Ask them if anyone else has shown an interest. Let them do the talking. Things to help you make the deal sway your way might include:

☐ offering to pay their legal fees;

☐ letting them name the exchange and completion date;

☐ showing off your credentials. Show them a bank statement indicating you have the cash to buy the property or proof that you have a ready bank of investors lined up already to take the property.

Once you have agreed a price it is then time to secure the deal.

Secure

Be prepared, and bring paperwork to secure the deal with you. The paperwork will depend on how you wish to sell the deal (see below).

You want a signature there and then. People can change their minds all too quickly. The act of signing a piece of paper cements things in the vendor's mind.

If they wish to think about it before signing, agree but inform them that you are seeing other properties and since you have limited funds you may not be able to buy theirs when they do decide to give you the call.

Now if you are lucky enough to have secured a deal you just have to get rid of it – fast!

MONETIZING THE DEALS

Now you have a deal all signed up, you need to sell it. Speed is everything. You do not have the luxury of not being able to sell it. Compare this with the more traditional property trader method, where you own the property and if it does not sell then you just wait until the next auction.

With deals the clock is ticking. You need a sale as quickly as the contract you signed. So if you agreed a completion in eight weeks you need to find a buyer who accepts the price *and* can complete in eight weeks. If there was ever pressure in a property business then this would be it!

Let me explain. Deals can be sold by one of three ways: **assignable contracts**, **sub sales**, and **option agreements**.

Assignable contracts

An assignable contract is a contract that you can assign to someone else. Let's say I have secured a property for £100k. I can then sell this contract to another investor for a fee. All that needs to be in the contract of sale is that the contract is assignable.

So if you have bagged a deal and want to get rid of it quickly and simply you just assign the contract to another investor for a fee. They will then step into your shoes and perform the contract.

If you have structured the deal as a 'no money down' deal you can still assign this contract to another investor.

Sub sales

A sub sale is where A contracts to sell a property to B who then contracts to sell the property to C before completion of the A to B contract.

You are B. The middleman. B's transaction never gets registered on the land registry. There are ways you can do this so the purchaser C does not fall foul of the six-month rule. I have heard you need two fax machines and two people faxing at the same time to stay the right side of tax law!

For example, you have found a property you can buy for £50k, and you have found a buyer for £70k. You would:

  ☐ have a contract to buy for £50k;
  ☐ have a contract to sell for £70k.

The purchase and sale would occur simultaneously, netting you a £20k profit. Nice! Now if you were able to get a valuation for £100k then you would be able to structure the purchase for the end user no money down.

Option agreements

As explained earlier, basically an option gives you the right but not the obligation to buy. So you can sell an option on to another investor.

If you are willing to provide bridging deposit finance (by teaming up with a bridging finance company) then you can structure the deal no money down which makes it very attractive. This again requires a valuation in excess of the purchase price.

Now you have to find a solicitor who understands these types of purchases and sales, which are quite fiddly. Some deals will fail. Lenders change the rules all the time, vendors don't understand what is going on, and certain rules need to be followed with precision. It is natural that some deals will fail. However, it is worth the persistence as the rewards can be very high.

FINDING BUYERS

Now you need to find buyers for the deals. Generally they will be investors. You may be able to find owner-occupier buyers but I warn you, they are *very* difficult to deal with. They need a lot of hand-holding and they will be buying based on non-financial reasons which can be difficult to grasp when you just want a quick sale! So my advice is stay away from them. The clock is ticking when you are a property sourcer so you want people who know what they want and can buy fast.

I have my own hierarchy of buyers. They are ranked as follows.

1. Cash buyers.
2. Credit-worthy buyers with deposits.
3. Credit-worthy buyers with no deposits.
4. Soon to be any of the above.

Cash buyers

Not a lot can go wrong with these buyers. They do not need finance as they have the full asking price to put down in cash. Deals can be done quickly and neatly. Some buyers can complete in seven days. Now cash buyers are well aware that they have the highest status. Do not expect them to pay the price you want. They hold all the negotiating power. However, if you can agree on price and you are not greedy you can make regular hassle-free profits.

A lot of cash buyers have facilities with commercial banks. They can simply write cheques for the full amount as the bank has security over their portfolio. They have what are called hunting licences, which enable them to go out and search for deals and pay cash so they can complete quickly. If you can get to deals before them then they are forced to pay your fee.

Credit-worthy buyers with deposits

This is the next best buyer. They are at the mercy of a lender but nevertheless able to buy. The good thing is, they do not need any complex 'no money down' structure so they are able to purchase in the normal fashion. Their deposits may be tied up in equity in their current portfolio so be sure to classify how much they have in liquid reserves and how much is equity tied up in their properties.

Expect a buyer like this to take anywhere between four and 12 weeks to complete on your deal.

Credit-worthy buyers with no deposits

At least these people can get credit! They will need to use a 'no money down' scheme so the transaction will be a bit more fiddly, but they may be less fussy on the deal you have got. As long as the deal is 25% BMV then it can be done without the need for the investor to put in a deposit. Because the nation is not overflowing with these sorts of deals this buyer will usually jump at such a deal as they do not come up very often.

We specialize in deals like these for our investors; 90% of our buyers fit into this category. That's not to say that they do not have the money, it is just that they want to get the highest return on any cash input they have to put in, so they want near 100% financing as possible. Very sensible in my opinion!

Soon to be any of the above

You may come across people who are potential buyers. That is to say, they are not in a position to buy at present but will be soon. These buyers are your pipeline. So keep in contact with them; when their circumstances change you can start offering them deals.

So how do you find these buyers? Well, you have to become a property sourcer (client facing) or contract with a property sourcer (client facing). My organization is a property sourcer (client facing). We work with plenty of property sourcers (property facing) and are always looking for more!

PART FOUR: BUSINESS ADVICE

17

STARTING YOUR OWN PROPERTY BUSINESS

Now all your passion and energy needs to be channelled into starting your very own property business, by doing the following, loosely in this order.

1. Getting the tools
2. Getting educated
3. Promoting your business
4. Informing the authorities
5. Controlling cash
6. Understanding your competitors
7. Understanding your customers
8. Building alliances

GETTING THE TOOLS

Get whatever tools you need to do your property business from the start. The key word in the last sentence is *need*. It's nice to have a laptop, pager, filofax and personal assistant, but is it necessary if your choice of business is renting out a room? The more cash you can save in the early days the better.

Certain primary tools are needed depending on what type of business you are starting. But my advice is that if you are in doubt on whether you need it or not then forget it. Preserve cash by not buying unnecessary items. Let's look at the possible tools *needed*:

1. **Office equipment**
   Telephone, fax, computer, printer. Some of this can be very expensive, so where you can avoid getting the latest technology. Older, outdated models do the same thing but just a bit slower. Don't drain your cash when you need it to invest.

   If your prospective property business requires minimal paperwork generation, then consider whether office equipment is really necessary. You'll be surprised how far pen and paper go. Acquiring office equipment may make you feel as though you're in business but their worth may be limited to start with.

2. **Office space**
   Office space is expensive, and only necessary if you are going to have meetings with clients. Otherwise the spare room, a corner in your living room or even your garage or shed will suffice.

3. **Stationery**

   Fancy business cards, invoices and compliment slips may make you feel good but it's your first sale that's the most important thing. If your letterhead is likely to be a key 'calling card' of your firm then invest in a good letterhead. If your image is a key representation of your firm then invest in a good suit. Have the sense to know whether fancy stationery will drum up business or not.

4. **Car or van**

   I knew a guy who wanted to start a property business around 100 miles from where he lived. The crazy thing is he didn't know how to drive. I'm not sure how he expected to go from one property to the other but the costs of transport would have eroded his profit to nothing!

   Evaluate whether a car is necessary. Running a car is expensive, but if you need one then get one. There's nothing more frustrating than to have a customer waiting and you can't get to them.

5. **Information sources**

   If you need to have access to trade journals, websites or newsletters then subscribe to them. Factor this cost into your plans as this information will be key to you keeping abreast and ahead in the market. Be selective. There will be a few standard primary information sources that everyone refers to.

6. **Website**

   Websites can either be cheap or expensive to set up – it depends on who you know. Consider whether your type of property business demands it. I would hunt down a cheap web designer or learn how to do it yourself.

7. **Employees**

   If you are going to need staff immediately then start recruiting early. The right people can make or break you. Don't employ the first person that comes along, or a family member or friend out of duty.

8. **Listing**

   Be sure to contact *Yellow Pages*, *Thomson* and directory enquiries (118 118) to get a listing. You will be surprised how many calls you will get if you are in a niche business. This is FREE! Do not be tempted to pay for an advert in any of these directories – as they are hugely expensive – although once you're established you might think about it. Remember – you need all the cash you've got.

This is not an exhaustive list. It depends on what type of business you are considering, but carefully evaluate whether they are necessary now or can wait until you are more established.

GETTING EDUCATED

This is very important. I have fallen foul of this. I entered the bar and nightclub business without any real understanding of the liquor trade, and learned the hard way, losing £250,000. With hindsight I should have found out a lot more. To get educated you can do the following:

- ☐ **Chat to people**. Who better to speak to than someone in the industry. But make sure it's not a potential competitor. Ask to shadow them if possible on a typical day.

- ☐ **Read up on it**. Look out for books on your proposed property business. The cost of a book is a tiny fraction of what you could lose if you don't follow the advice given. There are also many trade journals. If you can't afford to subscribe to them yet see if you can borrow them from your local library.

- ☐ **Use the internet**. I don't have to tell you that the internet is a great resource for information on anything – especially business.

PROMOTING YOUR BUSINESS

It's no good starting a business unless you let people know you're in business. You must promote yourself. The following tools are available.

1. **You**

   You are your best promotional tool! You are the key representative of your business. Your ability to speak, act and deliver/carry out the products/services of the business is paramount. The most effective way to promote your business is to do a good job. If you do then people will tell others. Word of mouth is everything. If you say you are going to do something then *do it*!

2. **Work for nothing**

   If you believe that you are better than the rest then initially work for nothing. People will soon cotton on if you are better. Once you've proved yourself they will come to you. A common trick is to do a job for a well-known company for a notional £1 fee. This well-known company is then technically a customer. This customer can be added to your list of satisfied customers, thus improving your profile.

3. **Free advertising**

   Make use of all the free advertising you can get. Tell everyone that you are in business, put your posters in the right places, send target emails and get press attention if you can.

4. **Mailshots**

You need a good letterhead on quality paper with quality envelopes. Target your mailshot to prospective customers. Make sure it is well drafted. Run it by someone whose opinion you trust.

One of my businesses, my accountancy practice, was kick-started by a targeted mailshot to 100 mortgage brokers offering my accountancy reference service. I had about six responses which resulted in work. I got referred to other mortgage brokers and now my business grows from recommendations only.

5. **Newspapers**

Before spending a small fortune on a regular display advert in the local or national press consider who you are targeting. Many people don't even glance at the ads. If you're in quite a niche market then the mass press may not be suitable. Carefully selected trade mags, newsletters and journals could be better and cheaper!

6. **Leaflet drops**

Leaflet drops save on postage. For mass marketing, like property sourcing or hunting for BMV properties print up some cheap leaflets and deliver them yourself!

7. **Website**

Websites can be cheap to set up. If your property business demands one then make sure it's well set up. If you need one just as a calling card make sure you link it to as many search engines as possible. It really depends on your type of business. Do your competitors have a website? If they don't then maybe this could be a way of differentiating yourself from them.

8. **Promotional discounts**

This can be a powerful promotional tool. You could supply your product or service at cost for the first few deals on each customer. If you get them hooked in you may have them for life.

9. **Introduction fees**

Offer a commission to anyone who brings you in business. If I get a deal from an introduction from someone I pay them 10% of what I get. It's a great encouragement to your contacts to bring business to you.

INFORMING THE AUTHORITIES

Apart from letting your potential customers know you're in business, you have to inform the authorities. The following will be interested in your new business venture.

1. **Inland Revenue**

   Unfortunately we all have to pay it – tax! Write to your local Inland Revenue office, whose address can be found in the *Yellow Pages*, to let them know you've started in business. They will send you a tax return to complete, which you can fill out yourself or employ a local accountant to deal with.

   Shop around if you need an accountant. If you are running a small uncomplicated business, a competent book-keeper may suffice, and will be half the cost or less of a chartered or certified accountant.

   The Inland Revenue informs the National Insurance Contributions Dept who will then contact you to set up a £2 per week contribution from your bank. The rest of your NI contributions will be paid when you pay your tax.

2. **VAT**

   This really only applies to serviced apartments and property sourcing. If you expect your turnover to be greater than £15,000 per quarter then you may have to be registered for VAT – it depends on whether your product or service is subject to VAT. Contact HM Revenue & Customs (www.hmrc.gov.uk).

CONTROLLING CASH

As I've mentioned before cash is king. Everything to do with the cash that comes in and out is the most important thing – *not profit!* You pay bills with cash, not profit. Profit is a notional, expected figure based on the agreed terms of your purchase and sale. If your customer defaults then the profit turns quickly to a loss. Let's look at this in more detail.

1. **Credit control**

   This is probably the most important side of the business when it comes to financials. If you can, never give credit. My accountancy practice demands payment upfront even though many accountants give credit. I don't worry about losing the business and I would never worry about customers not paying!

   If you do have to have debtors then make sure you keep tabs on them. Make it clear on your invoices when you expect payment, e.g. 'within 7 days of the date of this invoice'. You need a system for payments not received on time. It may be a phone call after one day, a letter after seven days and court action after a month.

   Have credit limits for customers. Set it at zero for new customers, rising to a figure that is no more than 10% of your working capital. Stay abreast of a customer's financial situation. If you know that one of your customers is struggling then consider reducing their credit limit. You don't want them going down and taking you with them.

2. **Credit periods**

   I'm telling you not to give credit to your customers, but at the same time do try to get credit from your suppliers! This is simply the way business works. Wherever you can get credit then take it. If you can get paid for a job before you've paid your supplier then you've cracked it – you are generating cash without any cash! Then the only limit on how much cash you can make will be purely the demand from customers.

3. **Pricing**

   Be sure to factor in unseen costs such as phone calls, postage, parking or any cost that is not directly attributable to your product or service. You would be surprised how many people fall foul of this. They make a profit after variable costs (known as gross profit) but make a loss after all the overheads are taken into account (known as a net loss).

   You can avoid this by setting your price by the technique of skimming. Skimming is going in high and then shaving off a little bit if demand is low. You have to be competitive, though. If you are charging a higher price than your competitors you need to be offering a little more, like better aftersales care or a more robust product or service.

   If your intention is to crush the competition by setting the price low then ensure that you take into account the losses you may incur and how long you can sustain this for. Consider setting the prices for some of your range higher than the competition to compensate for this loss. This strategy is called loss leadership. Large supermarkets do this all the time.

4. **Budgeting**

   You don't need expensive budgeting software to track every expenditure and calculate fancy statistics, but you must have an idea of what things cost. This is a game of money. Know how much *everything* costs and budget for it. You don't want any nasty surprises to catch you out and put you out of business.

   A calculation on a piece of paper will suffice. Be sure to include every possible expense. Things such as:

   ☐ **Mobile phone calls** – they can work out very expensive if you are calling across networks.

   ☐ **Postage** – you'll be surprised how much a mailshot can cost if you send out over 500 letters.

□ **Printing** – ink cartridges for printers are a scandalous price. I pay £27 for a black ink cartridge which lasts me about two months. That's nearly £200 a year!

□ **Travel costs** – be sure to include parking costs, potential fines, extra servicing costs due to higher mileage, taxis and congestion charges.

□ **Bad debts** – some customers will not pay you. I always budget 20% bad debt loss for my property business.

UNDERSTANDING YOUR COMPETITORS

It's not just you out there, you know. Others are doing exactly what you're doing – trying to make a living. The key thing is that you know who, what, why and where – and how and when!

1. **Know who they are**

   Every business has competitors. If there's money to be made in a market then there will always be several players fighting over market share. So know your competitors *and* potential competitors.

   We've all heard the expression 'keep your friends close and your enemies closer'. In business this is even more significant. The competition are your enemies as they threaten your lifestyle. Beware of what they're up to and their future plans. If you find that you are losing business due to an offer by one of your competitors then you are able to react with full information.

2. **Copy them!**

   You've found out who they are – copy them! If you're struggling for innovative ideas then copy them. It's difficult to reinvent the wheel, copying is not illegal! Use your competitors' ideas for your own inspiration or just improve on their ideas. There are no rules and regulations that govern the copying of ideas as this is what keeps business progressive.

3. **Differentiate**

   If copying is not the best strategy then do something different. You could offer something additional, or a completely different product that does the same thing. You need to keep up with the latest developments in your market and the products or practices that are more appealing or more efficient.

   Branding is a key way to differentiate. Easyjet, the low-cost airline, succeeded by offering basic air travel to limited destinations without any frills. They stood out with a very striking style of branding (bright orange and white), and nearly brought down the institution we know as British Airways.

An obvious differentiation will make customers choose you over others. The worst thing for your business is that you blur in with the rest of them, and there is no solid reason why someone would choose you over others.

Consider differentiation by one of these means:

- **Price** – be at the top end or the bottom end of the market. Either be the cheapest with no frills or the most expensive with all the frills.

- **Niche** – be a specialist in one small part of the market, thus eliminating most competitors. You can charge premium pricing for your expertise.

- **Quality** – offer the best! People will come to you as you are offering the best in the market.

- **After sales** – you offer the best back-up service for any issues arising after the purchasing of your product or service.

UNDERSTANDING YOUR CUSTOMERS

1. **Know who they are**
   This seems obvious. You're thinking, well I sold to them, of course I know them. What I'm saying is, *really know* your customers. Understand where they're heading and if your products or services will be required in the future be sure to guarantee supply. If their requirements are going to change then change with them if possible.

2. **Avoid being reliant on a few customers**
   The classic way of businesses going down is a customer going down. If you have only a few customers then your business is very fragile. You are reliant on the success of these few customers for your success.

   Do whatever you can to minimize your exposure to just one or a few customers. Reread the section on promoting yourself above to gain more customers, so you can be less reliant on just a few.

BUILDING ALLIANCES

This is something I need to get stuck into. It's all about teaming up with non-competing businesses and selling each other's products and services. We've all heard about lastminute.com. The key to their success of being the first internet site based in the UK to make a profit was their aggressive alliance programme. Their name was everywhere on the internet and the high street. The great thing is that even if none of these alliances worked it still got their name out there. It just so happened that aligning themselves with household names made them a household name, which meant more hits to their site hence more sales.

Depending on what your business is, there will be non-competing businesses that could sell your product or service and you theirs! You may find that selling their product or service could be more profitable than your own product or service.

18

DON'T GIVE UP! METHODS OF MOTIVATION

I have come up with four methods to ensure that you never give up. Use all of them together to keep you motivated.

1. Fear and greed method.
2. Negative positive method.
3. Competition method.
4. Goal setting method.

FEAR AND GREED METHOD

Now we all have drives. We are all driven to eat, sleep and have sex. These are actions that require little motivation. Anything else outside of these three drives requires motivation – including setting up *and* persevering with your own business. So how do you stay motivated? Well, to be blunt, we are all motivated to do things for two reasons only: out of **fear** and out of **greed**.

You don't have to be literally fearful and/or greedy . What you have to do is create the fear and the greed in your mind to motivate yourself. This will make you stop procrastinating, get up and do something! It's the ability to picture the fearful situation or the abundance that comes with greed.

Fear and greed are subjective and will be based on your personal circumstances. Don't hold back – let your mind be free to create the absolute worst and best scenarios that really motivate you to avoid or to strive for. Here are some general ones to get you going.

1. **Going back to the 9 to 5 grind.**
   This is my biggest fear. It's not having enough money or time, it's just going back to work! Really remember what trap you've escaped from. There is no way I'm going back to that.

2. **Missing out on key events as you're not a master of your own time.**
   You miss certain events by being at work: from simple things like football World Cup matches on TV to crucial things like hearing your child utter its first words. Think of the pain you've felt because you've missed out on things that you've found important.

3. **Going out of business.**
Can you imagine the stress of going under? You will be a disappointment to your friends, family and most importantly to yourself. When you're struggling to keep self-motivated, think of the shame and embarrassment you will experience if you become lazy and let your business go down.

4. **Working till you're too old to enjoy life.**
You may have to work until you are 65. There is so much that I want to do before I hit 40! Consider what you want to do and how working will prevent you from doing it. A surprising number of people work all their life and die within two years of retirement. It could be attributed to the dramatic change in life. Don't let this be you!

5. **Never having to take orders from anyone for the rest of your life.**
You can be the master of your own destiny. Few people in this world are in this privileged position. Whatever your situation is at any point in time is completely of your doing. No overbearing boss, no unachievable deadlines, no boring meetings. It's your business and you call the shots.

6. **Having all the time in the world to do things that are really important.**
What's important depends on you. But whatever it is you can do it. Going out for the day or travelling round the world for six months, if you've set your business up correctly it should be able to run itself.

7. **Having enough money to buy anything you or your family want.**
Successful entrepreneurs can do this. You can only reach this position by setting up your own business. Picture you and your family having the houses, cars and holidays you desire. It all depends on how much you want it.

8. **Having peace of mind knowing that you are completely self-sufficient.**
No one's ever going to make you redundant. You have full job security as you are your employer! The only threat of redundancy is from yourself. I am trying to make myself redundant through delegation – to get reliable people to run my business so I can do something else.

If those you employ to run your business are incompetent then it's they who have to go – not you. You still have your business. You just have to find other suitable people.

9. **Having an abundance of respect, adoration and accolade from society.**
If you want outside recognition then the only way to do this is by being the owner of the business. Owners get the praise – and rightly so! It was your idea and you

took it to the market. Picture yourself on the front page of the business section in *The Times*, on TV telling your story of success, on the radio promoting your product and at parties thrown in your honour due to record profits and bonus payments.

It's best to use extremes for this method. Some people find this easy. If you tend to make a mountain out of a molehill then now's the time to use this skill for fearful situations. Natural daydreamers can really let their mind run wild: picture an abundance of whatever you desire for greedy situations.

NEGATIVE POSITIVE METHOD

There will be setbacks – guaranteed. It's how you deal with them that will determine your success. It's a case of education. You simply learn from your mistakes.

Even though it's best to learn from other people's mistakes, nothing hits home like your own mistakes. One thing a book cannot give you is experience. You can follow all the advice in the book, but you'll still go through the process of making mistakes. For success you need to use the opportunity of a mistake to be a learning lesson.

You need to be able to turn a negative situation into a positive situation. You will then get wiser as time goes on. This is what experience is all about. There are many mistakes and misfortunes ahead. Here are some of mine and how I turned them around, followed by a few other misfortunes and how to learn from them.

1. Run out of money

Initial reaction (negative outlook)

Any self-respecting businessman would have faced this. It's known in the game as 'short term cash flow problems'. When you run out of cash it's called being bankrupt.

I ran out of cash as I had over-committed myself. I had assets but you can't pay your bills with assets – you need cash. I was forced to approach a bridging finance company who could raise the cash I needed but were going to charge me 28% APR.

Fortunately I was able to borrow £5,000 from my girlfriend which just about saved me. It was a stressful time as I had to stall certain creditors with lame excuses and I bounced a few cheques and direct debits.

Future action (positive outlook)

You will be sure, having experienced this, that you'll never go back to it. As a result of this experience I always have a cash float equivalent to six months' mortgage payments for all my properties.

I lived to tell the tale and I look back at that situation with a degree of humour. At the time I thought I knew everything about business and I couldn't understand how people could mis-budget, especially a chartered accountant like me. Let me tell you – it was a humbling experience.

2. Default by a debtor

Initial reaction (negative outlook)

When I started out I had a letting agent for one of my properties. I went to collect some rent and the owner told me that his partner had done a runner with the money. I believed him. As it turned out there was no partner. He was a compulsive gambler and had blown the lot on 36 black!

It can be very annoying and frustrating when someone takes your product or service and doesn't pay you. It's easy to think whether it's all worth it, especially if you've put a lot of hard work in to serving or trusting that customer.

Future action (positive outlook)

Question your choice of customer. Did you jump in too quickly because you were desperate for the business? Maybe you will reassess your choice of customer or readjust credit limits for customers so the same doesn't happen again.

Maybe it's time to be a bit sceptical of everyone you do business with. You've got a lot to lose if you don't adopt this attitude and even more to gain.

3. An unforeseen bill

Initial reaction (negative outlook)

I got hit for a £2,500 roof repair bill early on in my property investment days. Not everything can be budgeted for. A repair, an oversight or an accident can knock you for six.

Future action (positive outlook)

With time you will be more aware of unforeseen expenditure. You will budget for the unbudgetable because you have the experience. You will also question whether the repair is necessary as I do now – do not believe so-called experts. They are only after your money.

4. Court action

Initial reaction (negative outlook)

I was threatened by a letting agent that they would take me to court unless I paid a

£900 fee to come out of my contract. I had little knowledge of the law at that time and if I had had the money I would have paid it – but I didn't have the money.

I spoke to a solicitor friend, read a few books and wrote several letters to defend my situation. Eventually the letting agent gave up!

Future action (positive outlook)

I was forced to get educated! If it wasn't for this threat I would never have found out how I stood and now stand with letting agents.

Now I welcome court action in both directions. I recently took one of my tenants to court to evict her and I learned a lot.

Once you start enforcing the law you feel more confident in the deals you strike as you know that they can be enforced, if need be, in court.

5. Computer crash and loss of important data

Initial reaction (negative outlook)

I love computers when they work but absolutely detest them when they don't! You only realize how dependent you are on them when they let you down.

This happened to me. I needed to get certain letters out by a deadline and I simply missed that deadline. I think I looked amateur to the outside because my computer crashed and I had no back-up. I may have lost some future business due to the computer crashing as my business seems too fragile.

Future action (positive outlook)

Now I have a back-up computer. In fact I have two back-up computers! I have learned that the risk of being unable to print letters, access the web, check your email account or use my spreadsheet can have catastrophic consequences.

6. Not enough business to cover your fixed costs

Initial reaction (negative outlook)

Your initial reaction will be 'I'm going to go under!' You may start to look at ways of reducing your overheads but find that they're quite inflexible.

Future action (positive outlook)

This forces you to look harder within your business to find out why you're not getting enough sales. Having your mind really focusing on the most important side of the business, sales, can only be a good thing.

You may be surprised that after careful thought a few simple changes in your marketing strategy can have better returns than expected.

7. Get too stressed to cope

Initial reaction (negative outlook)

Running a business is a 24-hour occupation if you want it to be. The buck stops with you. So if you are facing stressful times within the business it doesn't stop when it hits 5 p.m.

Just being able to relax, and think clearly through the challenges your business throws at you, is difficult.

Your expectations are not being met due to others. It's these expectations that cause you the stress.

Future action (positive outlook)

Setting up a business is front-loaded. That is, you do most of the work at the start for a pay-off in the future. Every new business owner goes through this – you are not alone!

Over time you learn to deal with the stress. I used to get very stressed when a tenant did a runner without paying the rent or vandalized my property. Now it takes a lot more to get me stressed. Recently a tenant burned down my flat and I didn't bat an eyelid. I have become accustomed to these setbacks.

8. Market changes make your product or service obsolete

Initial reaction (negative outlook)

This can be very worrying. It can happen to anyone. Knowing your market and their fickle tastes is important.

Potentially all your stock is unsaleable and/or all your skills are redundant.

Future action (positive outlook)

The ability to be flexible and move with the market is key to success. This lesson really homes in on the fact that you can never stand still. You have to know what your customers want at all times.

You also need to be looking out for other opportunities that your existing market requires or in new markets.

9. An accident or sickness means you are unable to work

Initial reaction (negative outlook)

This can happen to anyone. If you're in a business that requires you to be there, sell the product or provide the service then having an accident or becoming ill is a major problem.

Future action (positive outlook)

If you can adjust the business to accommodate your setback then you've achieved a lot. Sometimes in life you are tested in situations where you think you cannot cope. When it actually happens you'll be surprised how well you do, thus making you stronger in the future.

COMPETITION METHOD

We all have a competitive streak. If you don't, then get one! A great motivator is to set yourself against someone else. It's like being back at school – being motivated to do better than your classmates. Do not be ashamed of or guilty about being competitive. My personal opinion is that it's extremely healthy. It forces us to get the best from ourselves.

Pick your competitors wisely, however. It's no good pitching yourself against someone too low or too high. If you can beat them then you will become complacent. If you can never beat them you'll become disheartened. Pick a competitor that's similar to you in some way. Typical competitor subjects could be:

1. **A business competitor you know**

   This is the most natural competitor. If you're not competing against your competitors then I would be worried! They're in the same line of business, their motivations will be similar and comparing your success relative to them will be easier to measure.

   Never be humble about your competitiveness to your competitors and never feel threatened by the competitiveness of your competitors. You're in the business of making money and every business should understand this. If they don't then they won't last long.

2. **A business competitor you don't know**

   Your natural competitor may be too big or too small for you to really feel that they are a competitor. It may make more sense to pitch yourself against a business that has been in business for the same period of time as you. So find someone that set up in business the same time as you, then use them to chart your success. You may choose one that is in the same general industry but is not a competitor, e.g. the internet. You could have a website business that wants to pitch themselves against another website even though you have different customers.

3. **A friend or family member**
   If you've always had a competitive relationship with a certain friend or family member then use it to your advantage. My father always used to put me down and in a way I thank him for that. This pushed me to prove myself at an early age.

   If this applies to you then don't let it get to you. Channel this energy in a positive way. Let it push you to do better than even them!

4. **Someone you know**
   There may be some people you secretly admire. You may not know them well, but you know what they do and what they've achieved. They're a sort of role model yet you want to do better than them. Remember that imitation is the sincerest form of flattery. So copying, competing and surpassing someone can only be admired – even by the person you do this too!

GOAL SETTING METHOD

I know you've heard about this one before but it really does work. This method helps people achieve success – including me. I have had many goals in my life and I continue to keep setting them. Some I have achieved, some not, some I have revised and some I have discarded. Here are some of the goals I've set, what's happened to them and why.

1. **To obtain my final salary when at work through self-employment in three years** ☑
   I had a realistic goal that was achievable in the time-frame that I had set. Because I had a set figure in mind I was able to plan my expansion of my business so that it could meet these targets.

   I used to study my Excel spreadsheets and play around with them so I would get my desired result. In fact I surpassed my goal, and earned a lot more than my final salary.

2. **To be a millionaire by the age of 30** ☑
   This was a goal that wasn't really thought through, it was just a goal that I had. A millionaire is someone who owns assets greater than £1m. As I owned property worth more than £1m then I was technically a millionaire.

Having a goal that is positive, even though it's not thought through, is not a bad thing. If it's making you strive forward towards a theoretical goal it's OK! The outside world creates these ill-thought-out goals all the time, such as being the richest person in the world or the largest company in the world, so having your own such targets is completely fine as long as they're positive.

3. **To have 50 properties by 2002**   ☑

This was another goal that didn't have much thought behind it. All I knew was that I wanted to own a significant amount of property and 50 seemed a decent round number. The key thing is that it was pushing me forward.

4. **To earn £50,000 per month by 2009**   ☑

I wanted £50,000 per month as I do not think I could spend more than £50,000 per month. This target ensures that I never have to go without when it comes to material goods.

5. **To own a Bentley Coupé before age 32**   Revised

I have adjusted this to age 40. It's my ultimate car and I will get one but currently I simply can't afford it.

You are not a failure if you do not achieve your goal in the specified time. It's fine to revise goals. If they're still things you want then obtaining them further down the line is still an achievement.

6. **To be a billionaire by age 40**   Discarded

I wanted to be a millionaire by age 30 and I achieved this. To be a billionaire is really a notional figure that has no real meaning. To be comfortable is an even better goal which I've equated to £50,000 per month, hence it's a goal. It's no good busting a gut achieving a goal when you really have no understanding why you want it.

You need to know when you are pushing yourself too much. Decide whether the goals you are setting are helping you or destroying you.

I hope you've noticed that all the goals had two common characteristics:

1. There was a timescale – by when?
2. There was a quantity – and how much?

So I wasn't saying just that I wanted more money or more time for myself. I wanted this amount of time or money by a certain date or age. So when you set your goals, be specific. Put a date and a specified outcome to your goals. Only by doing this can you monitor if you're on track to success. Monitoring builds confidence and we all know that having a confident attitude can take you a long way. Other characteristics that could form part of your goals could be:

3. With whom – having a goal to be supplying a certain customer or partnering up with a certain competitor.

4. Where – having a goal to be in a certain geographical region conducting business.

When setting your goals ensure that they push you. Do not set easily achievable goals. It could be the biggest, the richest, most ethical, the champion or the toughest. Whatever it is, be sure that you're heading to be at the top of your game.

19

STAYING IN BUSINESS

Staying in business involves:

1. Increasing cash inflow (business) – always growing the business to increase profit.
2. Controlling cash outflow (personal) – controlling personal spending.

So you've got out of the rat race, all you need to do now is ensure you stay out. This involves never being complacent. You have to learn one fact in business – if you stand still you lose. Nothing lasts for ever, especially in business. If your intention is to create a business that will provide you with a set level of income, with no growth or efficiency strategy, then you will be at the mercy of your competitors. If you decide to spend every penny of your profit on fancy cars or houses then you'll be at the mercy of your creditors!

INCREASING CASH INFLOW (BUSINESS)

I have identified two ways to increase cash inflow from your business: **duplicate** and **diversify**, or D&D as I like to call it. Let's look at what each one means.

Duplicate

Duplicate means exactly what it says. If you have an idea that works in one market then just simply duplicate it in different markets. Examples of this are all around. McDonald's is probably the most famous duplication ever. They had one idea of selling the Big Mac and just took this idea to every country in the world.

Gap mastered the art of providing trendy clothes at reasonable prices for adults, then they just entered the children's market and repeated the process.

I duplicated the idea of renting of properties in Essex and transferred it to the renting of properties in the whole of the UK. I found that I didn't need to be close to any of my investment properties as it wasn't me who had to repair them if anything went wrong. So I just duplicated the rental property idea a hundred times around the UK!

Is your idea capable of being duplicated or is your business very centred around you? Does your service or product require you and you only or can you delegate your role to someone else? The key to duplication is taking yourself out of the business and getting other trained individuals to run the business for you.

For duplication to occur you need to:

1. **Ensure that profitability is large enough to take on an employee or employees**
   If you want to duplicate then you need to be sure that the business profits can afford to pay for someone to do your job. You will be moving out of the original location and on to another location, so you will have to pay someone to do your job.

   The costs of employing someone are:
   - ☐ their gross pay;
   - ☐ employer's National Insurance (around 10% of gross pay);
   - ☐ employer's liability insurance premiums;
   - ☐ employees' expenses while doing their job;
   - ☐ other benefits you want to give and/or the employee expects.

   Remember that your employee gets paid before you do so if you make £2,000 profit for the month and your employee's pay is £2,000 per month then your pay is NIL! As a rule of thumb, if you can get an employee to do what you do for one-fifth (20%) of net profit, then consider duplication. So if your profit is £100k without an employee and you can get an employee for £20k p.a. then duplicate. If your profit is £50k then forget it. Focus on building your profit to £100k before duplicating.

2. **Train up staff**
   The type of business you have will determine the level of training you'll need to give to any potential employees. One thing is for sure, though – they will need some form of training. But do not even consider sending them to any kind of day course, college or residential training programme. The best person to teach them the job is you. I would say that for someone to do a good job requires training *and* experience in a ratio of 20:80. So training is a key part of the process but so is experience – allowing the employee to make their own mistakes. See below.

3. **Delegate well**
   No one can ever do all that you do as well as you. You have to accept this. Errors will be made by the people you have delegated to, and the reasons for that will sometimes be down to you and sometimes be down to them. It doesn't matter whose fault it is as long as lessons are learned.

   You must have reasonable expectations of your employees. They could be new to the business and inexperienced, but as long as they:
   - ☐ are loyal and trustworthy;
   - ☐ are hard-working;
   - ☐ have the intelligence to do the job;
   then they have the capacity to take your business very far.

4. **Adjust to the new skill requirements from yourself**
   The transition from being a one-man-band to employing several people is a big one. You have to let go of some skills and replace them with others. Skills that you should let go of are as follows.

   ☐ **Day-to-day operational activities** – things like admin, individual customer queries, cleaning and anything else that doesn't require much thought power or skill. You need to put a value on an hour's worth of your time. If an hour spent with a prospective customer can generate £500 of profit then evaluate it to the cost of £7 per hour for an employee doing a day-to-day activity – it's a simple case of maths!

   Skills you should be focusing on are as follows.

   ☐ **Choosing the right employees** – a business's success is dependent on the people who work for it. If you have the skill of picking the best employees, such as a book-keeper, manager, sales person and technical person, then you have won half the battle. The skill of recognizing talent will ensure your success.

   ☐ **Choosing new markets** – the success of your business requires you to know where's a good deal and where isn't. Your own livelihood depends on it and so do your employees'. Over time your ability to assess risk will be the most important skill you acquire. It is this ability that separates you from the layman in your chosen field.

   ☐ **Raising finance** – a business's ability to raise finance and deal with the financiers will ensure that you never go bankrupt.

   ☐ **Being the face of the business** – to grow the business requires you to be the best promotional tool there is. So if you can home in on tricks you know of to gain further business, then perfect them! This will involve meeting the decision-makers of your customers and suppliers.

   ☐ **Motivating your workforce** – you have to be able to manage your staff and this means getting the most from them. The granting of responsibility, the paying of bonuses and treating them with respect is key. John Cauldwell, the boss of Phones4U, hit the press by making the top ten branch managers millionaires by paying them a £1m bonus due to a staggering year of business as a result of their hard work.

5. **Create and implement control procedures**
   If you do manage to duplicate then you will need to create and implement procedures that:

   ☐ Control cash outflow so that you receive all the cash that is generated from your business and it is not spent on bogus expenses.

☐ Ensure that all the cash resulting from a sale is recorded and collected so that fraud or theft cannot occur.

☐ Make sure that all laws are being followed surrounding your business including employment law. All this can be found from any good business book.

Diversify

This means to branch out into a business different from the one you are actually doing. The beauty of diversification is that it lowers your overall exposure to business risk, because you are not dependent on one market. So for example, if you only sold luxury items such as fine wines or cherished registration number plates, then you would be exposed to the general state of the economy and a recession would potentially put you out of business.

My property portfolio and my property sources (client facing) businesses function, as much as they can, independently from each other, yet are complementary. People always need somewhere to live and there will always be property investors wanting deals.

My portfolio was my first business and I had already identified the supremacy of property above all other investments. It is relatively low risk and provides me with a solid income irrespective of the state of the economy.

So once you've set up a business that's making money then look into doing something that's different. Don't put all your eggs in one basket. Many start-up entrepreneurs put everything into one idea. Some make a lot of money but the majority go down at some point. Nothing lasts for ever! You need to mix and match as much as you can.

Keep abreast of several markets that interest you. Scan the newspapers, talk to people who own their own business, talk to customers, suppliers, competitors (if you can!) and anyone else doing business. Do not be afraid of asking direct questions about what they're doing. You'll be surprised how upfront some people will be, including me. I want to collaborate with others so that we can take the idea further.

Apart from D&D (duplication and diversification)

Another way to increase cash inflow is to control business expenditure – more precisely, the overheads of the business. The effect of this depends on how profitable you are. If you're making £200,000 per year and you reduce overheads by £10,000 then it's no big deal. But if you're making a £5,000 loss per year and you reduce overheads by £10,000 per year then it is a big deal – as you go from making a loss to making a profit. Consider trying to reduce the following fixed overheads.

- ☐ **Rent**. Talk to your landlord. If your lease is due for renewal and you've been a good tenant then tell them you want a reduction. But if you're in a long-term lease this may not be possible.

- ☐ **Wages**. Are you getting the best out of your employees? Think about subcontracting and only paying for work done rather than having the fixed cost of an employee.

- ☐ **Telephone**. Consider switching networks, taking advantage of deals or other promotions that keep your phone bill right down.

- ☐ **Interest cost**. If you've got borrowings then shop around for a better interest rate. Depending on your borrowings and the payback period, moving lender can have a dramatic effect on the repayments.

- ☐ **Bank charges**. Many banks offer free business banking for the first year. Even better, find a bank like mine that never charges you. This is because they do not offer business banking so they just accept your banking activities as personal banking.

CONTROLLING CASH OUTFLOW (PERSONAL)

If this is this final lesson I teach you, let it be the one that stays with you. I could go out now and buy myself a brand-new top of the range Bentley Coupé *and* an Aston Martin. So why don't I? The first reason, and the golden rule, is: *'I will spend my income not my capital'.*

So how do you identify the difference between income and capital? I use this basic rule:

- ☐ **capital** is an amount of money that can be invested to return an income;
- ☐ **income** is an amount of money earned as a result of an investment made.

What you deem to be capital is based on your personal circumstances and what you are willing to sacrifice now to invest for the future. For me, a sum greater than £1,000 is a suitable amount to invest. But even £10 is worth investing – it depends on your circumstances.

When I started my first job I earned £14,000 per year. I decided to invest half of it (£7,000 a year). Over the five years that I worked this consistent £7,000 p.a. investment (total £35,000) now returns me an annual income in excess of £200,000 per year. I was able to buy five properties in three years which returned me an income so I could leave my job. During the next four years I was able to buy a further 65 properties. I will buy these cars when I earn enough for the purchase not to threaten my lifestyle. This means when the total HP payment on both of these cars is less than 5% of my disposable income.

The second reason is that I know my income will be irregular. It may even be a loss for certain months. It's no good having liabilities when you could be using this money to fund your business through the hard times. I spend only 30% of the profit generated from my business on things I need. So if your business generates £3,000 per month then spend only £900 per month. This means that £2,100 is saved either for the hard times or for future investment. Typical expenditures you should avoid, unless you are sure you can meet their payments, are:

☐ mortgage payments for a house beyond your means;
☐ HP payments for a car that you struggle to even get a service for;
☐ personal loans for personal expenditure for such things as holidays, clothes and high-street goods.

In other words, avoid buying liabilities – that is, goods where you have to pay for them over a long period of time. This only serves to increase your fixed costs and thus the risk of bankruptcy. It will be difficult to go back to living like a pauper and looking at ways of minimizing costs once you've become accustomed to this lifestyle.

To get more helpful guides, videos, audio, spreadsheets, software and advice all for free, visit my site www.ahuja.co.uk

I wish you luck with your goals.

Ajay.

INDEX

actual price, 50, 51, 52
admin costs, 44
advertising, 91, 107, 117, 122, 139, 171–3, 239
affordability, 87
agreement, 94–7
alliances, 244–5
amenities, 88
anticipated revenue, 100–3
assets, 24
assignable contracts, 230
auctions, 115–16, 122, 220, 226

bad debts, 44
boom, 39–41
borrowing, 25
bridging finance, 120, 132
bubbles, 52–3
budgeting, 242–3
buyers, 232–3

cleaning, 90
commercial finance, 119, 132
competitors, understanding, 244
consumer price index, 66
conversion, 123, 125, 129, 131–2, 133
cost of living, 22–8
crash, 41
credit cards, 28
credit check, 92, 175, 202
credit control, 241
credit periods, 242

decorating, 89
developers, 226
diversify, 259
duplicate, 256

employed, being, 7–14
employment cost index, 66
endowment policies, 24
estate agents, 73, 122, 134, 140, 219, 226
expenses, 44, 48

fear, 197–9
foot flow, 105, 106
furnishing, 89, 168–9

GDP report, 66
ground rent, 44
growth, 37–43

house in multiple occupation (HMO), 93
house price inflation, 67
house rules, 90

Inland Revenue, 241
insurance, 44
interest rates
    fixed, 87
    global, 66
    home, 66
    tracker, 88

variable, 88
internet, 73, 91, 117, 169, 219, 227
investor, 18–21

lead providers, 220
leads, 139–40, 226
leafleting, 117, 139, 227, 240
letting agent fees, 44
local press, 73, 91, 117
lodger agreement, 94–7

market value, 113–14
Mortgage in Principle (MIP), 70
mortgages, 86–8
    buy-to-let, 86, 118
    residential, 86
motivation, 1, 246–55

negative equity, 63, 67
negotiating, 140–1

occupancy, 99
option agreements, 231

planning permission, 134
power of attorney, 142
presenting the deal, 222
profile, 200–4
profit forecasting, 93
property clock, 31–6, 55, 78
    cold spot, 36, 62–7, 72
    cooling spot, 36, 57–62, 72
    drivers, 35
    hot spot, 36, 55–7, 72, 73
    lifetime, 74–8
    warm spot, 36, 67–71, 72, 73
property finders, 220
property investor, 18–21
    buy to let, 153–63
    lease options, 209–15

pension, 177–208
    property, 183–7, 188–91, 193–6
    traditional, 179–83, 188–91,
        192–3, 199–200
    serviced apartments, 144–52
    student/HMO lets, 164–76
property price cycle, 31–79
property prices, 50–4
property sourcer, 216–33
    client facing, 216–24
    property facing, 225–33
property trader, 18–19
    enhance, 123–35
    options, 136–43
    traditional, 110–22

real price, 50, 51, 52
references, 92, 202
refurbishment, 123, 124, 126–8
regulations
    fire, 108
    food and hygiene, 108
    health and safety, 108
remortgaging, 162–3
repairs, 44
repossession, 63, 64, 67
    county court, 228
residential owner
    bed and breakfast, 98–109
    rent a room, 83–97
Return On Capital Employed
    (ROCE), 46
risk, 155, 197, 199, 203, 205

savings, 24
self-employed, being, 14–17
service charges, 44
serviced apartments, 144–52
shares, 24
solicitors, 221, 227

starting capital, 22–8, 158, 159
strategies, three core, 205–8
sub sales, 231

tax, 45
tenants, 90, 170–5
    choosing, 91
    finding, 91, 170–4
tools, 237–8
trader, 18–19, 21

unemployment rate, 67
USP, 105–6

VAT, 241
venture capital, 121
void periods, 44

website, 107, 148, 238, 240

yield, 43–50, 84–5, 103